Undone Science

Undone Science

Social Movements, Mobilized Publics, and Industrial Transitions

David J. Hess

The MIT Press
Cambridge, Massachusetts
London, England

Set in Stone Serif and Stone Sans by Toppan Best-set Premedia Limited. Printed and bound in the United States of America.

Library of Congress Cataloging-in-Publication Data

Names: Hess, David J., author.
Title: Undone science : social movements, mobilized publics, and industrial transitions / David J. Hess.
Description: Cambridge, MA : MIT Press, [2016] | Includes bibliographical references and index.
Identifiers: LCCN 2016016504| ISBN 9780262035132 (hardcover : alk. paper) | ISBN 9780262529495 (pbk. : alk. paper)
Subjects: LCSH: Science--Social aspects. | Technology--Social aspects. | Science and industry--Social aspects. | Industries--Technological innovations--Social aspects. | Social movements. | Political participation.
Classification: LCC Q175.5 .H473 2016 | DDC 303.48/3--dc23 LC record available at https://lccn.loc.gov/2016016504

10 9 8 7 6 5 4 3 2 1

Contents

Acknowledgments

This book weaves together my own research with that of my colleagues who work at the frontiers of science and technology studies and social movement studies. It is a good exemplar of the proposition that research is a social endeavor that is made possible by participation in the social and intellectual networks of a research field. Rather than cite my intellectual debt to individuals here, my best acknowledgment is to discuss their work, which I do in the pages that follow. I rely heavily on the work of a group of researchers who have advocated political sociological approaches to science and technology, but I also draw on the projects of many other researchers who would not necessarily identify themselves with this approach.

The book was made possible by a sabbatical leave from Vanderbilt University. The research presented draws on diverse projects over the course of my career, and many of the projects were partially or completely funded by the National Science Foundation's Program in Science, Technology, and Society, which has helped me to train students and to develop research over two decades. Although I discuss the research from these grants only in summary form, they deserved to be acknowledged as providing the foundations upon which this broad theoretical project has been able to develop over the course of my career. The first grant, "Public Understanding of Science: Expert and Lay Reconstructions of Science in the Alternative Cancer Therapy Movement" (SES 9511543, 1996–1998), allowed me to begin work on the problem of public understandings of science with respect to the movement for complementary and alternative medicine approaches to cancer, and I have reprised and updated some of this work in a new perspective in chapter 6. The grants "Sustainable Technology, the Politics of Design, and Localism" (SES-00425039, 2005–2006) and "The Greening of Economic Development" (Science and Technology Studies Program,

SES-0947429, 2010–2012) helped me to transition into environmental studies, and research from those grants is summarized at various points, including chapters 1, 3, and 5. Finally, "Conditions Favoring Consensus in State-Level Energy Policy" (STS Program, National Science Foundation, SES-1329310, 2013–2015) provides the basis for much of the empirical research discussed in chapter 5. Any opinions, findings, conclusions, or recommendations expressed herein do not necessarily reflect the views of the National Science Foundation. I also would like to thank the two anonymous reviewers for their comments on the manuscript. Scott Frickel, Abby Kinchy, Daniel Kleinman, Rachel McKane, and Sainath Suryanarayanan provided comments on portions of the first draft.

In the pages that follow, I discuss many of the research projects that I have completed either alone or with students since the 1980s. In some cases I summarize results from published work; reuse of that material is allowed under contract. Aside from inadvertent overlaps, the material presented in this book is unique. Sources are credited in the appendix and in the references.

Introduction

Many of the political problems of the day—climate change, industrial pollution, nanomaterials, new technologies of surveillance, and the products of molecular biology—involve complex scientific and technological issues that can provoke sharp divisions in public opinion. Often environmentalists and other advocates of change call for policies that address public concerns with new and existing technologies, and often industrial corporations reply that such concerns are unwarranted and that their technologies are safe and broadly beneficial. Legislatures, regulatory agencies, executive offices, the courts, and voters find themselves caught in the middle, and sometimes they also become divided over how best to develop and to regulate industry.

This general problem—the contentious nature of the politics of industrial innovation and technology regulation—is best analyzed from a transdisciplinary perspective, and in this book I investigate the insights that can be obtained by bringing together two relevant research fields, which are themselves transdisciplinary enterprises: social movement studies (SMS) and science and technology studies (STS). My goal is to sketch out some approaches to the integration of the two fields. I approach this problem of theoretical synthesis with the assumption that it is best conducted by avoiding the facile solution of syncretizing concepts from each field. However, exploring the opportunities for synthesis requires nudging both fields toward each other and exploring new concepts and research topics at the intersections of the two. Fortunately, this task is made easier by changes going on in both SMS and STS.

SMS has undergone a shift away from the confines of the traditional social movement, which is generally understood as organized collective action that uses extra-institutional repertoires of action to gain changes from governments. One influential approach to broadening the topic of the field is "contentious politics," which expands the scope of inquiry to include a broad range of challenger-incumbent relationships, including some that involve protest-based mobilizations and others that work through existing institutions (McAdam, Tarrow, and Tilly 2001). The nudge toward STS takes place as follows: in a world of increasing technological complexity, social movements must often grapple with complex issues of scientific expertise and technological design that are involved in the regulation of our industrial systems. Frequently, there are sharp disagreements over the meaning of scientific research and its relevance for policy, and sometimes industry and public interest groups can point to different networks of researchers who produce opposing findings. Thus, I argue that the study of contentious politics, which itself represents a broadening of the scope of SMS, can benefit from further diversification to include these issues of "contentious knowledge." (See, e.g., Diani 2003; Scoones 2005; Seidman 2013.)

The field of STS underwent a similar shift during the 1990s, when some leaders suggested a "public turn" that involved exploring the sociology of scientific knowledge not only from within the confines of research fields but also as it circulates through society. (See, e.g., Downey and Dumit 1997; Wynne 1995.) In this book I build on the public turn but nudge it toward a more diversified set of questions that extend beyond the focus on the public understood as the layperson or a community of people with lay knowledge who are engaged with experts. The nudge toward SMS occurs as follows: I expand on the public turn by exploring the idea of the "mobilized publics," or organized groups who mobilize for changes in support of the public interest. (See, e.g., Brown and Mikkelson 1990; Epstein 1996; Eyerman and Jamison 1991; Moore 1996.) Moreover, these mobilized publics often point to the problem of "undone science": the systematic absence of research identified by counterpublics when they seek to document potential risks and uncertainties of technologies and industrial processes, and they find that the desired research has not been done or has been significantly underfunded. This absence of scientific research is often in contrast with the much higher quantity of research funded by industry in support of the safety and efficacy of technologies and products (Hess 2007a: 22).

In short, the field of SMS has moved beyond the traditional state-oriented, protest-based unit of analysis, and the field of STS has moved beyond the idea of the sociology of knowledge as a product of networks internal to the scientific field. The idea of "undone science," like the broader concept of "contentious knowledges," suggests the general method that I will follow in this book: to avoid simply juxtaposing concepts from SMS and STS and instead to encourage the development of new concepts and research frameworks that emerge from the perspectives of both fields. SMS and STS have their own conceptual toolkits, but at this point the two research fields are often like ships passing in the night. In SMS, the concepts of repression, political opportunity, framing, mobilizing structures, and outcomes are salient; in STS, the concepts of interpretive flexibility, boundary objects, heterogeneous networks, enrollment, and sociotechnical systems are frequently central points of reference. In this book I develop the thesis that work at the frontiers of the two fields requires its own conceptual toolkit.

At one level the book provides an overview of a research field that is emerging at the intersections of SMS and STS, and it might be read as a long review essay. Because much of the empirical work in this intersection involves controversies over environmental and health issues, the book can be read as a survey of work on social movements, publics, science, the environment, and health. But at another level the book is a theoretical project that charts out some new concepts that are emerging in this interdisciplinary field. I do not see the articulation of new concepts as an exercise in creating jargon. Rather, like Weber's ideal types, the concepts facilitate empirical research on specific historical and ethnographic cases. Furthermore, comparison of cases leads to generalizing knowledge about the conditions under which types emerge or change, and in this sense they can also become variables in causal models. By understanding these explanatory factors, it is possible to develop a social science of science, technology, and social movements, and in turn it is possible to develop insights into effective and ineffective strategies for collective action and social change.

Theoretical Convergences and Divergences

The dominant frameworks of SMS and STS emerged in parallel during the 1970s and the 1980s, when researchers in both fields rejected theoretical assumptions that can be described in broad terms as functionalist or structural-functionalist. In both fields there was a shift to the study of the agency of actors and of accompanying systems of meaning, such as frames or research programs, which define and motivate action. In some cases, metaphors of entrepreneurship also became important, and the fields emphasized the processes of making, mobilizing, or constructing.

Merton (1973) had advanced an approach to the study of science that viewed it as an autonomous institution with norms and a reward system. This approach led to significant insights into the functioning of the scientific field, such as his important work on cumulative advantage in scientific careers. The functionalist approach also produced research on the extent to which science as a social institution was universalistic, a concern that was linked to policy issues such as affirmative action (Hess 2013b). But functionalist analysis tended to ignore the problem of the meaning of scientific knowledge to scientists, the social conditions under which knowledge changes, and the modes by which it gains credibility among the broader public. Functionalist analysis also tended to underplay strategy and agency, and in this sense its mode of explanation was highly structural.

By the 1970s the sociology of scientific knowledge had emerged as an alternative to the functionalist approach of studying science as an institution (Barnes and Dolby 1970; Mulkay 1976). One of the first exemplars of the new sociology of scientific knowledge utilized the concept of interests to explain positions in a scientific controversy as rooted not only in rival networks but also in the broader social structure. The term "social structure" will be used here to refer to the enduring forms of social stratification and conflict categorized by class, gender, sexuality, race, ethnicity, world system position, and so on (Hess, Amir, et al. 2016). We might also think of society as having an "institutional structure," which refers to the relations within and among the various social fields or institutions (the state, the economy, religion, science, the media, and so on). Interest theory sought to relate positions in a scientific controversy to different positions in the political field and in turn to social structure conceptualized as class conflict. (See MacKenzie 1978, 1981.) This approach suffered a setback when some STS researchers argued that the analytical strategy could not convincingly show the causal influence of the class positions on the technical positions in the controversy. (See Woolgar 1981a,b.)

Thus, the first program in the sociology of scientific knowledge offered a highly structural explanatory framework. Unsatisfied with the results from trying to draw causal connections between conflicts in social structure and in the political field to positions in a scientific controversy, many STS researchers moved on to the more manageable microcausality of the strategies that scientists use to convince others of their knowledge claims (Collins 1983, 1985; Knorr Cetina 1981; Latour and Woolgar 1986). During this period STS researchers developed new approaches to the study of meaning and agency within the scientific field, and they tended not to study the relationship between the scientific field and other social fields and social structure. Literatures on race, gender, and postcolonialism emerged (see, e.g., Harding 1998), and Bourdieu (1981, 1990, 1991) proposed a methodology that combined the analysis of meaning with that of influence from the political field, but these research projects tended to remain outside the core concerns and dominant networks of STS.

There was a parallel but somewhat different transition in SMS, where researchers rejected frameworks that had portrayed social movement mobilization as an outcome of societal strains that produce a disruptive psychological state. Among the variants of this "dysfunctional" approach were explanations of mobilization based on the idea that social isolation triggers alienation, status inconsistency (such as differences in wages for similar work) produces grievances, and stressful social change leads to ambiguity and questioning of norms. (See, e.g., Smelser 1962.) These explanations assumed a direct causal connection between a social condition and movement mobilization regardless of subjective meanings attributed to the social condition. The functionalist approaches also tended to miss the role of agency in building and making a social movement.

The next generation of SMS researchers drew attention to the analysis of resource mobilization, collective action frames, movement strategy, and coalitions—approaches that, like the constructivist accounts of STS, focused on agency and meaning (McAdam 1982; McCarthy and Zald 1977; Snow et al. 1986). Structural analysis, especially in the form of the study of political opportunities and threats, retained an important place in the formulations of postfunctionalist SMS theories. (See, e.g., McAdam 1982; Tilly 1978.) In contrast with STS, where the focus on the social negotiation of knowledge claims favored the analysis of networks and social conflict within the scientific field, in SMS the analytical frameworks retained a more prominent role for both social structure and institutional structure. The latter was focused on the "opportunity structure" for movements directed at the state and industry.

There are various strategies that one might choose to explain both the parallels and differences in the history of the two fields. With respect to the parallels, the focus on agency was consistent with the broader cultural transformations at the time, which emphasized individual agency and the enterprising of the self. (See, e.g., Hess 2013b; Rose 1999.) With respect to the different weight placed on structural explanation between STS and SMS, a biographical approach might show that the SMS researchers were influenced by experience in social movement mobilizations, where Marxist, feminist, and anti-colonialist structural analyses were in the air that they breathed. In contrast, the STS researchers may have had a different background that in many cases involved training in the sciences. However, the intellectual history of these two fields remains to be written, and we do not yet know how the biographies of the two groups of social scientists affected their theoretical preferences. Another approach would focus on the differences in the kinds of analytical frameworks that were best suited to problems studied. SMS researchers focused on political conflict between elites and largely disenfranchised challengers, a topic that makes the issue of structural inequality salient. Often there were instances of state repression, and the social movements themselves drew attention to structural inequality by articulating social change goals related to race, class, gender, colonial position, and sexuality. In contrast, STS research during the 1980s focused on conflicts involved in the fact-making and fact-adjudicating processes within the scientific field, which is a relatively autonomous social space. Although Collins (1983) called for attention to the analysis of exogenous factors in the resolution of controversies, in general there was little attention to the issue after the demise of the interests analyses during the early 1980s.

During the 1990s and the early 2000s both fields underwent additional changes. In STS there was a turn away from the laboratory and controversies to expertise and publics (see, e.g., Collins and Evans 2002; Irwin 1995; Wynne 1995, 1996) and to the study of science and policy (see Jasanoff 1990). These changes tended to open up STS inquiry to science and society issues that could potentially bring more attention to social inequality and power. For example, Wynne led a critical appraisal of the dominant approach of the public understanding of science literature, which he argued was "confined to measuring, explaining, and finding remedies for apparent shortfalls of 'correct understanding and use'" (1995: 362). He criticized political and industrial elites for adopting an empirically flawed deficit model that defined the public as lay opinion. This definition used public opinion polls about new technologies to show that the public suffered from a lack of knowledge about basic science and technology. The solution from the elites' perspective was public education and the transmission of knowledge to the great unwashed under the assumption that better knowledge would lead to greater public acceptance.

In contrast, STS researchers such as Wynne, as well as anthropologists of science (see essays in Downey and Dumit 1997), argued that public opposition to industrial technologies is often based on legitimate concerns and on lay knowledge, both of which cannot be reduced to scientific illiteracy. They showed that the lay public makes its own assessments of the credibility of expert sources by drawing on rational processes such as previous experiences of lies and punctured credibility. This approach reconfigured the problem of the public as understanding the decision-making process that laypeople use to come to conclusions about the trustworthiness of government officials and scientists (Wynne 1995). Rather than advocating better public education, the approach advocated bringing laypeople into policy deliberations through public engagement and participation.

To some extent this view of the public made its way into the policy process, especially in Europe, where there were various efforts to develop public trust through consultation exercises and other mechanisms of public participation. In response to these developments, STS researchers developed a critical analysis of this second-order issue of direct public participation in policy making. They suggested that public consultation exercises served to legitimize or at best to tweak technological trajectories already determined by elites (Wynne 2005, 2007; Irwin 2006). Thus, the first-order critique of the deficit-and-transmission model grew into a second-order critique that drew attention to the shortcomings of public engagement mechanisms.

As STS underwent a change of focus from the construction of knowledge in the laboratory or research field to the role of expertise and publics in the media and political fields, SMS diversified from its focus on protest movements. In *The Dynamics of Contention*, McAdam, Tarrow, and Tilly argued for a broad view of SMS that represented by the category of "contentious politics," which they defined as occurring when "(a) at least one government is a claimant, an object of claims, or a party to the claims, and (b) the claims would, if realized, affect the interests of at least one of the claimants" (2001: 5). This definition is consistent with the focus of much of SMS, in which a government is not responsive to the claims of challengers, who then engage in extra-institutional action such as street protest and civil disobedience. Importantly from an STS perspective, McAdam, Tarrow, and Tilly also broadened the scope of comparative inquiry away from protest-based or disruptive collective action. They challenged "the boundary between institutionalized and noninstitutionalized politics" by arguing that contentious politics includes two broad categories, contained and transgressive mobilizations (2001: 6). They suggested the importance of studying social movements and reform movements as well as their interaction.

Another strategy for relaxing the boundaries of the definition of social movements was to argue that they need not have the state as the object of contention. For example, Goodwin and Jasper argued in favor of moving away from the state-as-target assumption but maintained the extra-institutional repertoire element in their definition of a social movement as "a collective, organized, sustained, and noninstitutional challenge to authorities, powerholders, or cultural beliefs and practices" (2004a: 3). Consistent with "new social movement" studies (see, e.g., Melucci 1980, 1996; Touraine 1992), they suggested that SMS should also analyze movements that make claims on "universities, research centers, corporations, retail outlets, trade unions," and so on (Goodwin and Jasper 2004b: 81). When one combines both relaxations in the definition of the object of study—the inclusion of reform movements and the target of authorities other than the state—then the topic of study is not defined either by the repertoire of action (disruptive or institutionalized) or by the target of mobilization (states, corporations, religious authorities, and so on). Instead, SMS broadens its scope of inquiry to the incompatibility of the challengers' proposals with the policies and projects supported by incumbents in a particular social field such as the state or industry. Contention in this broader sense involves mobilizations by those located in a subordinate position—in the broad social structure or in the social fields where action takes place, and often in both—who find that incumbents have not responded adequately to their concerns, grievances, and perceptions of public interest.

As these two research fields developed in parallel, opportunities for their synthesis emerged. STS moved out of the microsociology of laboratory studies and scientific controversies to science in public, and SMS moved from the focus on state-based protest movements to a broader array of targets and repertoires of action in the challenger-incumbent relationship. The two fields also moved toward recognition of the need for balanced analyses that take into account structure, agency, and meaning. As an increasing number of researchers began to draw on both fields of research, the conditions ripened for a more systematic inquiry into the relationship between the two fields.

The Idea of Mobilized Publics

The term "public" is often a common point of reference in conflicts over optimal future political directions, but it is a notoriously slippery idea. One common image of the "public" is the person on the street whom a journalist may ask to comment on an issue of general importance. This "person on the street" image of the public assumes that the individual will have an opinion, albeit not always a completely informed one, and that the individual is neither an interested party in a policy conflict nor an expert on the topic. Thus, we use the term "layperson" rather than stakeholder or an expert to describe this concept of the public. Furthermore, the opinions of individual laypersons can be aggregated to become public opinion, which can be discovered and interpreted via polls, focus groups, surveys, and voting.

But there is a second meaning of the term "public." We can also think about the public as debate or contention that involves an interaction of collective actors who do "have a dog in the fight" and who have some knowledge of the issue (Bourdieu 1993). These mobilized publics contend with each other to gain broad support—to influence public opinion and public policy—in favor of a particular vision of the public good. Thus, the public in this sense of mobilized opinion is a dimension of the political and media fields where agents struggle to define a vision of desirable futures that are defined in terms of a broad public interest.

The idea of mobilized publics serves as an exemplar of a bridge between the two fields that also moves the object of inquiry somewhat in both fields. With respect to STS, both the mainstream science communication literature with its transmission paradigm and the STS critique draw opposing conclusions, but they tend to reinforce a notion of the public as individualized and accessible through public opinion methods, through public consultation exercises, or (in the critical literature) through ethnographic and qualitative methods. Thus, the concept of the lay individual public underlies the deficit model in this literature, but the critique of the deficit model does not always thoroughly interrogate the underlying concept of the public as the individual layperson or as an aggregation of such people. Furthermore, the lay individual public also tends to underlie normative theory of public opinion formation, which relies on a comparison between political practice and an ideal public sphere or a representative public sphere, in which individuals discuss their viewpoints on a topic in a rational-critical manner (Habermas 1989, 1992).

In SMS, the idea of a mobilized public can offer similar advantages. The idea of contentious politics opens the field to institutionalized action, and other approaches open the targets of mobilizations to institutions other than governments. Both approaches tend to focus on collective action from activists, advocates, and organizations that are challenging incumbents. However, incumbents must also develop campaigns that publicize their positions and explain to the media and to the lay opinion public why their positions are aligned with the general public interest. Thus, a term ("the mobilized public") is needed to encompass mobilizations from both challengers and incumbents that struggle for the legitimacy and credibility of favorable public opinion. As with the STS work on expertise and publics, this approach is largely consistent with SMS as the field has developed, but it is somewhat different in focus.

A mobilized public is a group of people and organizations that use various repertoires of action (institutional, extra-institutional, or both) to influence institutions such as business, science, the media, or government by making the case that their approach is of broad public benefit. The latter referencing of public benefit and public opinion is important, as Bourdieu clarifies:

> We know that every exercise of power is accompanied by a discourse aimed at legitimizing the power of the group that exercises it; we can even say that it is characteristic of every power relation that it takes on its full force only in so far as it disguises the fact that it is a power relation. In a word, the politician is someone who says "God is on our side." The modern equivalent of "God is our own side" is "Public opinion is on our side." (1993: 150)

Thus, the mobilized publics vie for the legitimacy of public support in the form of public opinion, but they do so by configuring their views as aligned with public benefit.

I will use the terms "counterpublic" and "official public" to designate two ideal types of mobilized public that map roughly onto the challenger-incumbent relationship. Frequently, I will use the term "counterpublic" as shorthand for "mobilized counterpublic," with the understanding that I am interested in the counterpublic not merely as a discursive position but as a network of organizations and persons that has mobilized for a social change goal framed as serving a broad public interest. In the media, political, and to some degree scientific fields, actors articulate competing visions of the general public good and of future political and economic directions. There are often divisions within official and counterpublic articulations of these visions, and there are complicated alliances built among segments of the incumbents and challengers. Thus, this initial binary distinction should be seen as a starting point for empirical research that uses more subtle distinctions. Increasingly, this approach to the public is gaining traction within STS. (See, e.g., Hess 2011c, 2015b; Welsh and Wynne 2013.)

The outcome of the conflicts among mobilized publics is support for or against a change in the policies and practices of governments, industry, scientific research, and other institutional fields. To mobilize support, the official publics and counterpublics construct a vision of public interest that is made meaningful by its similarities and differences from other positions, which together constitute a field of positions. Part of that meaning-making activity involves defining one's own position as representing a general or public interest rather than a special or sectional interest. A great deal of public debate, especially among political parties, involves attempts to tarnish other positions by suggesting that they will fail for various reasons, such as cost to society, unwanted side effects, or lack of feasibility. Actors also attempt to paint opposing positions as masking specific sectoral interests that the opponents hide under the rhetoric of broad public interest. In other words, they imply or state, "You claim to speak with the public interest in mind, but actually you are hiding your special interests." Public opinion—as measured by polls, by elections, and (indirectly) by policy outcomes—is relevant because it can arbitrate such disagreements, and it can affect strategies that the mobilized publics employ. However, public opinion from this perspective is also an outcome of attempts by different mobilized publics to gain support for their approaches to the definition of public interest.

It is helpful to provide a little more detail about the official public and counterpublic. The official public is the articulation of public interest by a network of incumbents in the political, industrial, and other social fields. Although in some historical circumstances there is a single, monolithic network that could be described as an elite or a dominant class, often it is more fragmented, and the term "elites" is more appropriate. Thus, leaders of segments of industry, government, and sometimes civil society form alliances to support a position on a specific issue. But they support their position not by arguing about how their own interests will be advanced; instead, they argue that their position is the best road toward the goal of producing an outcome in the broad public interest.

To convince policy makers and the lay opinion public, the official publics have powerful mobilizing structures. When there is the full support of the government, a potent juridical and repressive apparatus is available to weaken challengers and, if necessary, to repress protesters. But the organizational forms of official publics also involve what Barley (2010) has called "an institutional field" that can affect the broad contours of government policy and public opinion, and it can be mobilized for conflicts over specific issues. Barley's list for the United States includes peak organizations and trade associations, political action committees, government affairs offices within companies, public relations firms, law firms and lobbying firms, ad hoc organizations (issue specific), think tanks and foundations, and advisory committees and administrative appointments. Dunlap and McCright (2011) provide a somewhat different but overlapping list that draws attention to information transmission: foundations, think tanks, front groups, the media, and "astroturf" organizations. Together, these studies point to the significant resources that official publics can mobilize when they face challenges from counterpublics.

In contrast, counterpublic mobilizations tend to draw on grassroots and community organizations and on existing social movement and reform organizations. Often these organizations are anchored in broad structural inequalities of race, class, gender, sexuality, and global order, as described in counterpublic theory (Fraser 1997; Warner 2002). However, counterpublics can also have subordinate positions in various social fields, including in the industrial and scientific fields. Although these positions often map onto structural inequality, there are exceptions, and these exceptions can be important in research at the intersections of STS and SMS. For example, mainstream environmentalism and various professional reform movements often have a middle-class address in the social structure even if they occupy subordinate positions in the political and industrial fields. Furthermore, although counterpublics may take the form of social movements, they may also be anchored organizationally in professions, religious organizations, the media, networks of public intellectuals and scientists, community groups, and challengers in the industrial field such as entrepreneurs. Thus, although the insights of social movement theory will be an important guide for the analysis of official publics and counterpublics, the idea of a counterpublic is also broader than what we traditionally think about when using the phrase "social movement."

Mobilized Publics and Industrial Transitions

Assuming that one can bring together two central concepts, publics and social movements, how relevant are science, knowledge, and technology in the study of mobilized publics? Since the foundational work of Eyerman and Jamison (1991), researchers have noted the value of studying the epistemic dimensions of social movements. Social movements have broad cultural effects on research priorities, forms of education, and industry. For example, Jamison argued that the Romantic movement of the nineteenth century led to socialist experiments with new forms of industrial organization and to the growth of "people's high schools in the countryside, where populist approaches to science could develop" (2006: 53). In the other causal direction, scientific research can play an important role in social movement mobilizations. For example, scientists sometimes become activists and step into the public limelight (Moore 2008), activists engage science and technology by becoming lay experts (Epstein 1996), occupational reform groups work for changes in their industrial products and practices (Hess 2005), and entrepreneurs and inventors can contribute to social change through design innovations (Hess 2007a). More generally, scientific knowledge has played a major role in many social movements, even movements that are not specifically oriented toward industrial processes or technological issues, including the following:

• debunking racist, sexist, and homophobic ideas about biological difference and inequality,
• showing the value of community-based approaches to poverty reduction and economic development,

• overcoming medical concepts that pathologize structural inequality as psychiatric diseases,
• showing the benefits of worker ownership and unionization, and
• charting the links between democracy and economic well-being.

Science, especially social science and biomedical research, is far from irrelevant for many social movements of our day.

However, it is also hard to argue that science was central to signature social movement events such as the Montgomery bus boycott, the Salt March to Dani, the fall of the Berlin Wall, or the "Arab Spring" of 2011. The great paradigmatic examples of SMS—the movements in favor of social equality and democracy—were against authoritarianism and particularism and in favor of universalism in the sense of human equality and human rights. Epistemic claims played a role in the movements to end the "isms" (racism, sexism, heterosexism, ethnocentrism, colonialism, authoritarianism, traditionalism, and so on). However, these movements were not primarily about science, technology, and industry, and it is a formidable challenge to put science and technology at the center stage of the analysis of such movements.

A subsequent generation of social scientists may yet achieve the task of making STS perspectives central to the study of the universalizing social movements. However, the goal here is a more modest one. The topical focus of this book is on a particular target of mobilized counterpublics: the structure of our industrial processes and technological systems. More concretely, the focus is on the study of movements associated with industries such as buildings, chemicals, energy, food, medicine, transportation, and information technology. There is a type of counterpublic mobilization—both reform movements that work within established institutions, such as efforts to build sustainable food systems, and social movements that utilize extra-institutional repertoires of action, such as protesting mountaintop removal for coal—that deserves a name of its own. The simple phrase that I use is "industrial transition movements."

I use the term "transition" to describe this type of movement in order to flag a connection with "transition studies," a field of research at the intersections of STS and innovation studies that analyzes the causes and effects of long-term transitions of technological systems. Much of this work involves the study of the paramount industrial transition of our time: making our industrial systems more sustainable. It focuses on the challenger-incumbent relationship within an industry, which is epitomized by conflicts between advocates of niche technologies and the response from organizations associated with an industrial regime. The literature examines the various patterns of challenger-incumbent relationships and the dynamic processes of how they change over time (Geels and Schot 2007). Some of the studies point to a social movement as a factor that affects industrial transitions, especially sustainability transitions, but at present there is no systematic treatment of the topic, at least not in the breadth and depth presented here.

Industrial transition movements attempt to reform society by changing technologies, products, and industrial processes. They also attempt to change the social relations of industry to improve basic access to material goods or to alter the social organization of industrial production. Thus, as a type the industrial transition movement is analytically distinguishable from the universalizing movement. However, there are important intersections, and I will discuss interesting continuities between the civil rights movement and subsequent struggles for environmental justice and transit justice in African-American communities (Bullard et al. 2004). But there are also important differences between the two types of movements, among which is the greater salience for science and the politics of knowledge in the industrial transition movements. The movements also place the question of what Winner called the politics of design at the center of contestation, and they recognize, also to use his phrase, that "technology is legislation" (1977, 1986). For example, if a government decides to build a massive interstate highway system and to sanction a zoning regime that promotes suburban sprawl, it has in a sense secreted a shell which the society must, at least for some time, call home. These movements aim to transform the shell, and with it the snail that secretes it and inhabits it.

As I will argue, the study of industrial transition movements is likely to become more important for a variety of historical reasons. As the world becomes increasingly mediated and interconnected by technology, and as innovation becomes increasingly central to the economy, the societal implications of these changes become more visible and politicized. However, my argument is not identical to that of the risk society and the subpolitics of consumer boycotts and industrial opposition (Beck 1997). The industrial transition movements can include opposition to and responses to risks and hazards, but they are also about innovation and the development of alternatives, often from a grassroots perspective (Hess 2007a;

Seyfang and Smith 2007). The central actor is not necessarily an activist or a politicized consumer; it may also be a researcher, an inventor, an entrepreneur, or even—within the incumbent organizations—an "intrapreneur."

Field Theory

Field theory provides an overarching social theoretical framework for studying the politics of industrial transition movements and the associated politics of expertise and design. There are different versions currently in use, and my approach is to utilize them strategically as a broad set of tools (Bourdieu 2005; Fligstein and McAdam 2012). Field theory offers significant advantages over other general theoretical and methodological frameworks. With respect to cultural analysis, we want methodologies that look over the shoulders of informants to understand their symbolic worlds and how they construct meanings. However, a wholly semiotic analysis becomes a project akin to the interpretation of texts, and it is difficult to develop adequate explanatory accounts of social change that take into account social structure, field structure, and the strategies of agents. At the other extreme, political economy approaches are also an important starting point because we want to understand the capitalist global order and structural inequality. However, there is a tendency for such approaches to engage in what Bourdieu (1990) called the "short circuit" of explanatory reasoning, that is, to attribute differences in intellectual positions too easily to those of class position or to other social structural variables. In the tradition of Weber (1978), field theory is a middle ground that recognizes the relative autonomy of social fields and the crucial role of power differentials within and across fields; the importance of cultural meaning in the shaping of social action; and the need to have a methodology that balances the social theory triangle of social structure, agency, and meaning.

Furthermore, because power is a central problem in the study of mobilized publics and their conflicts, field theory provides a good resource for thinking about power in a systematic and precise way. The idea that agents can accumulate different "tokens" of capital and that they can exchange one form of capital for another is a much broader basis for examining power than semiotic hierarchies or class conflict. From a field theoretical perspective, power is the capacity that collective or individual actors may exercise, with varying degrees of skill, in order to attempt to influence outcomes, including the agendas of other actors, social structure, and field structure. (See also Lukes 1974.)

I depart from a strictly Bourdieusian approach to social fields in several ways. The concept of habitus—the acquired schemes and dispositions (roughly also the models of and for action in more anthropological language)—is far too individualized in most cases to provide a satisfactory basis for the analysis of meaning. One alternative, the concept of skill in strategic action theory, can serve as a valuable complement to the idea of the habitus, but it also does not provide the appropriate level of analysis that I am seeking. Like Bourdieu, I rely on a semiotic concept of culture, but I am also interested in the ways in which contrasting systems of meaning form a unit, something like the episteme of early Foucault (1970) but more interactive and contentious. I will develop an approach that draws on the idea of institutional logics, with the understanding that each field generally has multiple, contending institutional logics rather than a single overarching logic (Friedland and Alford 1991). These contending logics vary by field type: in the scientific field there are competing and complementary systems of research programs (bundles of theory, methods, and problem choices), whereas in the industrial field there are systems of design (for products, production, and consumption), and in political field there are systems of ideology. These systems of meaning represent another level of the semiotics of fields than habitus and skill, and they are more relevant for the particular questions addressed here.

The second departure is the autonomy assumption of fields. Fields have their own rules, and actors in a field share the sense of what is at stake. prestige in the scientific and cultural fields, profits and market share in the economic field, audience and credibility in the media field, and votes and legitimacy in the political field. Bourdieu's theoretical work on science tended to assume a fairly high level of autonomy encapsulated in his phrase "a world apart" (2001). To the extent that his analysis of science focused on the field itself, it was continuous with the work of both Merton and the constructivist studies of the 1980s and at odds with the public turn of the 1990s. However, Bourdieu was not limited completely by the autonomy assumption. As Camic (2011) noted in a special issue of *Minerva* that was dedicated to recuperating field theory in STS (Albert and Kleinman 2011), Bourdieu also recognized the importance of interfield dynamics in his writings on education. Likewise, his public intellectual writings on neoliberalism also examined the increasing influence of the field of power on the cultural fields. (See, e.g., Bourdieu 1998.) Fligstein and McAdam (2012) also provided an important contribution to the study of interfield relations by developing a systematic examination of how an event in one field can affect the opportunity structure in another field. Thus, there is a need to recognize the relative autonomy of some fields, especially the scientific field, but also to think through the dynamics of interfield relations, a topic that some of the recent work in the political sociology of science and technology has begun to address (Hess and Frickel 2014).

The third departure from Bourdieusian field theory involves field position and conflict. Fligstein and McAdam (2012) draw on SMS to emphasize the challenger-incumbent dynamic rather than Bourdieu's dominant-subordinate dynamic, and there is a need to track both sets of field tensions. Not all persons or organizations in subordinate positions are challengers, and in fact many do not harbor ambitions of subverting the established order. Scientists in subordinate positions may simply see their chosen research programs as relatively obscure and reasonably undervalued in comparison with those of the dominant actors in the field. Likewise, some firms may be happy in a niche market position such as occupying the discount or luxury end of a broader market. Conversely, incumbents can also become divided, with some of the incumbents providing challenges to the prevailing way of doing things. In some industries, especially in the technology industry, disruptive innovation often comes from large, incumbent organizations, thereby making the niche-regime relationship also distinct from the challenger-incumbent relationship. This is also true in the political field, where there are often crucial divisions within ruling coalitions and networks. So it is necessary to track various types of divisions that a flexible approach to field theory enables: subordinate-dominant field positions, challenger-incumbent field relations, and niche-regime relationships for technological systems.

In summary, although I advocate field theory as a general framework for building a theoretical synthesis of SMS and STS, my goal is to use it with some of the adjustments flagged here and to contribute to thinking that is leading it in new directions. There can be no "illusio"—that is, no belief in the game (Bourdieu 2001)—in participating in a research field where theoretical concepts are left as unmoved movers.

Contention and the Scientific Field

The concept of the scientific field will be central in the pages that follow because it focuses attention on the contentious aspects of scientific knowledge, including the politics of ignorance and undone science. Here I am expanding the meaning of the word "contentious" by focusing less on contention over policy and more on the intellectual contention that is a hallmark of modern science. Both practicing scientists and STS researchers acknowledge that making scientific knowledge is a contentious process. Scientists develop strong, sometimes even emotionally charged, intellectual commitments to their research programs, and they develop deep social loyalties to their networks of colleagues. Conversely, they also develop relations of fear, loathing, pity, and disdain for their opponents. We know from our own life experience as social scientists that the very definitions of intellectual and social positions acquire meaning in the context of distinctions among different research programs and social networks. Of course, there are areas of taken-for-granted knowledge, of "doxa," that remain unquestioned in the clashes among methods, concepts, and research priorities. But at the research front knowledge is usually contested, often heatedly. It is fair to assume that the making of scientific knowledge is contentious in the broad sense of involving interwoven relations of cooperation and competition among networks of researchers and organizations.

To recognize the contentious quality of science is also to recognize, at least implicitly, that the making of scientific knowledge takes place in social fields. Hagstrom (1965) summarized the relations precisely with the phrase "competition for recognition," but Bourdieu (1975, 2001) brought out the important idea that the scientific field is a structured social space with some actors in more dominant positions and others in more subordinate positions. He defined the relative position of individuals and organizations (and, by extension, networks) as based on the volume of types of capital, which in the case of science I generally divide into five major groups: symbolic capital (the esteem of a researcher, indicated by citations, prizes, and other rewards), social capital (the networks of allies and contacts), cultural capital (the scientist's knowledge about the specific research field and the scientific field in general), temporal capital (the organizational positions that a scientist holds), and financial capital (access to resources that can fund research, postdoctoral fellows, and students). The field perspective also draws attention to the idea that the dominant networks control the major graduate departments and research institutes, the editorial boards of the leading journals, the committees that allocate prizes and other rewards, and often sources of funding and funder priorities. Through this control of resources, the dominant networks can define good taste in a field as a sense of the "best" or "most interesting" bundles of research problems, methods, and conceptual frameworks. The word "paradigms" can be used to describe these bundles provided that it is used in the plural to recognize the conflictual and networked nature of scientific fields. The networks associated with the paradigms can also ensure that their sense of taste is passed on to a new generation of researchers who can reproduce, even as they modify, the dominant views of what counts as important.

Although the dominant networks set the agenda for the field and provide other forms of leadership, the participants in a dominant network can also become overcommitted to their research programs. They can ignore innovative ideas and insights from the B teams of the research field and can become a conservative force that defends a sclerotic paradigm. Kuhn (1970) popularized this situation with his concept of paradigm revolutions, whereby a research field undergoes a major change in methods, concepts, and agendas. These fundamental shifts are rare, but the more modest form of change—the scientific controversy—is more common. Challenges to the dominant paradigm or paradigms can come from the subordinate networks of the scientific field, or they can emerge from divisions within the dominant networks. Challenges may also first emerge from the subordinate networks before being embraced and appropriated by a segment of the dominant networks.

As noted above, researchers located in subordinate networks are not necessarily challengers. They may be in teaching colleges where their focus is on pedagogy, or they may be in industrial or government laboratories where they conduct applied or translational science. Researchers in these positions may be working on problems and with methods that are consistent with the dominant paradigms; consequently, the social position as dominant or marginalized does not necessarily predict the intellectual position as incumbent and challenger. But often the deeper, more significant challenges to standard assumptions about methods, concepts, and research problem priorities come from researchers located in subordinate positions in the research field. The B teams can undergo institutionalization by forming new research fields where they become the new A teams, or the A teams may decide that they can absorb and expand by incorporating and transforming the research of the B teams. But the A teams can also actively shun or ignore the voices of those in subordinate positions in the research field. As Collins (2000, 2004) has shown in detail for the case of gravitational waves, in some cases, such as for the persistently vocal and heterodox challengers, the dominant networks can actively marginalize them.

Although it is important to begin with an understanding of how the scientific field, even as a relatively autonomous institution, is contentious, it is also necessary to move beyond the confines of the scientific field to examine how claims about the way the world is, and therefore the limitations on what is possible and desirable, circulate through and are disputed in other social fields. As with the scientific field, the other social fields are also generally characterized by challenger-incumbent relationships. In some cases individuals, organizations, and networks in subordinate positions seek to challenge those in dominant positions; however, as in science, the actors located in subordinate positions are not always challengers, and likewise challenges to incumbents can come from other incumbents. Thus, the other social fields are characterized both by vertical contention (challenges from those in subordinate positions) and horizontal contention (challenges from those in dominant positions, such as from one leading firm against another). This point may seem technical but it will become important later in the analysis of countervailing industrial power and movements.

One way of thinking about interfield relations is to fall back on concepts of simplistic hegemony that can be traced back to Marx's chiasmus: the ruling ideas of the day are the ideas of the ruling class (Marx 1970). Sometimes there are clear homologies where an institutional version of Marx's perspective is insightful. For example, cancer researchers prefer to develop new therapies that are aligned with the standard of patented, testable drugs supported by the pharmaceutical industry, regulated by the government, and routinized in oncology practices. Those who challenge the industrial regime by advocating the less lucrative but potentially also less expensive and less toxic alternatives of high-dose nutritional supplements and changes in diet and lifestyle tend to be in a subordinate position, and they may even experience intellectual suppression (Hess 2004a).

However, one cannot assume that there is always a one-to-one mapping of dominant and subordinate positions in the scientific and industrial fields. Because the scientific field is a relatively autonomous social space, the problem of interfield relations cannot be reduced to simplistic formulations of hegemony. Most of the top scientists in the world do not take marching orders from the captains of industry and from the leaders of the government, and sometimes their research provokes opposition from powerful elite coalitions. For example, in the case of climate science, the dominant networks, in fact nearly the entire research field, have formed a strong consensus in support of the claim that anthropogenic greenhouse gases significantly contribute to global warming. They are also quite clear about the need for government and industry to take action to avoid disastrous consequences. Nevertheless, in the United States and some other countries the dominant organizations and individuals in the energy industry have supported climate science denialism and skepticism, and they have built powerful coalitions with political parties and segments of the media.

So although the sociology of scientific knowledge should begin with the relations of conflict and cooperation among scientists and networks within a research field, it also should be expanded to include interfield relations. We need to move out from the scientific field toward the relations with other social fields, the circulation of scientific knowledge, and the relations of support and opposition from other social fields. These exchanges involve mobilized publics that seek to shift the direction of the political and industrial fields to coincide with their visions of public interest, both in support of and in opposition to industrial transitions. No matter how hard scientists work to preserve political neutrality and the boundaries between the "is" of science and the "ought" of policy, their research nevertheless circulates through the other social fields, and sometimes the scientists themselves do as well. In this process of circulation the mobilized publics interpret the research, reinterpret it, and debate it.

In summary, I use a field theoretical approach, but I do so with fundamental clarifications, amendments, or modifications. They include the concept of contention among cultural systems or institutional logics, a relaxation of the autonomy assumption of the scientific field as a world apart, and attention to the lack of correspondence between the challenger-incumbent relationship and field position as dominant or subordinate. But I am also drawing attention to the analysis of the connections between the intrafield and interfield dynamics: intrafield distinctions among paradigms are in some cases linked to distinctions in other social fields among their

institutional logics such as political ideologies or design styles and to conflicts between actors in the other social fields. These ideas are fairly abstract
at this point, but they provide a general background for the analysis that
will follow.

Plan and Rationale of the Book

Although each chapter discusses examples and cases based on significant
empirical research, this is a theoretical book. My goal is to provide an overview of a way of thinking about the SMS-STS relationship that neither
translates concepts across fields nor imposes a framework from one field
on another. The strategy of presentation is to begin each chapter with a
theoretical problem in the study of science, technology, and industrial transition movements. Each chapter has a brief opening section that outlines
the theoretical and empirical problem area, a review of relevant literature
and concepts in SMS followed by a parallel review for STS, an outline of an
emergent concept that bridges the two fields, and case studies that demonstrate central aspects of the emergent concept. Rather than end the analysis
with the parallels between SMS and STS based on an inventory of existing
concepts, I suggest ways to move the conversation forward by developing
new concepts that are unique to the interdisciplinary terrain.

In developing the new concepts, I draw on the empirical work that I
have been doing, either alone or with students, and that my colleagues
have been doing. Thus, by the end of the book there is also broad coverage
of a wide range of mobilized publics with respect to science, technology,
and industrial transitions, and there is also a fairly comprehensive review
of the literature of SMS and STS. The book is based on six major topics in
the literature. In each chapter I develop a new concept or new perspective
on an existing concept based on the conversation between the two literatures and the empirical research base that has been developed: undone science and industrial transition movements, the epistemic dimension of the
political opportunity structure, the analysis of design conflicts as a material
perspective on the study of framing and meaning, the organizational forms
of counterpublic knowledge, regime resistance and processes of industrial transition, and the double movement of liberalization and epistemic
modernization.

In chapter 1, I develop the informational and epistemic aspect of the analysis of social movements and counterpublics. I begin with the SMS literature on the strategies that incumbents use to respond to challengers. I focus on how important it is for elites to control the flow of information in the media, especially coverage of repressive acts, by discussing work on backfire and its management. Some of this control involves the manipulation of information that creates ignorance, a topic that is shared with STS. I then discuss the analysis of ignorance in STS and the idea of the systematic production of nonknowledge. This analysis becomes the basis for the discussion of the concept of undone science and its relationship to industrial transition movements. I outline four basic types of industrial transition movements, the role of undone science in these movements, and the pattern of routinization or accommodation. Thus, in chapter 1 I outline the basic concepts of undone science and industrial transition movements and begin to make the case for the value of new concepts that have emerged at the intersections of STS and SMS.

In chapters 2–4, I discuss the fundamental social theory triangle of social structure, cultural meaning, and collective agency with respect to SMS, STS, and their intersection. In chapter 2, I discuss the SMS concept of the political opportunity structure, then show how researchers subsequently broadened the concept to include the industry opportunity structure for movements that target firms and industries. Next I argue that the theory of the opportunity structure can be further broadened by consideration of its epistemic dimension. This dimension has two basic features: the structure of decision-making criteria and the structure of evaluation preferences. In the case studies, I summarize the work of colleagues on genetically modified food and colony collapse disorder, and I discuss my work with students on the smart meter movement, climate denialism, and nanotechnology policy.

I open chapter 3 by discussing the concept of framing and the problem of meaning and culture in SMS. I then review some similar concepts in STS and argue for the parallels between framing in SMS and interessement and boundary objects in STS. Rather than stop with conceptual parallelism, I then suggest the value of materializing the analysis of cultural meaning via the study of design conflicts. I discuss three main types of design conflicts: those based on social structural conflicts of race, class, and gender; those based on industrial conflicts between incumbent firms and challengers; and those based on the environmental conflict between sustainability and resilience. In this chapter I use examples from my work on the greening of diesel buses, on the solar energy and organic food movements, and on tradeoffs between resilience and sustainability at the household and regional levels.

In chapter 4, I examine organizational perspectives in both SMS and STS, then discuss the need for an organizational approach to the construction and dissemination of counterpublic knowledge. I review work on four main types of organizational forms of this knowledge: scientific and intellectual movements, scientist-founded organizations for advocacy and activism, citizen-science alliances, and citizen science. I then discuss the relations among these different types of mobilizations associated with counterpublic knowledge. I summarize a wide range of research projects by people working at the intersections of SMS and STS, including a project of mine on civil society research by environmental organizations.

In chapter 5, I focus on the processes of industrial change that involve industrial transition movements. I build on two literatures, one from institutional theory and the other from transition studies, to develop an analysis of power and regime resistance. I argue that the next step in the literature should be to study how industrial transition coalitions can maneuver effectively when the regime organizations have closed down the opportunity structure for policy reform. I suggest three strategies based on research that I have completed with students and a postdoctoral fellow on the politics of energy policy reform in the United States: countervailing power, ideological judo, and dual-use design.

In chapter 6, I discuss the problem of developing a historical sociological perspective on science, technology, and social movements. I suggest that, because the literature on new social movements situates the historical sociology of social movements based on a type of movement rather than on historical processes of change, it is not helpful. Instead, I suggest that there is a need to focus on liberalization and reflexive modernization, which together form a dynamic similar to Polanyi's (1944) double movement. I then argue that there is a more specific dynamic of the liberalization of regulation and the epistemic modernization of policy and knowledge production. I analyze the dynamic in a case history that draws on my research on the movement for complementary and alternative cancer treatment.

Although my goal is to develop theory, the analysis uses many case studies drawn from my own research and that of colleagues. Most of my research has taken place in the United States, and likewise the networks of people who work in STS and SMS are mainly based in North America and secondarily in Europe. As in much of the broader STS and SMS literature, the preponderance of empirical research takes place in these two areas. I have looked for opportunities to discuss research based in other regions, and I have discussed such projects where relevant to the broad theoretical argument of each chapter. Developing a global perspective on undone science and industrial transition movements remains a challenge for future research.

1 Repression, Ignorance, and Undone Science

The politics of contentious knowledge is, at its core, a two-way interaction between official publics and counterpublics. But this interaction is mediated by the third face of the public, general public opinion, which affects how both incumbents and challengers work to change the structure of opportunities, to make their action meaningful, and to build organizations and coalitions. Activists and advocates strive to convince others to embrace their definitions of a situation and their prescriptions for action, and their task of persuasion entails getting the information out to them and making the information credible. This chapter will develop the informational and epistemic dimension of the relationship between STS and SMS with respect to the issue of mobilized publics, and it will develop a typology of industrial transition movements anchored in this dimension.

Repression, Cooptation, and Information in SMS

Social movements that utilize protest and other extra-institutional repertoires of action arise because the standard channels of action have not worked. If the incumbents view the proposals of challengers as at least partially legitimate, they may engage the challengers and work out changes through institutionalized channels. However, sometimes the proposals for change are incompatible with the direction of action that the incumbents wish to pursue, and the incumbents develop strategies for rebuffing the challenges. Often the first strategy is to ignore the proposals for change; if that strategy does not work, incumbents can shift to repression and cooptation. Repression can include using the police and the military to limit protest events, but it can also involve control over the flow of information and the public perception of the challengers' credibility. The informational dimension is the site in the repression literature where the bridge to STS can be built.

There is ample evidence in the SMS literature to suggest that repressive tactics can be effective. Repression can dampen protest (Olzak et al. 2003), and it can drive the more radical wings of a movement underground (Zwerman et al. 2000). Conversely, periods of time when there is an absence of repression are associated with long protest waves (Della Porta 1995). However, the use of repression creates complicated dynamics that in some situations may weaken the movements and in other situations strengthen them (Earle 2011). If the public perceives the repression to be illegitimate, then the movement may be able to recruit supporters more easily (Opp and Roehl 1990). Violent repression of a peaceful movement is especially likely to lead to public outrage, which in turn may generate more mobilization, whereas institutionalized responses based more on cooptation may weaken mobilization (Barkan 1984; Koopmans 1997). Thus, repression is arguably most effective when it is combined with a strategy of cooptation of movement moderates that accommodates some of their demands (Koopmans 1993; Titarenko et al. 2001; White 1999). For example, in some cases the government recognizes the moderates and brings them into the political process, which the moderates view as a victory but the radical flanks view as cooptation. Thus, movements themselves change as they gain some concessions from incumbents (Amenta et al. 2010; Jaffee 2012; Zald and Ash 1966).

Because incumbents may lose legitimacy if they ignore or repress the demands of mobilized groups, they pay attention to the media and to public opinion. The media tend to be more sympathetic to protesters who have a rights-based or instrumental agenda in contrast with a countercultural one. When the media spotlight is on the repression, the authorities may reduce their reliance on the strategy (Wisler and Giugni 1999). When there is media attention to the repression of a movement, it is easier for activists to gain support from the moral shock or backfire against the government (Jasper 1997, 1998; Jasper and Poulsen 1995). Thus, public opinion in the form of backfire is an important element in the three-way interaction of incumbents, challengers, and public opinion. Martin (2007) argued that two conditions must be met in order for backfire to exist. First, the public must perceive that the repression is unjust, a situation that occurs when the protest is nonviolent, the repression is violent or excessive, and the claims of the protesters are perceived to be just. Second, there must be effective communication of the repressive events to the public, and the size of the public that is reached by the communication and outraged by it must be substantial enough to trigger a response from the authorities.

Authorities will attempt to manage the informational flow of backfire with diverse strategies, a process that Martin calls the "dynamics of backfire" (Martin 2007; Hess and Martin 2006). One strategy is to cover up the situation and to attempt to control the media coverage. Another strategy is make statements in the media that stigmatize the protesters and their leaders in order to make the repression appear to be legitimate and in the broad public interest. Incumbents can also produce disinformation campaigns to discredit the movement and to manage public perceptions about the legitimacy of repression (Marx 1979). Authorities sometimes also reinterpret the repressive event and present it as self-defense or as legitimate law enforcement, and they may set up formal inquiries or commissions to investigate possible wrong-doing. The latter strategy tends to defuse public anger directed at excessive repression by focusing blame on a few police or military actors who are deemed to have used excessive force. Finally, authorities sometimes intimidate and bribe witnesses.

Thus, through the analysis of backfire, the SMS literature points to the important role of information. Incumbents manage the events of movement mobilization and repression by downplaying them or by spinning them in various ways. In turn, the constructions affect the ability of challengers and incumbents to mobilize public opinion to their side. Of the different types of information, scientific information can be important especially in the case of industrial transition movements. Thus, there is some potential to build a bridge to the STS literature.

Publics and Ignorance in STS

As indicated in the previous section, incumbents have an interest in ensuring that media reporting of their repressive tactics is both minimized and sympathetic. An ideal condition for incumbents occurs when there is little reporting of repressive tactics, and if there is reporting, the protesters are portrayed as threats to the society. Likewise, incumbents benefit when there is more reporting of accommodation tactics, and the portrayal shows that the incumbents are attempting to compromise with the challengers.

However, gaining favorable reporting of accommodation tactics may not be easy to achieve, and doing so may require manipulation of the media or, if the government is authoritarian, the silencing of portions of the media. If the goals are achieved, then the lay opinion public may be consuming a diet of incorrect facts and half-truths about the strategies of incumbents and those of the social movements. Under this circumstance we can say that there has been an active production of ignorance.

Although there is a long line of studies of ignorance, there is as yet no systematic theory about it in an information society, and only recently has research on ignorance begun to emerge in systematic form as a research field. (See, e.g., Gross and McGoey 2015.) A central distinction in this literature is between knowable and unknowable unknowns. The former can be subjected to the methodologies of risk assessment, cost–benefit analysis, scenario planning, and constructive technology assessment. Moreover, they can be politicized as worthy or unworthy of research funding. In contrast, the unknowable unknowns are made known only in retrospect, after a surprise (Gross 2010). These surprises often take the form of public health and environmental crises that emerge when a substance that was previously assumed to be safe turns out to be dangerous.

Most of the research on scientific ignorance does not address the issue of mobilized publics, but there are a few projects that point to some convergences. One example is the role that mobilized counterpublics play in identifying undone science and the countervailing role that official publics play in repressing the production of such knowledge and its dissemination in the media. For example, environmentalists wish to have more research on the risks of new nanomaterials and genetically modified foods, whereas chemical companies generally think such future knowledge is quite undesirable. Despite this difference in perspectives, both sides have specified a knowable unknown, and they agree that more research is possible. They disagree on how valuable it is to address this knowable unknown, and they may also disagree on the likelihood that unwanted surprises—unknown unknowns—may await future knowledge.

Some of the research has begun to explain the factors that lead to the generation of ignorance regarding scientific research. Frickel (2014) demonstrated that one general process is "knowledge sequestration," in which existing knowledge is prevented from circulating. A body of research on intellectual suppression has shown how government and industrial organizations have sometimes acted to stop the flow of information in the media and in research (Delborne 2008; Martin et al. 1986; Martin 1996; Stocking and Holstein 2015). This work became the basis for Martin's subsequent, broader analysis of the dynamics of backfire and the strategies by which people and organizations can overcome repression (Martin 2007). Frickel (2014) also pointed out that knowledge sequestration can be caused by less overtly political practices such as poor methods and lack of storage of data.

Kempner (2015) and Kempner et al. (2005) argued that another mechanism for the production of ignorance is a collective policy decision not to undertake certain kinds of research. Rather than sequester existing knowledge, funders of research decide not to pursue a possible research field that could answer questions of knowable unknowns. In some of the cases that Kempner discussed, mobilized counterpublics have led to decisions to prohibit future research. For example, some kinds of research involving animal and human subjects are no longer permissible, as are some types of research using human stem cells and cloning technologies. In addition to funders' decisions to block research, scientists themselves may boycott certain types of research, such as work on weapons and armaments (Moore 2008). Motivations for banning or boycotting research can come from civil society organizations, such as religious groups and advocates of animal rights, but they can also come from an industry that wants to have a type of research banned or reduced, such as work on greenhouse gases or on the health effects of microwave radiation from mobile devices. In some cases research is not explicitly banned, but scientists learn informally that others who have undertaken the research have lost funding or experienced other kinds of suppression.

Another mechanism for the production ignorance emerges from regulatory practice of extrapolation (Frickel 2014). This approach may appear to be politically neutral, but it can result from political priorities that underfund regulatory review processes. For example, the US Environmental Protection Agency's analyses of soil contamination after Hurricane Katrina identified 141 contaminants in flood sediment and soil. However, Frickel and Edwards (2014) found that for 70 percent of the chemicals the regulatory scientists calculated risk standards through extrapolation. Regulators would argue that the strategy was necessary because there is no government funding to provide for additional regulatory research, but the absence of documentation and research on risk is favorable to industry. A similar situation occurs with respect to nanotechnology, where chemicals at the nanoscale are presumed safe if they have a similar structure to existing chemicals (Hess 2010a; Lamprou 2010). Frickel noted that "risk standards generated from extrapolated carcinogenicity values—rendered as numerical values indicating lifetime cancer risk—become indistinguishable from risk standards that are generated from actual studies" (2014: 271). "This," he continued, "is one way that ignorance is simultaneously produced, hidden from view, and institutionalized as meaningful regulatory science."

Kinchy (2014) describes a fourth mechanism for generating ignorance, which is based on the effects of shifts in scale. She notes that at a broad national or global level the switch from coal to natural gas is viewed positively because it is a cleaner and more efficient fuel source, and she showed that some of the leading environmental organizations at first supported natural gas as a necessary bridge to a low-carbon future. However, at the local level movements against hydraulic fracturing technologies emerged because of the local knowledge about the harmful effects of extraction. Thus, there is a gap between the local scale, where effects can be known and knowledge can circulate in a community, and larger scales where political decisions are made. Landowners who have faced contamination of their water wells sometimes find it difficult to prove the relationship between local contamination and hydraulic fracturing, partly because there is no systematic collection of water quality data from the state government. Sometimes the landowners achieve settlements that are also accompanied by gag orders. Industry and regulators tend to treat the incidents of contamination as isolated, and there is a failure to build up a database of groundwater quality and contamination. Thus, there is a scale effect where local knowledge is not aggregated and systematized for use at higher geographic levels, where policy is produced. Frickel and Kinchy (2015) also noted that the scale effects can go both ways because data aggregation at too large a scale, such as tumor registries, can also mask local effects. (See also Allen 2005.)

In summary, the literature on scientific ignorance has identified various mechanisms by which ignorance is produced—the sequestration of knowledge, including through intellectual suppression; decisions not to pursue certain types of knowledge because of ethical questions that in some cases are linked to counterpublic mobilizations; extrapolation from existing data sets instead of new investigations, which is linked to the politics of funding priorities; and the mismatch between the scale at which knowledge is produced and the scale at which regulatory policy is made. This approach to knowledge takes us some distance from the more obvious forms of information control that occur when a government denies a repressive event, puts pressure on the media to avoid coverage of the event, and portrays activists in a negative light. It also takes us some distance from the vague idea of hegemony associated with the "breathing together" (etymologically the root of the word "con-spire") of a unified elite that dominates public opinion via the media, science, and religion.

Undone Science and Industrial Transition Movements

Bringing these two literatures into conversation requires thinking about the relationship between the control of social movements and the social production of scientific ignorance. The topic is potentially quite extensive, and in this chapter I focus on one possible bridge that links the study of one type of movement, industrial transition movements, and on one category of ignorance, undone science.

When counterpublics attempt to represent a broad public interest that they view as different from the formulations of official public interest that industrial and political elites project in the media and in the political field, the activists and advocates often run into a situation of absent knowledge. They find that if only they had more research about a specific issue, then they would be able to better justify their claims about the risks, dangers, and uncertainties of existing or new technologies and the benefits of pursuing an alternative course. New research might even discover surprises or unknown unknowns. Often the challengers find that industrial incumbents and their allies in the political field can cite studies that justify a claim of little or no risk. Likewise, the incumbents can also argue that there is not enough research to justify a regulatory intervention or the development of alternative products and production processes. Thus, undone science is not only about absent knowledge; it is also about a structured absence that emerges from relations of inequality that are reflected in the priorities for what kinds of research should be funded. It is about the contours of what funders target as important and unimportant areas of research.

The idea of undone science is continuous with the central focus of STS on the social construction of knowledge, but it shifts the level of analysis from the microsocial level of laboratories and networks to that of research fields and public debates over funding priorities. The two levels of analysis are complementary and can be brought together, but it is important to recognize that there is a field-level dimension of the construction of knowledge that involves the contours of done and undone science. The analysis of undone science is also perspectival; there are conflicts between incumbents and challengers in various social fields over the benefits of getting undone science done.

Research on undone science suggests important nuances beyond the first-level binary opposition between counterpublics and official publics (Frickel et al. 2010). First, the identification of undone science does not necessarily mean that it is "doable," at least within a time frame that is policy relevant. Howard makes this point with respect to the complex interactions of industrial chemicals and physiological processes that can make the assessment of chemical risk to organisms and ecosystems an extremely complicated, long-term affair (ibid.). Second, social movements that oppose a particular research method or industrial process can create undone science by arguing that we should defund a particular type of research, such as research involving animals or nuclear weapons (Kempner 2015; Moore 2008). More broadly, if funding is allocated to address concerns of undone science, then the allocation is a reallocation because of the constraint of limited resources. Third, there are divisions among counterpublics about what kinds of undone science are desirable and most worthy of immediate attention. Because movements often span a spectrum from radical flanks to insider reformers, and because countermovements sometimes arise in response to movements, the counterpublic definitions of undone science also can be at odds with each other.

Although the analysis of undone science draws attention to the understudied epistemic dimension of all social movements, the importance of this dimension varies by type of movement. A revolutionary pro-democracy movement may seek documentation of repression and corruption, and it may point to how the media systematically ignore these issues, but scientific research is likely to be less relevant than in a movement that is attempting to change an industrial technology. For the industrial transition movements, the problem of undone science is crucial because there are close connections between science and the evaluation of technologies and their innovation.

I divide industrial transition movements into four main types, which are associated with different goals, repertoires of action, definitions of undone science, and routinization patterns. This typology utilizes two dimensions or "axes of change" that are central in industrial transition movements (Hess 2007a: 239). On the one hand, industrial transition movements have the goal of changing the fundamental design of technologies. This material dimension of social change forms a continuum between two ideal types: the goal of sunsetting for existing, unwanted technologies (e.g., fossil fuels) and the goal of sunrising for the new, desired technologies (e.g., low-carbon energy sources). On the other hand, industrial transition movements can aim to transform the organizational and distributional dimensions of industrial systems. Although everything is in some way "social," one can think of this second dimension as the social dimension of the industrial transition movements. Again these goals form a continuum between two ideal types: the oppositional goal of ending the lack of access (sunsetting) of the poor to basic products associated with human rights and dignity (gaining access to clean air and water, affordable housing, clothing, and health care) and the pro-alternative goal of developing (sunrising) new organizational forms (e.g., B corporations, worker ownership, public ownership) and of reinvigorating old ones (e.g., locally owned, independent businesses). Using this two-way distinction, we can divide industrial transition movements into four main ideal types, with the understanding that many movements may involve a mixture of the types: alternative industrial movements, industrial opposition movements, industrial restructuring movements, and industrial access movements. (See table 1.1).

This typological approach to industrial transition movements has several advantages. First, it elucidates the focus of disciplines on different aspects of industrial transition movements. For example, sociologists tend to find the industrial opposition movements and access movements to be of greatest interest because of their continuity with the discipline's historical focus on protest movements and on poverty, whereas management scholars are more interested in the alternative industrial and industrial restructuring movements because they involve innovations in industry and business organizations. Second, the typology makes it possible to hypothesize patterns of mobilization, undone science, and outcomes that are specific to the type. These patterns can then guide empirical research and comparison.

Table 1.1
An overview of industrial transition movement types and associated undone science.

	Alternative industrial movement	Industrial opposition movements	Industrial restructuring movements	Industrial access movements
Type	Material sunrising	Material sunsetting	Social sunrising	Social sunsetting
Definition of undone science	Research on alternative technologies	Research on risk, uncertainties, hazards	Research on alternative organizational forms	Research on inequalities of access and remedies
Routinization pattern	Complementarization: redesign of alternatives to fit with regime	Partial moratorium on selected technologies, redesign of others	Incorporation of some elements but regime continuity	Transformation of activism into service provisioning organizations
	Examples (supporting)	**Examples (opposing)**	**Examples (supporting)**	**Example (opposing)**
Built environment	Green buildings, smart growth, new urbanism	Sprawl, local development projects	Cohousing, intentional communities	Lack of affordable housing
Energy	Renewable, low-carbon, efficiency	Nuclear, coal	Local public ownership, home power	High energy costs (support for low-income energy)

Table 1.1 (continued)

	Examples (supporting)	Examples (opposing)	Examples (supporting)	Example (opposing)
Finance	Socially and environmentally responsible investment	Financial fraud, industrial concentration	Credit unions, local currency, buy local, financial reform	Lack of access to loans (support for microfinance)
Information	Open-source, open access	Privacy, media concentration	Community media	Lack of low-income digital access
Food	Organic, slow food, vegan	Confined animal feeding, genetically modified food, pesticides	Localism, fair trade, cooperatives, community gardens	Hunger (supporting food banks, etc.)
Health	Complementary-alternative	Risks from medical technologies and practices	Community medicine, single-payer insurance	Lack of health care, lack of research on some diseases
Transport	Public transit, alternative fuel	Highway construction	Ride sharing, vehicle sharing	Inequalities of transit spending
Waste and manufacturing	Recycling, zero waste, reuse sector	Environmental damage from industrial pollution	Industrial ecology, eco-parks	Environmental injustice

The remainder of this section will chart out some of these patterns, drawing on my comparative work on the four types of industrial transition movements (Hess 2005, 2007a, 2009a). Each section will characterize the type, discuss the form of undone science associated with the type, and then suggest the pattern of routinization or outcome.

Alternative Industrial Movements

Alternative industrial movements can be divided into two main types. Technology-oriented and product-oriented movements aim to develop new technologies, and as a type they tend to be located in networks of small, entrepreneurial businesses that occupy a potentially disruptive niche in a broader industry. Examples include movements for sustainable, local food; rooftop solar and other forms of off-grid or distributed energy; alternative medicine for chronic diseases such as cancer; nonprofit recycling and reuse centers tied to community justice issues; open-source software; and community media. Much of the work in less developed countries that emerged from the appropriate technology movement can be classified under this rubric as well. (See, e.g., Smith et al. 2014.) Although the primary organizational form of these movements is the network of small business and nonprofit enterprises, it can also include household voluntary activity and research in independent institutes, universities, firms, and government settings. In general, these movements develop "grassroots innovation" and often have links to other kinds of community-building activities (Seyfang and Smith 2007, Smith et al. 2016).

The other subtype is the certification movement. The technology-oriented and product-oriented movements can also engage in certification activity, such as the development of organic food labeling, but in general the certification movements emerge from a different set of organizations, such as global justice and labor organizations. The certification movements encourage consumers to shift their spending to products that meet specified third-party environmental or labor standards, and they put pressure on global corporations to establish and implement social and environmental responsibility goals. In some cases the movements also aim to have consumers shift their purchasing to specific types of producers, such as women or rural cooperatives (Jaffee 2012).

Undone science in these movements entails the absence of support for new research fields linked to the alternative technologies and products.

Scientists may undertake research in these areas as a side project in larger portfolios, and some may leave research to become entrepreneurs. Advocates may also convince governments and foundations to support university-based research centers that become the core of new research fields such as sustainable agriculture research and solar energy research. In either case, the level of epistemic conflict with mainstream industrial science is lower than for the industrial opposition movements because the scientists are merely diversifying their research portfolios and following new opportunities. However, as the alternative research fields grow, scientists in the new fields can join with advocates and the niche industry firms to seek changes in the funding agenda for the broader field. For example, they seek changes in the agricultural research agenda to have more funding devoted to organic food and to small-scale sustainable agriculture, and they seek to gain more funding for nutritional and other complementary and alternative approaches to the treatment of chronic disease. As will be discussed for the case of complementary and alternative medicine (CAM), these efforts to build new research fields can become controversial and can trigger suppressive actions from the mainstream of the research field and from the industrial regime firms with which it is associated.

The intended outcome of the alternative industrial movements is the transformation of the industrial regime, but in the cases that I studied the more common outcome is incorporation and transformation (2007a). The incumbent organizations tend to accept elements of the innovations from the alternative industrial movements, and they blend the innovations into the industrial regime. This incorporation or absorption process can occur by developing new product lines that compete with those of the smaller companies, by purchasing the entrepreneurial companies, and by creating divisions within the incumbent organizations that support niche development. Often there is also a transformation of the design of the alternative products that makes them less alternative and more complementary to the technologies and products of the industrial regime. For example, CAM therapies in the United States have been integrated into some oncology practices and some of the large cancer hospitals but only as adjuvant or complementary therapies. A similar process has occurred with the solar industry, where in the US the utilities have to date incorporated the niche by creating centralized solar farms and distributed solar energy, both of which are a long way from the original visions of reformers to have off-grid power with on-site generation and storage. Thus, there are two processes in the routinization of the technology-oriented and product-oriented movements: incorporation of the products and companies into the industrial regime, and transformation of the design so that the alternatives are made complementary to the existing technological regime.

In the certification movements, the routinization pattern entails some acceptance of the new standard accompanied by attempts to weaken it. Incumbents may accept third-party certification and change their production processes and product lines, but they may also weaken the criteria of the original schemes. For example, the agro-food industry has made continual attempts to weaken the organic food standard in the United States. The national standard was focused only on technical issues and separated from the community and small-business orientation of many of the original advocates (Obach 2015). Thus, the term "organic" has itself become contentious, and some prefer other designations such as "sustainable, local food movement" to signal an approach that includes small farmers and networks of consumers and producers. Likewise, as Jaffee (2012) showed in an analysis of the fair trade movement, the proliferation of labels and divisions among the original networks of advocates weakened standards to the point that plantation agriculture has now been accepted under the fair trade label. In some cases industries also set up their own certification schemes that appear to have similar levels of assurance found in the original third-party schemes. The second-party certification labels can generate confusion in the marketplace by making it difficult for consumers to distinguish among "ethical" products.

Industrial Opposition Movements

Industrial opposition movements are the closest category to traditional protest-based social movements and thus present the strongest overlap with SMS. These movements often seek policy changes from the state, such as a new regulatory regime, but they may also target firms and consumers directly (King and Soule 2007). They seek fundamental changes in an industrial technology, industrial processes, or both. They are the "anti-" movements, such as those opposing nuclear energy, mountaintop removal of coal, and genetically modified food. When the movements engage in protest events, they can face government repression and the management of backfire as described above.

Undone science is defined for this type of movement as the need for more research on risk, safety, and uncertainty. Activists and advocates seek more knowledge to justify their claims that an industrial process or technology is harmful or risky and that more regulation, significant design changes, or even a complete moratorium is appropriate. The movements can generate intense epistemic conflict because their interpretations of risk differ from those of industrial scientists, and the movements also advocate investing in more research on risk, safety, and broader public implications. The scientists who document risks can find their work attacked by industry-funded scientists, and intellectual suppression can become intense, especially if only a few scientists are documenting risk. Communities that are exposed to toxic assault can also generate their own research either by themselves or in partnerships with scientists (Brown 2007; Ottinger 2010).

A second-order conflict emerges in the industrial opposition movements over the relationship between undone science and policy action. In the absence of proof of risk beyond reasonable doubt, the movements prefer a precautionary approach to scientific uncertainty and controversy, and their goal is to limit the technology until more information is available. The industrial opposition movements tend to generate political proposals anchored in the idea of a technology moratorium. The moratorium can be complete (such as to end all nuclear energy) or partial (to end only a class of chemicals or regulations in order to make an industrial product or process safer). Movements can also become divided between a radical flank that seeks a full moratorium until extensive undone science demands are met and a moderate wing that advocates a moratorium on some dimensions of the technology with a plan for regulatory review and approval.

In contrast, industry (or in some cases a segment of the government such as the military) often argues that risk is not demonstrated and that the public will be harmed by not having access to potentially beneficial technologies and products. Industry may also fund scientists who attack the evidence that movements publicize in the media. In response, movements argue that the lack of demonstration of harm is due to lack of political will to support the research—that is, to undone science—and they point to the industrial ties of contrarian scientists. The regulating agency must then balance the different perspectives and approaches to precaution and policy, but regulators are often heavily influenced by industrial lobbying and other forms of pressure. When regulators side with industry, the movements may view their decisions as tainted by the influence of industry and the failure to act in the public benefit.

In the routinization or outcome phase, the government may split the difference between movements and industry by enacting a partial moratorium. Where industry pressure for stasis is strong, there is often a weak or moderate regulatory response, such as the labeling of genetically modified food or the restriction of a small class of nanomaterials. Industry may also respond directly by developing new designs that enable it to keep the products on the market but also to address some of the concerns of the movements, such as by excluding known human allergens from genetically modified food. The government may provide funding for additional research on risk. These changes may coincide with divisions within the movement, where the radical flanks become marginalized.

Industrial Restructuring Movements

The third type of industrial transition movement involves the effort to create new organizational forms for industry. In practice this type often overlaps with the alternative industrial movements, but the epistemic politics and routinization patterns are different. The most radical form is based on the goal of government ownership of the means of production, that is, the socialization of ownership decisions and profits. There are still significant movements involving public ownership and opposition to privatization, and in some cases, such as conflicts over water privatization, these are protest-based movements (Perrault 2006; Robinson 2013). However, the trend in most countries since the 1980s has been against public ownership and in favor of privatization, and the industrial restructuring movements in developed capitalist societies tend to have more modest and reformist goals than the nationalization of whole industries. Thus, these movements often experiment with alternative organizational forms such as cooperatives, B corporations, social enterprises, socially responsible small family businesses, and employee ownership (Schneiberg et al. 2008; Williamson et al. 2002). Often the movements have a localist component that emphasizes community control and local ownership of business enterprises (Hess 2009a). The localist component can also include municipalization, such as attempts to bring about community ownership of investor-owned utilities (ibid.). Although the industrial restructuring movements can involve protest, they tend to be reform movements that seek a better organizational basis for the economy by utilizing institutionalized channels of action.

The level of epistemic conflict in these movements tends to be lower than in the first two types, and the call for undone science is less urgent. The relevant research fields are in the social sciences that are willing to study issues involving alternative ownership patterns for modern economies. Because these topics are not of great interest in the higher status disciplines of economics and political science, the researchers who study such topics tend to be in the lower-status fields of sociology and anthropology, or they may even be located in independent institutes and think tanks. Researchers in these lower-status positions who study topics such as employee ownership or agrarian cooperatives are not necessarily marginalized, but there has also been a decline of Marxist and socialist scholars at many research universities. In the case of STS in the United States, I have shown that researchers who study class, labor, and industry tend to be located in the lower-status universities and in the subfield of the history of technology (Hess 2011a).

These movements do not tend to produce profound social change, at least along the lines originally envisioned by advocates and activists. They may have a radical vision of a postcapitalist global society, in which production for profit is replaced by production for purpose. The proposed alternative economic order can be based on public ownership or on nonprofit organizations (a "civil society society"), and it can represent a fundamental modification of the modern industrial economy. However, there is little evidence that developed capitalist economies are going to convert to any of the alternative forms of industrial organization described above. Likewise, former communist countries have organized industry along lines that are commonly described as state capitalism.

Instead of achieving a profound reorganization of the ownership of production, the routinization process tends to involve shifts by which the large, publicly traded corporation has incorporated some of the elements of these reforms. For example, employee stock ownership programs, rather than employee ownership, have become more common. Corporations have also embraced social and environmental responsibility guidelines even as they pursue their mandate to provide good returns to shareholders. In the case of efforts to municipalize electricity in the United States, we found that new institutions emerged that were somewhere between municipal ownership and the investor-owned utility corporation (Hess 2009a). Community choice aggregation allows a city or other local political unit to aggregate its customers and to negotiate collectively with the utility. It allows enhanced community control over the electricity mix and the pricing, but it does not challenge the central role for the investor-owned utility in the way that municipalization movements do. Thus, other than the increasingly rare phenomenon of a socialist revolution and some cases of the return to public ownership after privatization failures or during an economic crisis, at present the industrial restructuring movements create an effervescence of organizational innovation at the grassroots, but they suffer from transition stasis.

Industrial Access Movements
These movements focus on the distributional issue of gaining greater access to industrial goods for the poor, and as such they are continuous with the universalizing movements in that they focus largely on the question of human rights. They can be classified by specific types of material goods that are defined as part of the bundle of rights. In the health field, these movements can include patient organizations that seek access to better therapeutic options for a disease constituency. (See, e.g., Epstein 1996; Klawiter 2008.) Mobilizations can take the form of protest movements when the situation is especially dire, but the movements also include charitable activities aimed at providing food, clothing, shelter, health care, transit, and clean air and water to the less fortunate. Thus, we can think of food banks, efforts to gain support for affordable housing, the growth of community development organizations, bus riders' unions, information technology provisioning for the poor, and other types of grassroots redistributional activities as a type of industrial transition movement. They aim to transform the patterns of access and distribution in the industrial system rather than the design of technologies themselves; however, as questions of the appropriateness of the technologies emerge, especially in less developed countries, the movements can include design innovation as well.

Again, the level of epistemic conflict is lower than in the industrial opposition movements, but there is conflict over the policy because neoliberal politicians frame the goals of these movements as giving handouts to the poor. Access movements can also overlap with the alternative industrial movements through syntheses such as community gardens and low-income farmers' markets; green affordable housing; the greening of public transit; and the development of low-cost, unpatented, nutritional therapies (Hess 2009a). But as an ideal type the access movement is concerned first with solving problems of unequal distribution rather than with addressing, for example, environmental and sustainability issues. As for the industrial restructuring movements, the undone science is also an undone social science, and again it appears in the lower-status social science fields, especially sociology, which has made poverty and its amelioration a central topic of inquiry. Likewise, anthropologists often draw attention to issues of poverty and access among rural and indigenous communities. These are higher-status topics in the lower-status fields.

The outcome of these movements can involve a positive response from the elites. Governments offer various anti-poverty programs, and business and civil society contribute to charitable programs for the lower-income segments of society. The responses from the government occur especially if the movements follow the strategy of engaging in tactics that are disruptive and sustained enough to overcome repression and to gain some accommodation (Piven and Cloward 1978). One of the responses has been to develop public-private partnerships for service delivery that also involve the recruitment of civil society organizations as vehicles of delivery. This opportunity may transform organizations and individuals from their radical roots of demanding resources toward service provisioning with government and private-sector support. I showed that this pattern can be found in a range of the access movements, especially in the hunger movement and in the urban housing movement (Hess 2007a). In the case of patient advocacy movements, in some cases the more radical organizations, which combined a demand for access to therapies with a call for more research on alternative and complementary medicine, have been marginalized in favor of organizations that are more closely linked to the pharmaceutical industry (Batt 2015; O'Donovan and Glavanis-Granthan 2005).

Conclusion

I use the concepts of undone science, epistemic conflict, and routinization pattern to develop an analysis of how industrial transition movements link the politics of knowledge to that of industrial change. This approach to social movements is continuous with the trend in SMS to think of mobilizations broadly, and in this chapter I have suggested that entrepreneurialism and charitable activities can be included as part of these mobilized counter-publics. I have also argued that by breaking down the industrial transition movements into four types, it becomes possible to examine the routinization patterns of each. Consistent with general knowledge in SMS, industrial regimes respond in a double manner that can involve rejection, repression, and suppression but that also can involve accommodation, redesign, and incorporation.

This introductory analysis provides one example of how the integration of SMS and STS might occur in a way that goes beyond the syncretism of concepts from both fields and beyond the application of concepts from one field to problems in another. Instead, a new conceptual framework draws on the insights of both fields but takes those insights in new directions that can make it possible to identify new categories of actors and new processes. This chapter has focused on the process of routinization in the Weberian tradition, and it does not look at the question of why and how the movements mobilize. Likewise, the chapter does not develop a theory of the conditions for successful and failed outcomes, that is, the problem of why some types of movements flourish and have broader effects than other types. To address that question we need to turn to the factors of social structure, meaning, and agency that will be discussed in chapters 2–4.

Although it is helpful to have an understanding of the industrial restructuring and access movements, in this book I focus on the material type of the industrial transition movements, that is, the industrial opposition and the alternative industrial types. Undone science is more salient in these movements, whereas in the "social" types of industrial transition movements the focus is less on epistemic conflict than on moral and justice issues that are woven into efforts to transform organizations, property relations, and the distribution of goods. It would be interesting to investigate in more detail the epistemic dimensions of the industrial restructuring and access movements, but that research problem will remain outside the scope of the present analysis. With the current body of completed research, the alternative industrial and industrial opposition movements—which are often intertwined biographically, strategically, and organizationally—provide better material with which to think through the relations between STS and SMS.

2 The Epistemic Dimension of the Political Opportunity Structure

As for SMS in general, one of the central theoretical problems for the analysis of industrial transition movements is to develop an explanatory framework for the conditions under which they emerge, fade away, and achieve effects. The social sciences have developed convergent general theory that draws on the triangle of structure, meaning, and agency. To paraphrase Marx (1970), men and women make history, but they do not make it the way that they originally planned or intended. This is because their historical agency is suspended in social structures and institutional structures. Furthermore, as Weber (1978) emphasized, both agency and structure are refracted through systems of meaning that enable actors to interpret their situation and to develop strategies for acting within it and for changing it. Thus, this chapter and the next two form a group that discusses structure, meaning, and agency with respect to industrial transition movements. This chapter focuses on developing the concept of the opportunity structure as a bridge across SMS and STS from the perspective of structure.

Opportunity Structures in SMS

Because the phrase "political opportunity structure" is notoriously slippery, it is important to give it as much precision as possible before moving on to other types of opportunity structure. The political opportunity structure refers not only to the enduring dimensions of government organizational forms and processes but also to the ephemeral positions of actors and their coalitions in the political field. As Tarrow (2011: 27) explained, the concept emerged as part of a broader critique of Marxist views of worker mobilization that focused on organizational leadership such as the revolutionary vanguard. Of course, Marxists were well aware of structural inequality such as class conflict as an explanatory factor for both movement mobilization and movement outcomes, but they tended to focus on social structure rather than on the institutional structure of the political field.

In SMS today, structural explanation that relies on some form of the concept of political opportunity structure is usually embedded in a more comprehensive framework that recognizes the role of meaning and agency as other approaches to explanation. This comprehensive framework has been in existence since McAdam's (1982) formulation of the political process approach and the joint use of the concepts of political opportunities, cultural framings, and mobilizing structures (McAdam, McCarthy, and Zald 1996). In this triangle of factors, opportunity structures and organizational strategies and structures are built and challenged within systems of meaning. As McAdam, Tarrow, and Tilly note, because opportunities and threats are "subject to attribution" (2001: 43), strategies that seek to change not only political outcomes but also government institutions are mediated by perceptions of those changes and by appropriate framing. Actors must make the goals actionable by showing how the goals resonate with the systems of meaning of existing organizations, potential coalition partners, and potential recruits. Thus, changes in political opportunities do not in themselves explain movement mobilization. Making that assumption would mean falling back into the mechanistic theorization of the prior generation of social movement theories (McAdam, McCarthy, and Zald 1996: 8).

The political process approach is broadly consistent with what later became the contentious politics framework, which examines the interaction of opportunity and threat, framing processes, mobilizing structures, and repertoires of contention (McAdam, Tarrow, and Tilly 2001). The contentious politics framework does not attempt to provide a unified explanation of all social movements in the vein of economic models. Rather, it provides a series of typological categories and sequences that can be used to guide empirical research. The approach balances structure, meaning, and agency, and it has some overlaps with one form of field theory (Fligstein and McAdam 2012).

Some SMS researchers have criticized the concept of the political opportunity structure as so vague that it can be meaningless. (See, e.g., Goodwin and Jasper 2004a.) However, like other concepts that rely on structural explanation, the political opportunity structure is made meaningful in its concrete applications, which require a comparative strategy across time or space. An early and influential example of structural analysis is Kitschelt's (1986) study of an industrial opposition movement in Sweden, France, the United States, and West Germany during the 1970s and the 1980s. Kitschelt argued that the political field tends to be more open to challenges by anti-nuclear activists under four conditions of the "input" structure: a large number of political parties, a legislature that is independent from the executive, pluralist and fluid links between interest groups and the executive branch, and the potential to build policy coalitions that aggregate demands and translate them into policy. He also argued that another important component of the political opportunity structure is the effectiveness of the "output" structure, which includes the degree to which the government is centralized, the government's ability to intervene in the economy, and the independence of the judiciary.

This depiction of the political opportunity structure as a combination of input and output structures enabled Kitschelt to develop a precise for-mulation of differences in the political opportunity structure across coun-tries. For example, in France the political input structures are closed but the output structures are strong, whereas in the United States the opposite conditions are found. The differences in political opportunity structure are then associated with differences in mobilization patterns and outcomes. In France confrontational repertoires of action are more prominent, whereas assimilative strategies are more prominent in the US. With respect to out-comes, in France anti-nuclear activists were not able to change policies to increase the cost of nuclear power plants, whereas in the United States the activists were more successful on this policy outcome, partly because there were opportunities available through state ballot measures and through liti-gation over safety policy.

Subsequent research distinguished other dimensions of the political opportunity structure. For example, Kriesi (2004) studied the difference between exclusive (repressive, confrontational) and integrative (coopera-tive, facilitative) strategies of elite response to challengers. In addition to these more durable elements, researchers also examined the more ephem-eral configurations of actors such as the party in power at a particular time. Furthermore, SMS researchers showed how social movements can change this more malleable aspect of the political opportunity structure. Koopmans noted, "Intense protest campaigns occasionally bring governments down and contribute to constitutional changes or even to the overthrow of entire political systems" (2004: 67). More modestly, movement mobilizations can legitimize and delegitimize parties, and they can play a role in shifts in public opinion and voter preferences. However, as Koopmans also noted (2004: 69), the dynamic relationship between mobilization and the political opportunity structure is more apparent in longitudinal, single-country designs than in cross-national research. Thus, the ability to recognize the ephemeral or configurational aspect of the political opportunity structure is connected with the choice of methods.

SMS researchers have increasingly paid attention to industrial transition movements, and as their focus has shifted, the concept of the political opportunity structure has tended to undergo modification. McAdam, Tarrow, and Tilly (2001) defined the focus of attention of the contentious politics framework as cases in which "at least one government is a claimant or object of claims." However, as Soule (2010) pointed out, this definitional restriction misses the tendency for social movements to bypass governments and to target corporations directly. McAdam and Tarrow (2011) agreed with Soule that their focus on the state was too narrow; they also argued that their approach could be used for any institutionalized system of authority relations. Soule (2012) then suggested that the "private politics" literature of activist-corporation relations could be brought into conversation with the contentious politics literature. She suggested that in addition to the political opportunity structure of national and subnational governments and the transnational governance opportunity structure, corporate activists also work at the levels of the corporate opportunity structure and industry opportunity structure.

We thus arrive at the first major reformulation of the idea of the opportunity structure. I will refer to this approach under the rubric of the industry opportunity structure; that is, I will treat what Soule called the corporate opportunity structure as one dimension of the industry opportunity structure. Whereas the political opportunity structure focuses on the political field, the industry opportunity structure is a parallel concept for activists and advocates who seek changes in the industrial field, with or without accompanying policy changes from governments. As for the political opportunity structure, we can think of the industry opportunity structure as having several dimensions. The first dimension involves the microlevel of the corporation itself as a field of conflicts over strategy and reputation (Soule 2012). For example, King (2008) argued that the effectiveness of movement mobilization depends partly on internal factors of a firm's political dynamics, strategy, and history. When a firm is undergoing a reputational decline, some actors within the firm may seek to highlight the problem of reputational decline and to resolve it through a change of corporate strategy. In this situation the firm may be especially responsive to media campaigns and social movement mobilizations that could negatively affect its reputation. King suggested that firms are more likely to concede to the demands of a boycott if they have experienced a recent decline in reputation, even if their reputation is high overall. Thus, King demonstrated how movement mobilization is connected with the internal politics of a firm and with its relative reputation within an industry.

Weber, Rao, and Kenny (2009) examined another aspect of the interaction of mobilization and internal firm processes. They argued that the location of a firm (local political factors) and strength of mobilization against a firm do not explain differential outcomes in a decision to respond to movement demands. Rather, like King, they found that internal coalitions of leaders within the firm have disagreements over the future direction of the firm. For example, when a firm shifts its strategy from a traditional pharmaceutical focus on organic chemistry to molecular biology and genetics, internal constituencies in the firm are affected, and people who oppose the shift can use the external mobilization to strengthen their arguments in favor of pursuing the firm's traditional strategy. However, the effectiveness of internal attempts to sway firm strategy depends in turn on the diversity of the firm's board of directors. In the firms that have boards with greater diversity of backgrounds, there is less commitment to the new direction of biotechnology investment, and the uncertainty generated by public pressure is more salient than in the firms that have a larger percentage of directors with a biotechnology or medical background.

The internal dynamics of the firm are connected with the second main dimension of the industry opportunity structure: the relationship of the firm to other firms in the industry. In an analysis of the movement against genetically modified food in Europe during the 1990s, Schurman (2004) provided a foundational contribution. She argued that if the industry has consumer products with brand names or if firms have a corporate culture linked to sustainability and social responsibility, it may be easier for social movements to put pressure on the firms because of concerns with consumer loyalty and with the competitive value of the brand. In the case of genetically modified food, activists targeted retail and consumer products firms, which were more responsive to consumer concerns than the large biotechnology companies. Furthermore, Schurman argued that if an industry structure includes challenger firms, social movements may be able to build alliances with those firms. For example, Iceland Foods, the first food company to shift toward the activists' position, was in a subordinate position in the industry and willing to challenge incumbent firms. Food companies also had readily available alternative products, so they were not dependent on "Frankenfoods," as the activists described genetically modified food. More generally, Shwom (2011) argued that divisions in the industry may be an important factor that enables a regulatory response from the state. Fragmentation of the industry was also an important factor in the analysis of the conflict between animal rights activists and fur farmers in Sweden, but Wahlström and Peterson (2006) found that a strong trade association can overcome some of the fragmentation.

In summary, the SMS literature has already begun a diversification process from the political opportunity structure to the industry opportunity structure. In doing so, it has recognized the growing importance of industrial opposition movements. However, there is a missing epistemic dimension to the opportunity structure that is especially important in the analysis of industrial transitions.

The Intellectual Opportunity Structure and Expertise

In STS there are also some signs of further broadening of the concept of the opportunity structure. In a discussion of reform movements within the scientific field, Frickel and Gross (2005) introduced the idea of the "intellectual opportunity structure" as the conditions that affect the ability of scientist-reformers to effect change in their research field. These conditions include employment opportunities, the capacity to earn prestige, and the availability of organizational resources. Waidzunas (2013) noted how one research field's intellectual dominance over others is an important aspect of the intellectual opportunity structure, and he extended the concept to the problem of nonscientist reformers who wish to influence scientific research fields. (See also Arthur 2009.) These approaches suggest a parallel concept to the political and industry opportunity structure but for reform efforts aimed at changing agendas and frameworks within a research field. Just as mobilized publics of advocates, activists, and businesspeople may target firms and industries directly, so they may seek changes in research agendas in the scientific field. The concept of an intellectual opportunity structure can be used to describe the receptivity of a research field to such calls for change, which can involve the identification of undone science and its remediation.

Although the idea of the intellectual opportunity structure is an important development in the conversation between SMS and STS, in this chapter I will develop a somewhat different direction of synthesis by moving back toward the political field. I argue that the theory of the political opportunity structure can benefit from greater systematic analysis of its epistemic dimension. A similar argument could also be made for the industry opportunity structure by analyzing the relative openness of a firm or industry to the knowledge claims of counterpublics and to their proposals for technological change. This intriguing topic will be left unexplored here, but I will return to it in a somewhat different form when I take up the issue of countervailing industrial power. The focus in this chapter will be on the epistemic dimension of the political opportunity structure, a topic that has a sufficient research base to develop a more systematic analysis.

STS research on the epistemic dimension of the political field has focused largely on the politics of scientific expertise. Political actors rely on scientific experts for information to inform decision making, but scientists who provide such expertise must negotiate a complex terrain of political conflict in order to retain their credibility. One might hope that scientists could serve as a neutral court for the political field, a source of arbitration to which deeply opposed groups could turn to adjudicate the facts of the case. However, because scientists often do not agree with one another, the role of experts in politics is much more complicated. Experts must exert considerable effort to handle partisan disputes and to fend off claims that they are not politically neutral (Bimber 1996), and sometimes it is better to produce a summary of disagreements than to attempt to compose a consensus statement (Jasanoff 1990). Boundary organizations have emerged to negotiate this complex zone between science and politics (Guston 2001), and the scientists in these organizations must avoid having their internal disagreements become public and thereby discredit their expertise (Hilgartner 2000).

By providing expertise, scientists exercise a narrow but important form of political power. They do not have huge amounts of financial and temporal capital that they can spend to influence political outcomes in a conventional way, and in this sense they are not politically powerful actors. However, scientists exercise considerable influence for some issues and at some junctures in the policy process, so much so that Jasanoff (1990) described scientific expertise as the fifth branch of government. This power is limited, just as it is for other branches of government. When political actors accept the credibility of the experts' advice, scientists have considerable political power because they can define crucial terms, such as regulatory standards, and they can establish the epistemic terms of political debate. In Bourdieusian terms, they can establish the doxa of political debate, or at least the epistemic doxa—that is, the area of agreed-upon facts that provide the basis for arguments over different policy strategies (Bourdieu 1977).

Similar problems of politicization plague scientists in academia or research institutes whose work documents risk and the potential need for regulation. Often both official publics and counterpublics can find scientists to support their arguments about the risks or potential harms of technologies. These conflicts can occur within the political process that involves scientific advice, but they can also occur in the media and other social fields as broad technological controversies (Nelkin 1992, 1994). The conflicts occur at three levels of intensity.

At the first level, some scientific researchers produce data that document risks or safety concerns that raise the possibility of a regulatory intervention. Industry may mobilize its own scientists to attack the methods of the first group of scientists and to produce alternative data. In this circumstance, a scientific controversy can emerge between scientists who publish research suggestive of technological risk or uncertainty and industrial firms that wish to defend the view that the product is safe. The controversies can remain polite and technical, or they can become more contentious.

At the second level, the differences become more public and involve other tactics. If civil society organizations such as consumer and environmental organizations advocate a regulatory response, if there is substantial media coverage, if researchers continue to produce more research that documents safety concerns, and especially if some of the researchers adopt a public profile in favor of a regulatory response (that is, they step out of the role of fact producer), the attacks on the researchers' credibility are likely to expand beyond methodology and data. The types of attacks include loss of funding and employment, mischaracterizations of the psychological stability of the scientist, and litigation (Martin et al. 1986). The development of intellectual suppression can lead scientists to abandon their public profile, their research programs, or even their careers. Scientists can lose status in their research field, and some of their colleagues may even shun them. Sometimes they become sick from the stress, and they may also become financially destitute. Even if they are able to maintain their work as researchers, they may find that the extreme stress that the attacks, especially the litigation, put on their lives makes it difficult for them to enjoy their work and to focus on it. Moreover, their story becomes a cautionary tale to other scientists who might be thinking about studying the problem.

However, scientists who face suppression are not passive victims, and increasingly the literature on the topic has examined their strategies of response. Scientists may opt to publicize the attack, and there are many advantages to taking the suppression into a public forum, even though doing so means surrendering a great deal of the privacy that scientists may have come to expect (Delborne 2008; Martin et al. 1986). By gaining media attention and the support of public opinion, the scientists can create a situation of backfire that may encourage the incumbents to revise their strategy to compensate for the loss of legitimacy that they incur from public outrage (Martin 2007). Public-interest organizations and their sympathizers may publicize the repression, and the incumbents may find themselves on the defensive and facing reputation loss.

At the third level, epistemic rift occurs when the credibility of the entire research field is subjected to attack (Hess 2014c). The term "epistemic rift" is derived from "ecological rift" in environmental sociology, which refers to a breakdown in the circulation of materials between humans and the landscape (Foster et al. 2010). In traditional agriculture, farm waste (e.g., human and animal feces and food waste) was returned to the fields to provide fertilization, but with the growth of cities the waste was deposited in rivers and landfills, and the virtuous circle of waste and food was broken. In a similar way, "epistemic rift" refers to the breakdown in the circulation of advisory knowledge from the scientific community to the political and industrial fields and of financial support in the return circuit.

Failure to act on scientific knowledge does not imply epistemic rift. It is only when policy makers and industrial leaders argue that there is no scientific consensus when in fact scientific consensus is strong that epistemic rift occurs. This situation can involve suppression, but it is much more systemic and extensive because it involves the accusation that an entire research field is politicized. As long as the scientist or scientists who are documenting risks are few in number, a strategy of intellectual suppression and of media attacks may be sufficient. But the level of contestation can go beyond suppression when the leaders of the research field, or the professional associations and boundary organizations, say that there is a consensus, that there is a problem, and that the problem should be addressed. When epistemic rift occurs, the research field can no longer establish the facts of the case upon which politicians of various persuasions debate appropriate policy outcomes. In turn, when political leaders who embrace science denialism gain political power, they work to cut the funding of the relevant scientific research field, and the cycle of advice and funding circulation is thus doubly severed.

Under the condition of epistemic rift, incumbents mobilize against the research field itself rather than against individual scientists. The incumbents are often industrial firms and trade associations such as chemical or biotechnology companies and their allies in government, academia, and the media. However, government networks can also mobilize against the research field in cases in which the technology is government controlled, such as nuclear energy or weapons. The incumbents can draw on their own scientists in industry or government to produce knowledge that suggests that claims of risk or uncertainty may be overblown and that there are methodological problems in the original research. Often industry retains "merchants of doubt" who are generally scientists of some stature, albeit in different research fields from the one in question and often with symbolic and social capital developed more from administrative and political positions. They mobilize to discredit an existing or emerging scientific consensus about the extent of the problem and the need for a policy response. Oreskes and Conway (2010) analyzed the primary cases of this phenomenon in the United States, and they showed continuity of organizations and personnel beginning with the case of smoking through nuclear winter, acid rain, secondhand smoking, and climate change. The tobacco and fossil-fuel industries have been especially prominent in producing epistemic rifts between a research field and the policy field.

In return, the credentialed scientists in the research field (those with symbolic capital in the specific research field rather than capital in other research fields) attempt to discredit the merchants of doubt as outliers who lack appropriate credibility. However, the capacity for the merchants of doubt to have an echo chamber in the media matters more for maintaining the epistemic rift than does the lack of credibility that the merchants of doubt have within the referent research field. Thus, epistemic rift is maintained through a strategy of mobilizing an official public that involves constructing favorable public opinion through the media. The strategy of building and maintaining epistemic rift has been quite effective in the case of climate research in the United States, where ample funding from the fossil-fuel sector and utilities, which work in coalition with wealthy conservative donors and the conservative media, has enabled the purging of Republican Party moderates in primary elections, the acceptance of climate denialism as a basis for the energy policy of many leaders in the party, and a disinformation campaign in the media. Some climate scientists have experienced intellectual suppression—for example, receiving suspicious white powder in envelopes, having to answer Freedom of Information Act inquiries, and being investigated by their universities (Clynes 2012). But the process goes beyond intellectual suppression. Members of Congress, as well as legislatures and governors' offices in state governments, attempted to cut funding from a range of research programs, including the Department of Energy, the National Aeronautics and Space Administration, the National Science Foundation, and the Environmental Protection Agency (Hess 2014c; US House of Representatives 2011). These cuts suggest a qualitative difference between intellectual suppression and epistemic rift, even though the two types tend to be continuous.

What factors trigger the development of epistemic rift? It is likely that a political field that is relatively open to the influence of campaign finance on elections and to business lobbying would be fertile terrain (Barley 2010; Jacques et al. 2008). This general condition would probably have to be combined with emerging scientific research that has potentially alarming policy implications for an industry that has the resources to influence the political system. The industry may see a threat to its future because the research suggests that there is a need to sunset basic industrial technologies and to transition to alternatives. Because there are industrial transition movements advocating the sunsetting of the industry, and because elected political leaders (usually of left parties) bring the issue into the political arena, the research cannot be ignored.

However, these factors alone may not be sufficient for epistemic rift to occur, and the case of regulation of chlorofluorocarbons to reduce ozone depletion is instructive. Scientific researchers identified a problem, and in 1987 forty-three countries signed the Montreal Protocol, which limited production of the chemicals. Several factors converged to allow a smooth conversion of scientific advice into policy: the potential health risk from skin cancer and the economic risk to agriculture, the potential liability to large companies such as DuPont for consumer lawsuits if they were to continue to produce the chemical, the relatively small size of the affected portion of the chemical industry, the role of civil society organizations as both policy advocates and technology developers (e.g., Greenpeace's alternative refrigerant technology), and the uptake of safer products by manufacturers. Although we do not have a good database of cases in which epistemic rift occurs or does not occur, this negative case suggests some possible variables that involve the industry opportunity structure as well as the political opportunity structure.

In summary, STS research provides the basis for developing an analysis of the epistemic dimension of the political opportunity structure. When standard conditions prevail, there is an advisory process based on boundary organizations that have methods for producing reports that summarize the state of knowledge in a research field. Political leaders may choose to act on the expertise, or they may decide not to act, but the scientist-advisers put a great deal of effort into maintaining their technical credibility and political neutrality. Industry can provide its own versions of expertise, and in some cases it may single out some scientists who are particularly threatening. A more extensive breakdown in the credibility of science occurs when industry-funded merchants of doubt attack the consensus knowledge of a research field and the consensus statements of boundary organizations. In this situation of epistemic rift, it no longer matters what the scientists determine to be credible knowledge; what matters is the volume of ignorance that the opposition can generate through influence on the media and political fields.

The Epistemic Dimension of the Political Opportunity Structure

Research on scientific expertise, intellectual suppression, and epistemic rift suggests the existence of an underrecognized dimension of the political opportunity structure. It is likely to be especially salient in the case of industrial transition movements, which must make epistemic claims about risk, efficiency, efficacy, and other aspects of technologies and products. However, there is still a gap between the two literatures: SMS does not focus on the epistemic dimensions of the political opportunity structure, but STS tends to focus more on scientists than on social movements and mobilized counterpublics. Thus, there is an opportunity to enhance the conversation between the two fields by examining more systematically the epistemic dimension of the political opportunity structure in the context of mobilized publics.

In the remainder of this chapter I will explore two aspects of the epistemic dimension of the political opportunity structure: the structure of decision-making criteria and the structure of evaluation preferences. A policy field may be relatively open to decision-making criteria that go beyond technical considerations of risk and safety or it may be relatively closed to them. When the latter occurs, we can say that the field is highly scientized. Likewise, the policy field may be relatively open to participation by laypersons or relatively closed to it, and it may welcome different forms of lay participation. With respect to evaluation preferences, the policy field may place a premium on methods that evaluate risk in a comprehensive, open way or in a narrow, closed way. Furthermore, the policy field may have preferences for precautionary approaches to incomplete evidence, or it may be more closed to those perspectives.

In the discussion that follows, I will provide an in-depth analysis and some examples of these two pairs of features of the epistemic dimension of the political opportunity structure. The analysis is not intended to be exhaustive, but it does provide a fairly complete summary of the state of existing research, and it helps to flesh out how epistemic politics work for mobilized counterpublics.

The Scientization of Decision-Making Criteria

Kleinman and Kinchy defined scientism as the belief that broad social values "should not be considered in decisions about science and technology"

(2003: 379). Under conditions of scientization, when decisions are made to allow new technologies to be widely used, the criteria are based on the analyses by experts who use formal analytical tools such as risk assessment and cost-benefit analysis. These analyses are guided by technical values such as improving safety, reducing potential toxicity, and weighing costs and benefits. The analyses are conducted in ways that are intended to be understood as politically neutral and are cordoned off from broader social values such as the effects of technologies on users, lifestyles, ecosystem preservation, social justice, jobs, or global competitiveness. Although scientized decision making is neither value-free nor politically neutral, it is often framed as both.

Winner was one of the first STS researchers to caution against a decision-making process that transforms the potential for democratic political debate into the technical analysis of risk. When this shift occurs, he argued, the "confidence in how much we know and what ought to be done about it vanishes in favor of an excruciatingly detailed inquiry" (1986: 143). Instead of allowing a broader public discussion of questions such as "do we even need or want this technology?" the field of debate is limited to the assessment of risks and benefits. This does not mean that risk assessment per se is politically favorable to industrial interests when they clash with counter-public articulations of public benefit. To the contrary, risk assessment could be a valuable adjunct to a vigorous and democratic process. But Winner was pointing to the problem of a scientized policy field. He argued that "deliberations about risk are bound to have a strongly conservative drift ... that upholds the status quo" (1986: 148). He warned that when activists and public interest advocates accept scientized decision making and attempt to maneuver within this terrain, their experience "will resemble that of a greenhorn who visits Las Vegas and is enticed into a poker game in which the cards are stacked against him" (151).

Although connected, scientization and risk analysis are not identical. The level of scientization refers to the extent to which decision making in the policy field is restricted to technical criteria such as risk assessment or is more open to evaluation that makes reference to the social effects and social desirability of a new technology. As the world has become technically more complex and more rationalized, the level of scientific and technical complexity has increased in many policy fields (Drori and Meyer 2006). With this change, policy debate can become more technical, and the role of experts from government, academia, and industry is likely to be more important in many issue areas. However, the importance of expert input and advice to a policy process is not the same as scientization. It is possible to have a broad policy debate that includes social values and also to make extensive use of technical expertise such as risk analysis; the two are not necessarily incompatible. Nevertheless, Sarewitz (2004) noted that technical analysis can give advantages to actors who wish to avoid a broad public debate about the potential social desirability of new technologies. In environmental controversies, the polluting firms can benefit from a policy process that focuses on narrow issues of environmental and health risks rather than on allowing a broad public debate about the social and environmental implications of a new technology. Thus, the relative weight of technical analysis and broad societal considerations is at the heart of the concept of scientization.

Likewise, scientism is sometimes equated with technocracy, but the equation is misleading. Technocracy refers to a situation in which policy decisions are dominated by technical experts—in the strong case, something like Veblen's (1921) ideal of government by soviets of engineers. In contrast, the concept of scientization does not presume that scientists or other technical experts have great political power outside the zone of establishing the facts of the policy issue. In most cases political leaders have the power to delegate risk assessment to technical experts and to shift the analysis to other experts, and thus in the final instance the political power of experts rests with the political parties and their allies in industry and civil society. Thus, the use of experts is different from the idea of rule by experts. In a technocratic government the scientists (including the economists) tend to dominate a party's control over the major departments of a government; thus, as a profession they gain political power, which means that they participate in the wide range of political debate as political actors. We sometimes see political leaders described as "technocrats" if they have emerged from the civil service or from a technical field such as engineering or economics, but having technocrats in political positions of authority is not the same as ceding decision making to experts.

The decision-making process of a particular policy field may be characterized as one of the following types: highly scientized, in which risk analysis is based on narrowly defined safety and health concerns; moderately scientized, in which there is room for socioeconomic impact statements and analysis; or vigorously democratic, in which there is open discussion of the deeper issues involving the social desirability and societal implications of the proposed technology. The degree of scientization varies not only across policy fields but also by level of government (from local to global) and across countries and subnational regions. We do not yet have a theory of the conditions of variation of scientization; however, one would expect that, when the policy process is more open to participation by social movements, civil society organizations, and the lay public, those actors will draw attention to decision-making criteria other than formal assessments of risks and benefits based on technical criteria of safety and health. For example, they may argue that they do not like the political effects of a new technology because it centralizes power in a few corporations, or they may prefer existing technologies because of familiarity, comfort, privacy, security, health effects, and cost. But this capacity to bring in broader social considerations and to move evaluation from narrow, technical analyses of risk and benefit in turn depends on the openness of the government to participation by the lay opinion public and by mobilized publics.

In some cases the policy process explicitly creates room for the inclusion of broader criteria in the decision-making process. In the case of the regulation of recombinant bovine growth hormone in the European Union, Kleinman and Kinchy noted, there was a "fourth" regulatory hurdle for veterinary drugs (after quality, safety, and efficacy) that involved "the idea that approval for market introduction of a new technology should be based in part on its likely socioeconomic impacts and the consistency of these effects with existing policy determinations and the values underlying those policies" (2003: 390; Kinchy et al. 2008). The idea of "social sustainability" was included in Austria's 1994 Genetic Engineering Act, but it was not clear what was intended or how it would be evaluated (Seifert and Torgersen 1997). In the end, the decision to ban the growth hormone was made without the hurdle. Although the development of formal recognition of social criteria could help broaden the basis of decision making, Kleinman and Kinchy (2003) argued that socioeconomic impacts can also be configured in a scientistic way if they are analyzed formally by experts through methods similar to risk analysis. As a result, the prospect of descientizing a policy field requires more than inclusion of social impact criteria; it means opening up the range of criteria to broad public debate.

One attempt to descientize a policy field involved an effort to include socioeconomic criteria in the Cartagena Protocol on Biosafety, an international agreement that allows member countries to regulate or ban the importation of living genetically modified organisms. Kleinman and Kinchy (2007) showed how a coalition of environmental and development organizations came together with representatives of less developed countries (collectively termed the "Like-Minded Group") to identify the potential threat to traditional trading patterns and to small farmers. Their proposals descientized the decision-making criteria by including socioeconomic impact. In contrast, the United States, Canada, and Australia formed a different group that worked with biotechnology companies to argue against the inclusion of any criteria that might restrict international trade, and they argued against the scientific basis of socioeconomic regulation. The inclusion of socioeconomic criteria remained unresolved at multiple meetings of the Conference of the Parties, and in the final agreement it was included only on the condition that it was consistent with existing trade agreements. "When the Biosafety Protocol was finally ratified after so many years of discussion," Kleinman and Kinchy concluded, "it reflected very little of the Like-Minded Group's demands for provisions to protect against negative socioeconomic impacts." (2007: 202)

In a subsequent study, Kinchy (2010) argued that critics of the scientization of a policy field can try to change it, but, as in the case of the Biosafety Protocol, she also demonstrated how difficult it can be to achieve a successful result. In the case of transgenic maize in Mexico, environmental and grassroots activists organized protests at a meeting of the expert advisory group for the Commission for Environmental Cooperation, which was part of a side agreement to the North American Free Trade Agreement. Scientists were initially surprised by the level of vehemence and anger that emerged at what they thought would be a meeting devoted to the discussion of papers, but in their final report to the commission they argued in favor of including cultural, political, and other concerns of rural communities in the policy-making process. Building on the work of Keck and Sikkink (1998) on the boomerang effect (the use of transnational networks by activists in less developed countries), Kinchy termed this relationship between activists and scientific experts an "epistemic boomerang." The metaphor describes a process by which local activists "throw" their concerns out to the international community, especially the international scientific community, which in turn throws the concerns back to the national government. On the return, the local concerns have become infused with the prestige of international science and the power of global scrutiny.

In the case of transgenic maize, scientists agreed with activists that it would be good to descientize decision-making criteria, but the national government and biotechnology industry portrayed the experts as having become biased by local political concerns. The advocates of genetically modified maize portrayed the scientific commission as having strayed from the role of scientists as interpreters of matters of fact. However, because of the industry dominance of the political process in this case, it is not clear if any strategy from the scientists would have altered the decision-making process.

Thus, there are limits to what scientists can achieve even when they throw their prestige behind efforts to descientize decision making. Stirling (2008) cited as an example the case of the European Union's Expert Advisory Group on Science and Society. The EAGSIS had criticized the European Commission's program of public engagement as veiled one-way communication and as innovation boosterism, and the advisory group had advocated a more democratic and citizen-based approach to participation that would be open to decision-making criteria that emerge from the more inclusive process. The experts' advice turned out to be unwelcome:

In this tiny example of a much more general pattern, the recalcitrant experts were disciplined in a succession of ways: first, by being ignored; then by being variously chastised as unwise, naïve or impolite; then by being threatened that future prestigious expert advisory positions would be jeopardized; and, finally, by being effectively fired. With EAGSIS thus disbanded and its offending reports sidelined, the ongoing programme continued without the fig leaf of legitimation-posing-as-oversight. The loss was not widely noticed! (Stirling 2015: 136)

To conclude, although scientization can be contested, the cases of the Cartagena Protocol, of the movement opposing transgenic maize in Mexico, and of the EAGSIS suggest that when activists, experts, or both attempt to contest it, their successes are likely to be limited. Governments that have become committed to a technological trajectory see little value in opening up decision-making criteria in ways that could cause them to lose control over policy. More comparative analysis is needed to show under what circumstances efforts to open up a scientized decision-making process are more or less successful.

Public Participation in the Policy Process

As was noted in the preceding section, the structure of public participation in the policy process is closely related to scientization because it brings a wide range of decision-making criteria into the discussion. There are two main types of public participation: by laypersons and by counterpublics. Although in principle enhanced public participation in the policy process can lead to better policy formulation, its effectiveness depends on the extent to which the government genuinely wants to change policy in response to participation. Fischer (2009) has examined some cases in which inclusion of lay participation in the policy process has been successful.

However, much of the research on public participation has been skeptical about its effects on political outcomes. For example, in the Windscale Inquiry, which concerned a nuclear reprocessing plant, the British government sought public participation, but it placed the burden of proof on the objectors, restricted discussion to the "facts" of the case (scientized the debate), ended up dismissing the objections, and left opponents wondering if they should have participated at all (Wynne 1982; Irwin 1995). Thus, there is considerable capacity to stage public participation as a legitimizing process for decisions that have already taken place. Wynne suggested that this capacity is put into practice relatively frequently when he commented that "virtually all of the mushrooming commitment to public citizen engagement" has been "something of a mirage" (2005: 68). Public engagement mechanisms often occur on the periphery of a policy process that has already settled on a policy outcome. As a result, the consultations can devolve into legitimization exercises that allow policy makers to fine-tune their policies and to show that the public was consulted.

Although the conclusions of STS researchers on the issue of public participation are as negative as they are for scientization, there are a few optimistic notes. Delborne et al. (2013) suggested a more optimistic perspective provided that the assessment of the outcomes of participation processes is not restricted to specific policies. (Also see Powell and Kleinman 2008.) There are various avenues of potential influence that a public engagement mechanism can access: involving policy officials in the deliberations as invited guests or opening speakers, disseminating the results to potential policy makers or to civil society representatives in a policy process, gaining a briefing before a policy-making body (in this case the White House Office of Science and Technology Policy), and gaining media coverage. As in the general SMS literature, the definition of an outcome is itself much more complicated than might appear at first glance (Giugni 1998).

Another potential way to open the opportunity structure is to question the definition of the public as consisting of individual laypersons rather than as including mobilized groups and coalitions. Defining the public in this limited way may coincide with a decision to exclude mobilized publics by classifying them as stakeholders. This approach equally excludes the official publics represented by industry trade associations and industry-friendly think tanks and the counterpublics of social movement organizations, activists, and the broader realm of civil society organizations. The outcome of a public engagement process can therefore come to represent a public interest that is built from a jury of individuals who are defined as a lay public that is untainted by having an explicit stake in the field of contestation over the public good. As such the engagement process can reduce the legitimacy of the counterpublics by arguing that their construction of the public interest is itself tainted by their "special interests" (Hess 2011c). The lay public statement that results from a consultation process such as a consensus conference may be at odds with the counterpublics and may reduce their credibility to speak for a general public interest. Of course, it can also go the other way and be at odds with the official publics. But it tends to delegitimize the capacity of counterpublics to speak for the general public interest against the sectional interests of elites.

One solution to this problem is to institutionalize participation from civil society organizations that claim to represent broad sectors of society and could potentially mobilize to form protest-based social movements. Where there is a role for these organizations, we would expect that, ceteris paribus, the political opportunity structure would be more open to the arguments that they raise about the need for regulation, funding to correct a situation of undone science, or other policy interventions. However, our research on the topic leads to conclusions that are not much more positive than those of Wynne discussed above. In the United States, there is an outmoded chemical regulation regime that has not been updated for nanochemicals, and civil society organizations participate in governance mainly through informal mechanisms such as working with sympathetic members of Congress and through informal ties to the regulatory agency (Hess 2010a; Lamprou 2010). American environmental organizations who advocate stricter and more precautionary regulation of nanotechnology have sometimes looked to Europe as having a much better opportunity structure for civil society participation.

In Europe, civil society organizations benefit from a more precautionary regulatory regime for chemicals (Registration, Evaluation, Authorization and Restriction of Chemical Substances, abbreviated REACH) and from official recognition of their status as participants in the policy process. They also benefit from institutionalized inclusion in the governance of nanotechnology. The European Commission funded the Nanotechnology Capacity Building NGO ("NanoCap") Project, which convened civil society organizations to help them to develop policy capacity (van Broekhuizen et al. 2011). The project provided unions, environmental organizations, and consumer organizations with the resources to participate in nanotechnology policy and to develop position statements. In addition, the European Union provided substantial funding for some of the civil society organizations, and it granted them official access to the policy process through observer status in the working groups and expert committees of the European Chemical Agency (Lamprou and Hess 2016). Furthermore, the civil society organizations enjoy access to the Directorate-General for Environment and to the European Parliament via the Green Party.

Despite the greater access that the European Union granted civil society organizations, interviews with the leaders of the organizations indicated that they were frustrated by their lack of influence on the policy process (Lamprou and Hess 2016). Although the organizations had official status, they lacked influence over the Directorate-General for Internal Market, Industry, Entrepreneurship and SMEs, which strongly influences the European Chemical Agency, and they were excluded from some crucial policy-making processes within the European Chemical Agency. Like leaders of civil society in North America, the leaders in Europe pointed toward the overwhelming influence of the chemical industry on the political process. The European Chemical Industry Council (CEFIC) is the largest industry association (Greenwood 2011), and the chemical industry in the United States donates substantially to Republican Party candidates (Center for Responsive Politics 2016a). Moreover, the issue of nanotechnology had not triggered the public reaction and mass protests that had occurred with genetically modified food, perhaps because food is much more closely associated with identity and health.

The comparison suggests that even if public participation is defined broadly so that counterpublics are included, it does not guarantee effective influence. When governments open up the decision-making process to either form of public participation, they also open the conditions for new questions to be raised. However, when the questions and perspectives include precautionary preferences, descientized decision-making criteria, and the identification of undone science, the industrial powers are likely to find such perspectives unwelcome, and they will develop other sites of decision making that marginalize the new mechanisms of public participation. As a result, the institutionalization of public participation can become a moving target, with decision-making authority shifting to sites that are insulated from both the lay public and counterpublics. More research is needed on the conditions under which public engagement mechanisms—either of the lay public type or of the civil society type—facilitate a genuinely more open political decision-making process or only serve as a mechanism for legitimizing decisions that have been made elsewhere.

The Epistemic Culture of Risk Evaluation

The second aspect of the epistemic dimension focuses on the structure of methodological preferences. There are two main types of preferences: those involving the mix of methods that are considered legitimate for evaluation of regulatory issues and those involving the strategy for making decisions in the absence of complete information. In this section I discuss the first of the two types of evaluation preferences.

The deepest analysis of this issue to date is a comparative study of colony collapse disorder among bees in France and the United States in which Suryanarayanan and Kleinman (2014) argue that the conventional tools of SMS provide good but incomplete explanatory power. With respect to political opportunity structure, the government in France is more centralized than that of the US, and there is a tradition of government responsiveness to street protest that is based in part on France's revolutionary tradition. In the US there is a tendency for mobilizations regarding environmental and regulatory issues to work through more institutionalized channels and for mobilized counterpublics to adopt multiple strategies. Suryanarayanan and Kleinman argue that the fragmented nature of the American state limits the strategy of beekeepers, who "could not direct their collective actions and resources against any single authority, and they could not hope that the action of a single government ally—the head of the [Environmental Protection Agency]—would transform their cause" (2014: 114). With respect to the industry opportunity structure, the difference between the two countries was minor for the pesticide industry because the chemical companies involved in the manufacture of the neonicotinoids are global corporations. However, there were significant differences in the structure of the beekeeping industry because in France most beekeepers derive their income from the production of honey and related products, whereas in the United States beekeepers tend to derive their income from professional pollination services.

There were also crucial differences in mobilizing structures and framing. The three main national organizations of beekeepers in France were unified in their opposition to the neonicotinoids, and the beekeepers also had support from the Fédération Nationale des Syndicats d'Exploitants d'Agricoles. The umbrella organization faced some internal opposition from the maize farmers but overcame the opposition and supported the beekeepers. The French movement also received support from the Minister of the Environment, the Green Party, and environmentalists. The French beekeepers framed the problem as "mad bee disease," a phrase that linked the problem to "mad cow disease," an especially salient problem among European consumers that made it easier to recruit allies and to win public support. In the United States the mobilizing structures were more fragmented. Some of the commercial beekeepers rejected the association between neonicotinoids and colony collapse disorder, and the two main beekeeper organizations did not support the group of beekeepers who called for more regulation of the chemicals. Likewise, the framing of the problem as caused by insecticides was contested because a group of commercial beekeepers blamed the problem on inferior beekeeping, and they framed the problem not as CCD ("colony collapse disorder") but as PPB ("piss-poor beekeeping").

The outcomes were very different in the two countries. After mobilizations and demonstrations in 1998, the French Minister of Agriculture implemented restrictions on one class of chemicals. A group of chemical companies sued the government, but the court ruled in favor of the ministry. Beehive losses continued, and in response to additional demands and protests from beekeepers for expanded regulation, in 2004 the ministry added additional chemicals to its suspended list. In the United States, beekeepers did not engage in street protest, and they focused more on getting the undone science funded. They agreed to develop a study with Bayer, but it "ended bitterly, with Bayer researchers suggesting that Movento had only benign effects on bees and participating beekeepers asserting that the data pointed to more pernicious effects" (Suryanarayanan and Kleinman 2014: 104). Beekeepers who sought regulatory restrictions launched a class action suit against Bayer, but it proved unsuccessful after a five-year delay. Another lawsuit led by the environmental organization Natural Resources Defense Fund was successful, but the Environmental Protection Agency later reinstated the chemical. The Environmental Protection Agency's primary response to the beekeepers was to form a "Pollinator Protection Workgroup," which focused on warning labels and educational programs.

To summarize the argument of Suryanarayanan and Kleinman, the traditional conceptual apparatus of SMS—the combination of political and industrial opportunity structures, mobilizing organizations and strategies, and framing of the problem and the solution—suggest a variety of factors that can contribute to the explanation of the differences in mobilization patterns and outcomes. However, they argued that the framework also misses the important role of epistemic cultures, and the two researchers provided the first analysis of this important element of the epistemic dimension of the political opportunity structure. Both the French Commission de Toxiques and the US Environmental Protection Agency rejected the beekeepers' call for a moratorium on the specific insecticides. In both cases the agencies cited the lack of conclusive evidence, which Suryanarayanan and Kleinman (2014) described as a regulatory preference for false negatives. However, when the French ministry overrode the decision largely in response to political protest and litigation, it based the decision on studies by government scientists that suggested that there were chronic sublethal effects from exposure. The ministry then established the Scientific and Technical Committee (CST) with government bee researchers, and the committee based its recommendation for the expansion of the moratorium on combined field, semifield, and laboratory research. These scientists were skeptical of field-only research because it was prone to fluctuations. Thus, the epistemic preference in France was in favor of multiple methods. The appointment of the CST advisory committee was, according to Suryanarayanan and Kleinman, a "game changer" because the beekeepers "would probably not have been able to sustain and expand the suspension of the insecticides without the CST's imprimatur, which itself was shaped by a culture of institutionalized skepticism regarding the reliability of field tox-icity tests on honey bees" (2014: 109).

American beekeepers criticized the Environmental Protection Agency's standard of toxicity, which they argued was based on rapid, lethal death rather than on the potential of more chronic, sublethal effects. However, no other governmental unit was willing to step in and to contradict the agen-cy's approach; thus, a situation of undone science emerged. An important study by the government scientist Jeff Pettis of the US Department of Agri-culture documented sublethal effects similar to the research of the French government scientists, but "the EPA questioned the 'biological relevancy' to bees 'under natural conditions' and cast doubt on such laboratory-based findings" (Suryanarayanan and Kleinman 2014: 109). Thus, the American government's bias against an inclusive methodology, which would have recognized the value of laboratory studies, weakened the capacity to docu-ment sublethal effects that would have favored a regulatory response.

In summary, Suryanarayanan and Kleinman suggest that the political opportunity structure for social movements includes the differential valu-ation of methodologies that lead to different interpretations of the same data. The French government allowed a wider range of methodologies into consideration in the evaluation of the potential toxic effects of the neonic-otinoids, whereas the US government did not. The methodological prefer-ence for a wider range of methods contributed to a more open political opportunity structure for regulatory intervention. The case also shows how the debate can become very technical and oriented toward the merits of different methodological strategies and their relationship to causal expla-nations, but these differences in the valuation of methods are also charged by the broader political conflict and by the willingness of a government agency to take a more precautionary approach in the face of inconclusive evidence.

Precaution and Sound Science

In addition to the structure of methodological preferences at the level of research methods, there are differences in the metamethodological struc-ture of preferences for decision making under conditions of incomplete evidence. In the case just discussed, the French government cited the pre-cautionary principle in its justification for the moratorium on some insec-ticides, but industry rejected the applicability of the principle. Although the precautionary preference of a government can be distinguished from its preferences for more or less inclusive methods of evaluation, Suryana-rayanan and Kleinman (2014) suggested that the two may be connected. In the case of colony collapse disorder, the preference for field studies in the United States made it difficult to document sublethal effects of the neo-nicotinoids, and with that form of evidence discounted, it became more difficult for the coalition of farmers and environmentalists to mount a pre-cautionary argument.

The precautionary principle in this context is the preference to delay reg-ulatory approval of a new product or technology or to hasten the restriction on a product already in use. The principle is invoked if suspected harms are substantial, but adequate scientific research to prove the suspected harms has not been completed. Thus, a precautionary preference can emerge as a response to lack of research, which in turn can include the systematically unproduced research associated with undone science. Of course terms such as "substantial" and "adequate" are subject to dispute, and thus the pre-cautionary principle leads directly into the politics of precaution that often involves clashes of interpretation and strategy.

One way of approaching the politics of precaution is to examine the opposing principle of "sound science." The term suggests that precau-tionary reasoning is either unsound or unscientific, and it travels well in the media as a discrediting strategy for research that industry opposes. A more accurate term is the principle of complete evidence of harm; in other words, industry argues that before regulatory intervention there should be extensive, peer-reviewed scientific research that documents the existence of harm. Disputes over a precautionary or sound science approach to risk can also involve the interpretive (or "interpretative") flexibility of data, that is, the meaning that different actors attribute to the same data and to the assessment of how complete the data are (Collins 1983). Thus, not only is the standard of decision making in question, but the meaning of the evi-dence is also at play.

Although the debate can proceed on theoretical and rational-critical grounds, the choice of which standard of evidence to apply can have sig-nificant implications for the legitimacy of the counterpublic or official public definitions of which policy outcome best serves the public inter-est. Whereas mobilized counterpublics in the colony collapse disorder case invoked the precautionary principle and called for a more open and transparent decision-making process, official publics represented by industry spokespersons, government regulators, and associated scientists argued for a "sound science" approach to incomplete evidence (Suryanarayanan and Kleinman 2014; Oreskes and Conway 2011). The dispute also reappears in the social science literature, where one social scientist has criticized the favorable approach to precautionary policy of other social scientists (Burgess 2003; Harremöes et al. 2002). Thus, a social scientific analysis that favors a precautionary approach runs the risk of becoming a captive of the controversy between industry and movements (Scott et al. 1990).

The preference for a more precautionary versus more sound science approach to policy varies by country, by level of government, by time period, and by policy arena. Although the European Union and some European governments tend to have a more precautionary approach than other countries, there are also cases in which the United States has a more precautionary outlook. For example, the American government has tended to have stronger policies than Europe when health issues are involved, such as from secondhand smoking exposure and from diesel exposure from vehicles. (The latter also converged well with domestic industrial interests because diesel-powered automobiles were generally European imports.) Furthermore, the state and local governments have sometimes exercised precautionary politics ahead of the federal government. When the subnational governments begin to show too much interest in precautionary approaches, industry may attempt to preempt the policies by gaining more favorable regulations at the national level or by weakening the capacity to regulate industry via international treaties.

There are also differences across international treaties. Whereas the Cartagena Protocol favors a precautionary approach to the regulation of living genetically modified organisms, the World Trade Organization (WTO) favors the complete evidence or sound science principle by requiring definite scientific evidence of harm. When the European Union declared a moratorium on genetically modified food, the producer countries won the case before the WTO by arguing that the moratorium was not based on risk assessment. The WTO panel reviewed the European Union documents and found that there was a lack of consideration of quantitative risk assessment (Halfon 2010). Because the producing countries have not ratified the Cartagena Protocol, its legal standing is weak in the WTO dispute resolution panels. Thus, the overall structure of international regulation favors both a scientized decision-making framework and a sound science (rather than precautionary) preference for decision making under uncertainty.

We do not yet have a good theory of the conditions under which the level of precautionary preference is higher or lower. If an industry is mobilized in support of a decision to allow a new technology on the market and if regulators are sympathetic to industry perspectives, it would be reasonable to expect that the level of precautionary preference would be low. In this case we might also expect that mobilized publics of activists, advocates, and technical experts would emerge to demand a more precautionary policy response from a government that is perceived to be captured by industry. The case of opposition to smart meters in the United States and Canada provides one example of this type of situation (Hess and Coley 2014; Hess 2014a).

Smart meters allow real-time monitoring of electricity consumption in homes, and they can allow utilities to develop time-of-day pricing schemes that can contribute to energy-efficiency goals. Thus, there is broad support of the technology both from environmental organizations and from industry. However, opponents in several countries have cited a range of concerns including privacy, security, fairness, and safety. Our research on smart meter opposition in the United States and Canada showed that health concerns with wireless microwave technology were the paramount reason given for opposition. Opposition organizations documented cases in which persons claimed to have suffered headaches, ringing in the ears, and more serious disorders after the installation of smart meters. Concern was strong enough that some people locked their older analog meters and engaged in civil disobedience. Entrepreneurs also developed a range of products intended to shield customers from the microwave radiation emanating from the new meters.

Our analysis of public testimony in opposition to smart meters showed explicit reference to the precautionary principle as a basis for the calls to end smart meter installations (Hess and Coley 2014). Many local governments passed ordinances opposed to smart meters and called for moratoria on installation until health and other questions had been addressed. However, in the United States these ordinances lacked authority because jurisdiction lies with the state governments. The utility industry and state government regulators rejected the claims of health risk, and they cited the general literature on microwave radiation. Nevertheless, in some American states and Canadian provinces the public utilities commissions, utilities, and legislatures responded to public mobilizations by allowing customers to opt out and to keep the old analog meter or to use a microwave-free digital technology for a monthly fee.

The conflicts among smart meter opponents, industry, and regulators all made reference to the scientific literature. Although there is undone science on the health effects of smart meters, there is substantial research on the health effects of the similar, microwave-based technology of mobile phones (Hess and Coley 2014). Within the research field, a group of credentialed scientists is challenging the mainstream view that nonthermal microwave radiation poses negligible health risks. Scientists who support the hypothesis of nonthermal risks also suggest that the no-risk studies tend to be funded by industry and that meta-analyses should take industrial bias into account. Some of the scientists have also become more publicly engaged by facilitating the public availability of research on health risks of microwave communication technologies. (See, e.g., BioInitiative Working Group 2012.) Responses from governments have varied significantly. The World Health Organization has recognized the risks of nonthermal effects of microwave radiation by declaring it a potential carcinogen (International Agency for Research on Cancer 2011). Local governments in the United States developed a precautionary approach for mobile phone towers by setting stronger electromagnetic emissions standards than those of the federal government, but industry-supported legislation by the federal government preempted the authority of local governments (Burgess 2002).

This case suggests the dilemma posed by the play of precautionary and sound-science approaches to risk and perceptions of risk. On the one hand, it would be a mistake to allow a potentially harmful technology on the market without a full analysis of the risks and a regime of risk management, but on the other hand, it would be a mistake not to allow a potentially valuable and beneficial technology on the market if public concerns with risk are unfounded. Ultimately, the precautionary principle cannot act as a simple decision rule. Stirling (2007) argued that for best practice, attention must be paid to the process of evaluation in addition to formal analyses such as risk-benefit assessment. This approach links the analysis of precautionary preference to the other epistemic elements of the political opportunity structure discussed above. His list of seventeen features of a good precautionary-based assessment includes both a broad scope of analysis (e.g., attention to the full life cycle of a product) and an inclusive decision-making process (e.g., general citizen participation). This approach articulates an ideal of good precautionary governance, and it can also be used as yardstick against which actual policies and processes can be measured.

Although such an approach suggests ways in which precautionary politics can be linked to the broader political opportunity structure, we do not yet have a good database of empirical studies that document whether a more open and democratic decision-making process will lead to precautionary outcomes. In our everyday lives, people are aware of health guidance (e.g., smoking is dangerous and exercise is healthy), but they often ignore it. Likewise, at broader scales of action, we also find that communities and countries ignore evidence about risk (e.g., continued high levels of greenhouse gas emissions are dangerous). As with most of the topics in this nascent field of research on the epistemic dimension of the political opportunity structure, we need more research on the conditions under which a government's preference for precautionary politics is higher or lower.

Conclusion

Because the contemporary global society is highly dependent on science and technology, policy issues that involve scientific and technological controversies have and will become increasingly salient in the political process. As this chapter has shown, industrial transition movements have targeted technologies for sunsetting, and they have suggested alternatives that might be substituted. SMS cannot dwell in the world of twenty-first century politics without grappling with the politics of industrial transitions. Doing so does not require jettisoning the insights of a well-worn concept such as the political opportunity structure, but it does mean expanding it to develop a more systematic analysis of its epistemic dimension. At the same time, the study of the politics of expertise in STS is diversifying from its historic focus on scientists and scientific advice toward expertise in the context of mobilized publics.

Thus, I have outlined an approach to the political opportunity structure that includes an epistemic dimension oriented toward the role of mobilized publics. The cases discussed include mobilizations to stop the unwanted spread of agricultural biotechnology, the diffusion of nanotechnology without prior regulatory review, the use of neonicotinoids in agriculture, and the installation of smart meters without public permission and review. In all of the cases, the counterpublics base their call for political changes on knowledge claims that they deem credible but that industries reject as unfounded. The counterpublics sometimes also point to the absences of research and the need to have funding to get the undone science done. As these conflicts appear in the political field, they are simultaneously struggles of contentious politics and contentious knowledges.

Research on the epistemic dimension of the political opportunity structure is not yet at the stage where general patterns can be gleaned. On the basis of the research discussed here, we would expect that the following would represent a more open political opportunity structure for these publics: a less scientized and more participatory decision-making process, and a preference for multiple methods of risk evaluation and for precaution in the face of uncertain evidence. However, researchers who are considering wading into this field should be careful about rushing to an obvious but oversimplified conclusion. An industry could utilize a descientized decision-making process in its favor by arguing that jobs will be lost, products will become more expensive, or other negative social and economic effects will occur if the product has to undergo a design change or be removed from the market. Likewise, the institutionalization of public participation, especially through consultations with laypersons, can discredit the legitimacy of counterpublics to claim that they speak for the public. The inclusion of civil society organizations in the consultation process can divide the more moderate organizations from the more radical grassroots. With respect to methodological preferences, a more open and inclusive methodological preference could make it easier for industry, with its vast resources, to develop convergent studies across a range of methodologies. The preference for precaution may protect society from the risky technologies, but it can also generate false positives for risk and slow down access to beneficial innovations. In summary, research on the epistemic dimension of the political opportunity structure probably will have to steer clear of simplistic formulas, and in doing so it will open up both SMS and STS to a new terrain of unanswered questions.

3   The Politics of Meaning: From Frames to Design Conflicts

Although the structural approach is an important strategy of explanation, activists and advocates must interpret the structures and then develop culturally and historically attuned strategies for action. Because the SMS and STS fields have well-developed literatures on the analysis of meaning, there are many possible ways to build a bridge between the two fields on this topic. After considering some of the dominant approaches to the study of meaning in SMS and STS, this chapter will outline one strategy for bridging the two fields—a strategy based on a material culture approach to design conflicts.

Frames and Cultural Analysis in SMS

In SMS the most influential approach to the analysis of meaning is frame analysis. In Bateson's (1955) original formulation of the concept, a frame is a metalevel of communication that indicates to actors what kind of game they are in, such as cooperation or conflict, and that provides a lens through which actors can interpret the actions of others. As applied to SMS, the narrower concept of collective action frames involves the core tasks of prognosis, diagnosis, and motivation (Benford and Snow 2000; Snow et al. 2014). To be effective, frames must resonate with potential recruits, and thus activists and advocates must align frames. There are various strategies for doing so, including bridging, amplification, extension, and transformation (Snow et al. 1986).

One underlying condition for the credibility of frames is that when they make references to empirical knowledge, they must rest on credible science. Benford and Snow (2000) recognized this condition in their discussion of empirical credibility as one of the foundations of frame resonance, but they did not focus on scientific and technical credibility. This aspect of credibility is especially salient in the industrial transition movements—where empirical claims about risks, uncertainties, benefits, and efficacy are central—and a portion of the SMS literature examines the issue from a frame-analysis perspective. For example, Lubitow (2013) described the partnership that developed between scientists and activists in the movement to regulate bisphenol-A in the United States. Scientists helped activists to develop a scientifically credible diagnostic frame involving children's health, and activists relied on the expertise of scientists to gain passage of state laws that banned some uses of bisphenol-A from children's products. Likewise, Frickel (2004) drew on frame analysis in a study of a network of scientists who founded the field of genetic toxicology. He showed how they engaged in frame amplification to interest the broader research communities of biology, medicine, and public health. Whereas Lubitow examined how scientists helped activists to frame their issues for policy makers and the public, Frickel focused on how scientists framed their reform efforts within the scientific field. Together, the two approaches suggested that frame analysis can be a fruitful way to analyze the relationship between social movements and scientific expertise both in the political field and in the scientific field.

Although frame analysis provides a well-tested method for the study of meaning and mobilized publics, some SMS researchers have argued that a broader, cultural approach can provide additional insights. (See, e.g., Goodwin and Jasper 2004a; Johnston and Klandermans 1995; Poletta 2004.) As they have argued, frame analysis focuses on the instrumental and cognitive dimensions of the politics of meaning (Goodwin and Jasper 2004a). In contrast, cultural analyses focus on a different unit of analysis, such as the story or narrative, which can include more emotionally resonant aspects of meaning. (See, e.g., Poletta 2009.) Furthermore, a story can be more than an interpretive scheme; it can also be a model for action or performance (Johnston 2009). A story or narrative is also a more multivocal unit of analysis that is amenable to an interpretive approach that can bring out tensions and layers in the analysis of meaning. To this point, work in anthropology on social movements also draws attention to the use of "cultural repertoires" such as historical narratives of colonialism and genocide (Hess 2007b). Like the story or narrative, the cultural repertoire is a multivocal unit of analysis, but it also connects social movement action with charged historical events that can provide a template for action. Cultural repertoires often dramatize relations among complex layers of oppression and inequality, such as among Anglos, Latinos, and indigenous groups in the American Southwest (Masco 2006). Importantly, cultural repertoires are configured in oppositional terms that are linked to conflicts between oppressed groups and elites, such as repertoires of sacred indigenous traditions versus those of secular progress. Frames can be constructed in ways that connect with cultural repertoires, and doing so may make frames more effective (McCammon et al. 2007).

It is not necessary to make a choice between frame analysis and the broader family of cultural methods. There are multiple units of analysis available—including frames, narratives, and cultural repertoires—that can be brought together. But as a whole this literature has a general limitation in that the analysis of meaning is focused largely on language-based cultural meanings. Thus, there is room for innovation if one looks also at how material culture provides a rich avenue for exploration, and this approach is especially relevant in the study of industrial transition movements. From this perspective, the STS literature can provide a valuable complement to SMS perspectives on the politics of meaning.

Frames and Cultural Analysis in STS

A good starting point in the STS literature is work on the social construction of technology, which provides a processual approach to technology controversies that uses the word "frame." The analytical strategy begins with the condition of interpretive flexibility (multiple designs and meanings attributed to a technological problem), then moves through social negotiation, and ends with the stabilization of a new technological design (Pinch and Bijker 1987). The model of technological change is continuous with similar processual models of scientific change, especially Collins' empirical program of relativism in the sociology of science (Collins 1983). The concept of frame comes into play because the relevant social groups build "technological frames" for an artifact, and when closure occurs after social negotiation, a new technological frame emerges.

From the perspective of the collective action frames in SMS, the construction of a technological frame could be viewed as a frame bridging. However, the comparison with collective action frames can go only so far. Bijker (2010) likens his use of a frame to Kuhn's (1970) concept of a paradigm, which includes goals, concepts, and problems. In contrast with the collective action frame of SMS, a technological frame is more related to a network of relationships among objects, inventors, producers, and users rather than to the strategic use of meaning in the conflict between challenges and incumbents. Although this difference of focus may make the two uses of the same word faux amis, the STS approach does offer an important insight with respect to the SMS literature: it draws attention to the issues of design and material culture in the politics of meaning.

A closely related approach in STS is the analysis of boundary objects. Star and Griesemer (1989) developed the approach in response to the analysis of interessement in actor-network theory (Callon 1986). Like frame alignment, interessement is the process by which an actor recruits allies by convincing them that in order to fulfill their goals, they benefit by going through the heterogeneous (sociomaterial) network being constructed by the actor. The concept of boundary objects addresses what Star and Griesemer argue is a two-dimensional limitation in the analysis of interessement. In other words, the actor-network approach focuses only on the relationship between a network builder and a recruit to the network. Drawing on their intellectual roots in symbolic interactionism, Star and Griesemer argue that in many cases "entrepreneurs from more than one social world are trying to conduct such translations simultaneously" (1989: 389). They propose an ecological perspective that does not give primacy to the scientist or to the administrator with respect to the enrolled allies. A good example of a boundary object is a database that can benefit from diverse contributions and that can be amenable to diverse uses. As new actors join the community of users, the database undergoes design changes. It becomes a shared resource that enables coalitions, alliances, and networks to be built. In the language of frames, the boundary object becomes an enabling mechanism for the alignment of frames.

As with SMS, there is also a body of research in STS that moves beyond the analysis of interessement and boundary objects to broader cultural methods. Examples of influential lines of cultural research in STS are studies of imaginaries and governmentality (Jasanoff and Kim 2013; Foucault 2008). These analyses often highlight a central symbolic concept, such as neoliberal governmentality, and show its deployment across a range of uses and social fields. Although the analyses provide insights that are appropriate for their purposes, they tend to have limitations for the study of industrial transition movements. By emphasizing the underlying cultural logic that appears across multiple sites or expressions—such as in media reports, in government policies, and in everyday practices—there is less attention paid to conflicts of meaning among actors. Rose et al. also suggest that such approaches can turn a cultural category such as "neoliberal governmentality" into a "more or less constant master category that can be used both to understand and to explain all manner of political programs across a wide variety of settings" (2006: 97). More relevant to the study of industrial transitions movements is the post-Geertzian analysis of conflict, contention, and innovation among the units of cultural analysis. (See, e.g., Gupta and Ferguson 1997.) The focus on conflict also tends to connect differences in meanings with differences in social positions, and it brings us back to a field theory approach. To this end, I have suggested the value of approaches to cultural analysis that focus on conflicts among institutional logics, a topic to which I will return later (Hess 2015b; Hess, Wold, et al. 2016).

In summary, through the concepts of technological frame, interessement, and boundary objects, one can locate a parallel universe in STS to that of frame analysis in SMS. To some degree there are also common intellectual roots, at least in the case of symbolic interactionism, which influenced theories of collective action frames and boundary objects. Likewise, there is also a parallel diversification in SMS and STS toward broader modes of cultural analysis, but the SMS approaches tend to be more relevant for the present purposes to the extent that they draw out conflicts among systems of meaning.

Toward a Synthesis: Design and Material Semiotics

Although one strategy of synthesis of these two diverse literatures might involve bringing together the analysis of collective action frames with that of boundary objects or some other syncretism, I will instead tack in another direction. Just as the previous chapter brought an epistemic perspective to the analysis of opportunity structures, so this chapter will bring a design perspective to the analysis of meaning. This approach is consistent with Johnston's (2009) discussion of "artifacts" as an important but understudied dimension of cultural analysis in SMS, but it is broader than his focus, which is mainly on nonmaterial artifacts such as music and texts. Closer to the approach that I adopt here is Pinch's (2010) analysis of Goffman's work (1974) that draws attention to the hidden or underappreciated role of material objects in the theory and analyses of symbolic interactionism. However, Goffman's analysis of symbols lacks the richness of semiotic methods, especially prominent in anthropological methods influenced by structuralism. (See, e.g., Bourdieu 1977.) These methods examine the co-constitution of social and material orders and chart out the systematic meanings of material and other cultural codes. Thus, material objects are made meaningful not only by their distinctions among each other but by the play of their similarities and differences with other cultural orders (Hess 1995). Rather than view technology and material culture as props for social action and or as instrumental resources for mobilization, I will develop an approach that views them as meaningful objects of contestation. This perspective places design conflicts at the center of analysis.

The analysis of material culture has implications not only for the study of meaning in SMS but also for STS. To some degree existing frameworks in STS bring us into this world through the analysis of the stabilization of networks or of collaboration through boundary objects. But in the cases analyzed above by Lubitow (2013) and Frickel (2004), the outcome is not necessarily stable or collaborative. Thus, we need an approach that combines attention to material culture and to the inequalities of social structure and institutional structure. I previously used the term "object conflicts" as a field-theory variant on the idea of boundary objects (see, e.g., Hess 2007c), but the term has not caught on in the literature, so I have tended to shift to the more common phrase "design conflicts."

Design is the intentional structuring or patterning of material objects from the scale of small objects to large infrastructures. Design is a process of making matter meaningful through the play of similarities and differences associated with physical objects. Although one can extend the concept to other animals to the extent that one can attribute intentionality to their activities, for our purposes design is a human activity, and the concept of natural design is a category error. Like the concept of power, the interpretation of design is linked to attributions to the intentions of an actor, which other actors interpret and misinterpret, and to the intentions of users who configure and sometimes alter design. Design is meaning that we give to objects by modifying them and by interpreting the modifications diacritically in contrast with other objects and choices. As in Bateson's

(1955) original formulation of a frame as metacommunication, design tells us what game we are in. Designs both enable and constrain action, but they are transformed by action as well. The focus here is on design conflicts, which emerge when actors have strongly different views of how material culture should be configured. The remainder of the chapter discusses three main approaches to the analysis design conflicts: structural inequality, industrial regime compatibility, and environmental.

Structural Inequality and Design Conflicts

This type of design conflict is based on patterns of structural inequality that haunt all human societies. Arguably the foundational analysis in this tradition is Mumford's contrast between two types of technologies: "one authoritarian, the other democratic, the first system-centered, immensely powerful, but inherently unstable, the other man-centered, relatively weak, but resourceful and durable" (1964: 2). In a precursor of new urbanism, a reform movement that emphasized the walkability of cities among other features, he pointed to the design of pedestrian-oriented cities as an example of the democratic type. Winner (1986) developed this analysis for the study of energy, where he discussed the centralized, bureaucratic requirements of nuclear energy. Also consistent with Mumford's approach is the work of Schumacher (1973), who drew attention to the design of organizations and technologies that emphasized local control, small businesses, and appropriateness to local needs. The appropriate technology movement led to a wide range of experiments in less developed countries that linked innovations in design to public participation and rural development (Smith et al. 2016).

In addition to work on democracy and design, a significant body of research in STS also draws attention to design conflicts that involve social structure. For example, Noble (1984) analyzed how the automation of manufacturing operations shifted power from the shop floor to the managers and resulted in deskilling labor and weakening the bargaining power of unions. However, unions pushed back, and in some cases companies adopted the technologies only after making compromises between unions and management. A better-developed literature in STS involves studies of gender and design, which encompass a wide range of material culture, including biomedical technologies, workplace and domestic technologies, and the built environment. (See, e.g., Layne et al. 2010; Rothschild

1999.) For example, feminists have developed a critical perspective on the new urbanist reform movement by arguing for a radical redesign of homes and neighborhoods that would allow women and men to share domestic labor and to create new paid labor within neighborhood settings. (See, e.g., Hayden 1980; Torre 1999.) The cohousing and ecovillage movements are examples of alternative industrial movements that implement some of these alternative design features.

Another area of research involving structural inequality is the design of software and information technologies. Eglash et al. (2006) translated ethnomathematics into culturally situated design tools such as teaching the concept of fractals to African-American schoolchildren via the use of cornrows, a type of hair styling. Williams (2013) has shown how clinicians and inventors in India have developed designs for cataract lenses and surgical techniques that are more responsive to the problem of cataract surgery in less developed countries. These approaches to design are high-technology innovations and distinct from the low-technology designs of the previous generation of appropriate technology advocates.

This work on the politics of design suggests that awareness of the different perspectives that are associated with structural inequality can lead to innovations that provide new approaches to everyday products and the built environment. We might call this "design from below" to expand on Harding's (2008) similar and widely influential analysis of knowledge and science. As Layne et al. (2010) have shown in their analysis of reproductive technologies designed to benefit women, the progressive aspirations of design from below must be tempered by an awareness of the complexities of how new designs are interpreted and used, often in ways that are not anticipated by the designer. Furthermore, designers must attend to how they can reproduce relations of inequality that they seek to undermine. Nevertheless, inclusion of perspectives of those located in the lower rungs of the social ladder can lead to more robust and inclusive design.

To extend the parallel with Harding's work, she argued that with respect to science the inclusion of perspectives of those located in subordinate positions in the social structure results in "strong objectivity" (Harding 2015). For example, when women have entered research fields, they have sometimes questioned the implicit cultural assumptions of scientific theories and methods. Examples include the "man the hunter" theory of human evolution and the idea of a passive egg and active sperm for human reproductive physiology (Haraway 1989; Martin 1991). When scientists query existing theories and data sets for their gendered or other implicit cultural assumptions, there can be an increase in the empirical accuracy of research programs. In a similar way, when designers or inventors include the perspective of subordinate structural positions in their design criteria (either by thinking about the needs of different users or by including users in a participatory design process), the result is that designers are better able to see the social meaning of design decisions. One outcome, universal design, enables the object or technological system to function for existing users, but it can also open up possibilities for flexible new uses or even reappropriation by users (Eglash et al. 2004; Oudshoorn and Pinch 2003). Thus, there is a process similar to strong objectivity that operates in the world of design conflicts that emerge from structural inequality.

The idea of universal design entails opening up our thinking about material culture to envision new ways to make it more flexible and usable for a wider range of users. It is most often associated with design for differently abled persons. In the case of city transportation systems, various design changes have made it easier for persons using personal mobility devices to board and to exit public transit vehicles. Design changes include automatically lowering the threshold of entrance for a bus, providing ramps instead of stairs, and building elevator access to underground trains. Often there is a history of political mobilization and conflict that leads to policy changes such as revised building codes. Once an accommodation is made for one group, other categories of users, such as persons with baby carriages or those with knee injuries or with arthritis, may find that the design change is helpful. As a result, political constituencies in support of the design change can expand.

It may perhaps be better to think of the outcome of design conflicts as "universalism" in design rather than universal design. In the Weberian tradition of social theory (see Weber 1978), universalism refers to norms that treat people according to the same standards regardless of particularistic traits such as race, gender, religion, ethnicity, and sexuality. Many social movements anchored in structural inequality have attempted to overturn particularistic norms and legal institutions (such as the lack of vote and the existence of employment barriers for women, indigenous peoples, or ethnic minority groups) and to replace them with more open, fair, and democratic alternatives. Sometimes these struggles involve design conflicts, especially regarding the rights of women and differently abled people. Although these issues of social justice and universalism are less salient in the industrial transition movements, they nevertheless transect the industrial movements in important ways.

One example where the issue of universalism and design is connected to the politics of industrial change is in the history of the design of the transportation system in the United States. *Plessy v. Ferguson*, a landmark Supreme Court decision handed down in 1896, was based on a challenge to a Louisiana state law that required separate rail cars for whites and for blacks and creoles. This is one of the most outstanding examples of particularistic design because it sorted people into different physical spaces by race. The railroad company opposed the law, which required the purchase of additional rail cars, as did a committee of citizens; thus, Homer Plessy's challenge to the law was planned. However, the state courts and the US Supreme Court upheld the law and the general principle of separate but equal facilities, thereby ensuring a particularistic built environment that encoded racial segregation. Changes in the material culture do not always coincide with those of the legal system, and there can be a lag. I remember visiting relatives in Florida during the 1960s and attending the greyhound races. At the dog track, the signs "whites" and "coloreds" had been painted over but were still visible. Although segregation had officially ended, whites and blacks maintained the distinction by sitting in the previously designated segregated spaces.

Transportation was the focus of one of the triggering events of the civil rights movement: Rosa Parks' act of civil disobedience regarding the seating rules for African Americans on buses. Here the seating design of the buses included a whites and colored section, but there was a sign on the seats that the conductor could move to allow the white section to expand and to force African Americans to give up their seats and move to the back of the bus or to stand. Her decision not to move led to a court challenge, and it also was the spur to the 381-day Montgomery bus boycott. After a Supreme Court decision in another case, the city repealed its discriminatory laws.

The examples of segregated rail cars and buses show how a transportation system can be designed in ways that builds in structural inequality. Although some may like to think that in the United States these issues have been resolved, structural inequality continues to plague the urban built environment and transportation system. For example, when Rosa Parks later became secretary for Congressman John Conyers, she became involved in another racially based design conflict: the destruction of Detroit neighborhoods that was caused by highway development and other policies. Conflicts over highway design were endemic to US cities during the 1960s and the 1970s, and the design conflicts over urban highway systems were often inflected by racial politics. Federal government funding for highway transportation was much higher than for urban transit systems, and urban highways often ran through African-American neighborhoods or ran along the "black-white line" in cities. Whole neighborhoods, such as Overtown in Miami, were weakened if not destroyed by highway construction (Mohl 2003). Anti-highway movements emerged, but they tended to be successful only in cities where powerful cross-racial coalitions could be built, such as in Boston (Mohl 2004).

In many cities, the white middle class took advantage of the highways and commuter rail to move to the suburbs, and the public transit systems of the cities, especially the bus systems, became increasingly the means of mobility for people of color and the urban poor. The design distinction between white and black rail cars or the front and back of the bus became transformed into a new distinction between commuter-oriented highways and rail versus urban bus systems. When jobs followed the middle class to the new office buildings of the metropolitan periphery, the transit systems failed to offer opportunities to connect the urban residents with jobs unless they had cars (Bullard et al. 2004). Investments in urban rail at the expense of buses were particularly contentious in Los Angeles, where the Bus Riders Union won a federal consent decree to reduce the discriminatory policies for bus riders, who in Los Angeles were largely low-income people of color (Moore and Rubin 2008). Conflicts did not end with this victory; they continued over the region's heavy investments in the rail system.

Even the relatively progressive politics of urban sustainability initiatives have involved a racial politics of design. One example involves conflicts over the greening of urban buses (Hess 2007c). Diesel exhaust contains a well-documented brew of toxic chemicals, and by the 1990s environmental and health organizations were calling for the reduction of emissions from diesel-powered vehicles. (See, e.g., Natural Resources Defense Council 1998.) The Environmental Protection Agency also designated nonattainment cities and mandated that they purchases cleaner buses beginning in 1998. This rule was a factor in the design conflict that emerged over two types of buses: emissions-controlled diesel (ECD) and compressed natural gas (CNG). Studies of emissions and health risks from the two types of fuels did not conclusively favor one over the other, but ECD was generally a less expensive alternative, and in most fleets the managers and mechanics were familiar with the technology and wary of conversion. My interviews with fleet managers indicated that the natural gas industry had lobbied forcefully to get some transit agencies to convert to CNG; however, fleet managers tended to resist the pressure, and in some cases the transit agencies were in open conflict with city council members who backed conversion to CNG. In the end, some transit agencies opted for CNG, others for ECD, and some tested both.

The changes in bus technology intersected with the environmental justice movement in Atlanta, Boston, Los Angeles, New York, and San Francisco, where groups mobilized against the emissions effects of diesel bus depots and dirty diesel buses in general. They drew attention to the location of most bus depots in low-income communities of African Americans and Latinos. These groups favored conversion to CNG, and in some cases the advocates reached above the city governments to have the state governments intervene. In Boston, New York, and San Francisco, the transit agencies eventually opted for conventional and hybrid-electric ECD. However, Atlanta and Los Angeles pursued CNG, partly because of the litigation by environmental justice groups and partly because of support from the natural gas industry for conversion (Hess 2007c). CNG remained a viable option for several cities particularly because natural gas prices were competitive with diesel prices, but many transit fleet managers remained wary of the conversion and the potentially higher repair costs.

In some cities the distinction between ECD and CNG became aligned with racial injustice politics, but the technology, fleet compositions, and urban political alliances were all changing. It would be simplistic to write out a semiotic equation of the design conflict as follows: ECD is to CNG as a conventional racist status quo is to a cleaner and more environmentally just alternative. The technology itself was in flux, and some studies indicated that the nanoparticles of CNG emissions were as toxic as diesel particulates. Some fleet managers also argued that because the purchase price of ECD was lower than that of CNG buses, it would be possible to retire the older, more polluting diesel buses more quickly if the transit agency were to remain with the infrastructure of diesel and shift to ECD. Thus, the analysis of design conflicts requires attending to how technical design distinctions are made meaningful in different and complicated ways that often resist simple equations of the type that Mumford articulated. These equations can be useful as a first approximation, but the analysis of design conflicts requires digging more deeply into the historical and ethnographic material.

More generally, the analysis of race and design in the urban transit system suggests the need for methodological caution. The connection between class and race distinctions and transportation design distinctions is not a simple relation of, for example, highways versus public transit. Rather, there are layers of distinction that come into play: commuter rail versus light rail and buses, rail of any kind versus buses, and types of "green" buses (e.g., ECD and CNG). The class and race differences reappear with each design distinction, and they vary significantly over time. Thus, a less "racist" design is not something that can be depicted with a simple formula, just as Layne et al. (2010) showed for the question of a more "feminist" design. In cities with extensive subway and light rail systems that run across diverse neighborhoods, the bus versus rail distinction may not be as salient as it has been in Los Angeles. Furthermore, many medium-sized American cities lack any kind of rail transit, or it is very limited, and thus the design conflicts tend to be within the bus system. Each city is unique, and the social movement mobilizations have tended to emerge only in cities with already mobilized environmental justice organizations.

The analysis of urban transit design conflicts helps to clarify the general argument of this chapter about the way in which STS perspectives might help to diversify the analysis of the semiotic dimensions of industrial transition movements from the focus on framing. In the policy conflicts that erupted over transit design decisions, the different agents involved (fleet managers, city council members, neighborhood groups, environmental justice groups, bus manufacturers, the natural gas industry) drew on a variety of frames, including economic calculations of costs and benefits, concerns with the health effects of emissions and air quality, and civil rights in a lineage that traces back to Plessy and Parks. So it would be possible to develop a conventional frame analysis of the environmental and racial justice movements with respect to the politics of urban transit. But such a perspective would miss the way in which the material culture is itself under contention, how material culture and social relationships are in flux together, how design distinctions become connected with social positions, and how design decisions become built into the structure of everyday life. The material form of a vehicle, transportation system, or city is secreted by the politics of urban life and, once constructed, becomes both an enabling and constraining factor for those politics. Furthermore, the design choices are themselves not only meaningful to the different actors but differently meaningful and contested. The outcome is that we end up living in a world in which material culture and social inequality are changing together.

Industrial Regimes and Design Conflicts

The second type of design conflict involves the relations among firms and industries, and at first glance it may appear to be somewhat distant from the concerns of either SMS or STS. In the traditional model of industrial innovation, the focus is on design innovation from the perspective of marketplace competition. Innovation may come from one of the large industrial corporations that dominate an industry (an "incumbent"), but these corporations have an interest in innovations that fit within the existing technological regime. For example, the hybrid-electric vehicle can be integrated into a petroleum-powered transportation system while providing environmental, economic, and (especially for urban buses) air quality benefits. However, radical innovations, which disrupt and challenge the underlying technological system and regime of an industry, often come from start-up companies that exist as a technological niche (Geels 2002). This is not always the case, and we sometimes find large corporations in one industry pioneering disruptive innovations that upset the regime in a neighboring industry, much as Apple's entry into the mobile phone market disrupted the regime of flip phones.

This type of design conflict is based on the distinction between regime and niche that has been central to the study of industrial transitions. As analysts of the transitions of industrial regimes have shown, often the more radical technologies are not market ready and thus require some protection from market forces (Smith and Raven 2012). Protectors may include venture capitalists, nonprofit organizations, universities, dedicated entrepreneurs, or even incumbent firms that wish to gain market share. Governments often step in to provide funding for niche development if the new technology is aligned with policy goals. The goals can include public health, national security, and environmental sustainability in addition to maintaining or building an industry so that it can generate good jobs and be competitive in global markets. However, when niches reach a price point that allows them to compete in markets, they can also represent a threat to the incumbent organizations. Thus, design conflicts erupt over how to alter the niche technologies so that they can be made compatible with the industrial regime. This section will summarize research projects on two industries where industrial transition movements are closely tied to design conflicts between challengers and incumbents in an industry: solar energy and organic food and sustainable agriculture.

Solar Energy Investor-owned utilities, publicly owned entities known as "public power," and cooperatives are the three main types of organizations that generate and deliver electricity in the United States. The mix of organizations is the result of a complicated history of government policies developed at different periods during the twentieth century (Hess 2011b). Although the investor-owned utilities are small in number relative to the other types of providers, they provide service to the largest number of customers. Public power is controlled by a local city government or by an independent metropolitan entity. Most metropolitan areas rely on investor-owned utilities for their electricity, but public power is the main form of service in dozens of large cities. Cooperatives are generally rural entities that came into existence during the rural electrification of the 1930s and the 1940s. The investor-owned utilities are regulated by state-government entities called public utilities commissions. Historically, the investor-owned utilities were vertically integrated entities that encompassed generation, transmission, and distribution, but after the restructuring of the industry during the 1990s, both generation and retail service have become separate entities in some states (Hirsh 1999).

The development of small-scale solar energy, such as rooftop photovoltaics, is a good example of a niche-regime design conflict. By the 1960s the American government was supporting solar energy research, and advocates of the technology sought more funding. During the 1970s they formed coalitions with environmentalists and others who emphasized local control, a vision that was in contrast with the utilities' goal of providing stable, baseload power from large-scale, centralized, generation plants (Laird 2001). Advocates also criticized the bias of government funding toward large-scale solar and pointed to the undone science of research that would support small-scale and off-grid configurations (Metz 1977; Reece 1979).

Thus, by the 1970s a design conflict had emerged over solar energy and its relationship to the grid and utilities, and this conflict has remained in place until the present day (Reece 1979). On the one hand, activists had visions of enabling households and businesses to generate and store their own electricity, and a home-power movement emerged in support of this vision (Tatum 1995, 2000). On the other hand, utilities were alarmed by the long-term threat posed by this configuration of solar, and they worked to develop a model that was more compatible with a centralized grid such as large-scale solar farms (Hess 2013a, 2016).

Often a design conflict between the technologies of the niche and the regime can be resolved by a new synthesis that incorporates the alternative technology but transforms its design. Distributed renewable energy is such an example. It enabled rooftop production of solar energy but with a grid connection and generally without on-site battery storage. This design innovation drove a wedge between the production of local solar energy and the aspirations of democratic, off-grid power associated with the home-power movement and solar activists. Net metering and interconnection laws provided the financial incentives and legal arrangements that allowed owners of solar panels to sell their solar energy back to the grid at retail prices, thus providing a stable economic model that enabled investment. As long as this niche remained a tiny portion of the market, the utilities could tolerate it as an experimental technology accessible to homeowners with adequate income and with technical resources.

A major drawback to rooftop solarization is that homeowners or business owners must accumulate the savings for the initial investment, or they must borrow money. Furthermore, there are significant transaction costs associated with gaining permissions for installations and with running systems. These hurdles presented an opportunity for another design innovation, this time in the financial products used to support rooftop solar. Property-assessed clean energy (PACE) financing allowed building owners to borrow funds and repay them as part of the annual property tax; these laws were passed in many state legislatures during the period 2009–2012. However, for homeowners the arrangement came into conflict with the Federal Housing Authority, which was concerned about their first-lien rights on mortgages. PACE financing continued to grow for commercial buildings, and various solutions, such as second-lien mortgages, emerged for residential buildings. Another solution was to allow people to buy shares in solar farms, which are controlled by cooperatives, city governments, private businesses, or public power agencies. This arrangement of "community solar" allowed persons to enjoy the income stream and the personal satisfaction of owning solar without the investment and transaction costs of ownership.

As the cost of solar energy declined, the technology and financial sector developed new solar financing products known as "third-party ownership." This form of financing can involve either a lease paid to a solar developer or an agreement from the building owner to purchase solar power from the installation company at a specified rate. In either case, the solar technology is owned by the third-party company, and there is usually an option to purchase the unit at the end of the lease period of fifteen to twenty years. Owing to the combination of decreasing costs and favorable regulatory policies, finance and technology companies poured money into this financing mechanism, and distributed solar energy entered a takeoff period after 2009. By 2011 third-party financing had become the dominant model of solar financing in several major markets (Hess 2013a).

Although the absolute level of solar energy was low in most markets (under three percent of customers), the growth rate began to alarm the utilities. The parallel improvement in energy-storage technology also began to make it easier for building owners to shift to use on-site batteries, which could lead to disconnection from the grid. Reports from the utility industry began to sound the alarm that the growth of distributed solar may have an effect on the industry similar to that of cell phones on land lines (Kind 2013). This reaction was similar to the original concerns raised during the 1970s with the solar democracy movement, but now it was in response to a more mature technology that had the backing of corporate investors from the financial and technology sectors. The design of new financial products was driving a scale shift by which the niche was becoming a potential threat to the industrial regime.

By 2012 the utility industry was mobilizing in state legislatures to limit or repeal policies in support of distributed solar (Hess 2016). In some cases utilities sought to gain monopoly control over third-party financing, but such efforts were not successful. Utilities were more successful at undermining net metering laws. They argued that the laws were unfair because solar customers who could generate most of their own power benefited from the grid connection without paying their share of costs to maintain the grid.

The utilities further argued that as the rate of solarization increased, the cost of grid maintenance increasingly fell to nonsolar customers, and net metering in effect became a transfer to distributed solar customers from all other customers. In reply, advocates of solar argued that distributed solar provided numerous other benefits to the grid, including the avoided cost of new facility construction, and a gray-literature scientific controversy erupted over methods for the valuation of solar.

A coalition of environmentalists, solar installation firms, and solar advocates—the alternative industrial movement—resisted attempts to modify the net metering framework for distributed solar. The coalition mobilized using demonstrations, petitions, media campaigns, and litigation. In some cases the utilities won the right to charge solar customers additional fees, and in some cases the coalition kept net metering rules in place. In a few cases, new compromise regulatory frameworks were based on calculation of the value of solar to the utilities rather than the retail price. These solutions gave to the public utilities commissions the problem of solving the epistemic conflicts over how to value the different contributions of solar energy to the grid (Hess 2016).

In summary, the analysis of the niche-regime form of design conflicts points to distinctions that go beyond the story of solar energy as a grassroots movement and entrepreneurial niche versus the utilities as the industrial incumbents that attempt to maintain a technological regime in the face of disruptive innovation. We see various configurations of solar energy with different social meanings. In the original visions of its advocates, solar energy would usher in an era of localized control of electricity and thereby democratize energy production. Advocates envisioned a world without the grid in which electricity would be produced and stored on site. However, the regime responded with design modifications that enabled it to include the technology in the complementary modes of large-scale solar farms and distributed solar energy, both of which are compatible with the continued central role of utilities as providers of electricity. The strategy effectively blocked the original visions of activists and advocates of a future of democratic, locally controlled electricity production.

Second-order design conflicts emerged over the financing products and the net metering policy structure that enabled the proliferation of those products. The emergence of the new financial products threatened a scale shift that could be destabilizing to the incumbent firms. The invention of the third-party ownership model brought a huge infusion of capital that could help spur the scaling up of a solar transition, but it also shifted ownership to third-party companies. As distributed solar began to scale up, the utilities attempted to modify the policy regime by ending net metering, which in turn would alter the underlying finances of the products that were triggering the scale shift. Thus, in addition to niche-regime design conflicts involving the configuration of the technology itself, there are metalevel conflicts (to invoke Bateson's approach to frames) over the design of financing models and regulatory models.

Organic Food and Sustainable Agriculture   On the surface, the case of organic food and agriculture has striking parallels with that of solar energy. This alternative industrial movement in the food sector began somewhat earlier than solar energy; the origins are usually dated to reform efforts in the United Kingdom and the United States during the 1940s (Hess 2004c). European immigrant gardeners to the US provided the first social address for organic food production, but by the 1960s it had become integrated into the counterculture and the movement to develop sustainable farming that served local communities. Just as some of the reform visions for rooftop solar and small wind rejected the regime of the centralized grid in favor of off-grid power generation, so the reform visions of the early organic agriculture movement rejected the "grid" of industrial agriculture with its industrial farms, long supply chains, and supermarkets. Instead of large-scale monocropping supported by synthetic pesticides and fertilizers, the organic farmers developed agricultural techniques based on small-scale multicropping with organic fertilizers and nontoxic forms of pest control. For consumers, the emphasis was on fresh foods available through farmers' markets, food cooperatives, and community-supported agriculture arrangements rather than on processed food and fast food. Thus, this alternative industrial movement was also an industrial restructuring movement that linked experiments in the design of products (food) and production technologies (agriculture) to organizational innovation.

Another parallel with the solar movement is that organic agriculture has to date remained a niche in its industry. In the United States as of 2015 organic food sales were only 4 percent of food sales (US Department of Agriculture 2015). As with distributed solar energy, the growth rate is high, and for some types of food it is in the double digits. Also similar to the history of solar is the change from the original design of small-scale, community-oriented farming to the industrial scale of production that has made the growth possible. The National Organic Foods Production Act of 1990 made possible a standardized label and a standardized production process that contributed to the severing of the category of organic from the broader movement for sustainable local agriculture and community food relations (Obach 2015). Large growers entered the market where they saw profit opportunities, and the association between organic agriculture and small, community-oriented farms broke down. The large growers who entered the market also tended to erode the ecological farming techniques and to reduce the category of organic agriculture to the minimal level required to meet the standard (Guthman 2000). Another important change was that supermarkets began to offer organic products, and food processing companies entered the market by developing organic product lines and by purchasing small organic food companies. By 2015, more than 90 percent of organic food sales in the United States were through supermarkets (US Department of Agriculture 2015). In addition to buying whole foods, consumers could also purchase organic packaged foods, an example of product redesign to fit with an existing industrial regime. Much like the development of solar farms and distributed solar energy, organic agriculture had become integrated into the grid of industrial agriculture.

The broad design conflict between industrial and sustainable agriculture plays out in various ways, one of which is over continuing attempts by the incumbent organizations to weaken the standards that define organic. For example, in 1998 the US Department of Agriculture proposed standards that would have included sludge, irradiation, and genetically modified organisms in the definition of organic, and the proposals also included increased fees and paperwork for farmers. The Organic Consumers Association was founded in response to the threat, and it launched the Save Our Organic Standards campaign. After mobilizing consumers through the networks of local organizations such as food cooperatives and farmers' markets, the campaign successfully turned back most of the proposed changes. However, agriculture companies have continued to attempt to weaken the rules. For example, in 2003 a poultry corporation added a rider to a larger bill that would exempt poultry producers from the organic feed requirement if the costs were twice that of conventional feed. The Organic Consumers Association (2015) successfully ended this attempt to render meaningless the organic label for poultry. Many organic farmers who remained faithful the original vision of sustainable, small-scale, community-oriented agriculture rejected the industrialization of organic agriculture, and some experimented with new labels (Obach 2015).

Comparisons and Summary Whereas in the case of distributed solar generation the utilities became alarmed at the growth of solar energy, this is not the case with the food-and-agriculture regime with respect to organic food. Instead, industrial agriculture has absorbed organic as an upscale product and at the same time weakened the standards. Even if organic food were to scale up to 50 percent of the market, it would not present a major threat to industrial agriculture. Organic has been redesigned to fit into the industrial regime of large-scale production, long commodity chains, processed foods, and supermarket sales. In this sense industrial organic is more like centralized solar farms because it is compatible with the existing configuration of the industrial regime. It would be as if the utilities were to scale up solar by building more large solar farms with centralized storage, and they were to offer this option to consumers as an upscale product choice or as an addition to the energy mix in response to renewable portfolio standards.

The deeper challenge to the utilities is from the potential convergence of rooftop solar with on-site storage. Consumers could disconnect from the grid and in effect make their own electricity. In the case of agriculture, a similar situation would occur only if consumers could purchase all or almost all of their food from local farms and gardens or from distant cooperatives via fair-trade networks. If this outcome were to occur, there would be a parallel threat of disconnection from the "grid" of industrialized food and agriculture. However, it would be expensive in many areas to produce food locally throughout the year, it is inconvenient to do shopping at both a farmers' market and a store, and few locations have a good food cooperative that connects consumers conveniently with small farmers. Furthermore, much organic food is now packaged food that is sold by large food-processing companies that have swallowed up the smaller entrepreneurial firms. In short, the threat of a consumer disconnection from the grid of industrial agriculture in the United States is minimal in comparison with the threat that utilities perceive with respect to the distributed solar energy.

Although this section has only examined two examples of design conflicts and industrial regimes, the examples draw attention to the need for a

comparative approach that would require additional cases of niche-regime
conflicts involving the alternative industrial movements. Likewise, a comparative approach that includes cross-national studies would be highly
beneficial. The degree to which the regime is able to absorb and transform
the challenger's innovations appears to vary considerably, and this factor
may affect the extent to which the conflicts become heated or modest. The
extent to which a challenger technology depends on consumer labeling
may also be an important factor.

The Environment and Design Conflicts

The third type of design conflict involves the choices with respect to the
environment-society relationship. When human societies encountered
environmental limits in the past, they engaged in technological and social
innovation, such as by domesticating plants and animals and by developing systems of storage and irrigation. Recognition of environmental limits can also lead to intensified warfare and trade among societies. When a
society breaches the local environmental limits, its very future can be at
risk. However, as Diamond (2005) has shown, the risk of complete collapse
has tended to be most acute in isolated societies such as the Northwestern
Atlantic (e.g., the Vikings in Greenland) or the Southeastern Pacific (e.g.,
the Polynesians in Easter Island). He also found that in some cases societies successfully responded to their perception of environmental limits with
social and technological innovation.

In today's global society, the issue of ecological limits has become
embedded in profound changes in all major social fields, where efforts are
underway to reduce the unsustainability of current technological systems.
Recognition of environmental limits leads to the proliferation of proposals
for design innovation from a sustainability perspective. As the previous section indicated, these proposals for industrial change can be analyzed from
the perspective of a niche-regime conflict, where there is a conflict between
actors who support the emergent green technologies and those associated
with the industrial regime. This section focuses on another type of design
conflict: sustainability and resilience.

Daly (1990, 1996) argued that a society is sustainable if the withdraws
from the natural environment are less than its capacity to replenish them
and if the waste injected into the environment is below the environment's
limits to process the wastes. Other definitions, such as that in the UN report

Our Common Future (World Commission on Economic Development 1986), bring in social criteria such as intergenerational equity. Despite the growth of institutions associated with ecological modernization, today's global society is far from achieving a transition that could be defined as sustainable under either definition. Progress on this front may be best described with the metaphor of a treadmill: there is substantial motion in the form of efforts to green institutions, but with a few exceptions there is no fundamental improvement in sustainability because of ongoing growth in the consumption of resources and deposits of wastes (Schnaiberg and Gould 1994). Owing to the lack of progress on sustainability transitions, social institutions face not only the challenge of becoming more sustainable but also that of developing the capacity to maintain basic functions when confronted by crises, disasters, and other general systemic stresses. The failure of sustainability policies and practices increases the likelihood that social institutions will have to engage problems of resilience. Resilience is understood here as the capacity of a system (a person, organization, institution, society, or world system) to maintain its basic functions when faced with a systematic disruption.

This third type of design conflict, described here as "environmental," involves the potential tradeoff between sustainable and resilient design. The tradeoff is sometimes described as the mitigation-adaptation choice: sustainable design is oriented toward reducing and transforming environmentally undesirable technology, whereas resilient design is about adapting to environmental change, which often is the result of the failure of mitigation efforts. Furthermore, sustainable design often involves improving and transforming materials, chemicals, and energy, whereas resilient design is largely oriented to transforming infrastructures and relationships with water. To oversimplify, sustainable energy is at the center of sustainable design, and adaptation to water-related problems—sea level rise, droughts, floods, and storms—is at the center of resilient design. In the world of adaptation to climate change and other types of environmental change, the problem is not just CO_2 but also H_2O.

The conflict between sustainable and resilient design is both an engineering design problem and a political issue. In the green bus case discussed above, the conflict involved issues of system resilience and sustainability. Even if one were to agree that natural gas is a cleaner fuel and the better option for urban bus fleets and urban residents, the conversion of such fleets to natural gas posed problems of system resilience that led to conflicts between fleet managers and environmental justice groups. Effectively, the fleet managers asked, "Even if CNG buses are cleaner than ECD alternatives, what good is a CNG system if it is plagued by higher costs and risks to our workers such as explosions in bus barns?" Likewise, choices between bus and rail systems can entail both sustainability and resilience tradeoffs. Bus systems have greater flexibility when infrastructure is destroyed, and they can be designed to run on multiple energy systems that provide resilience. Although rail may be more energy efficient and may also be more easily accommodated to efforts to increase urban and suburban density, both the transportation and electricity grid can face simultaneous failure if the rail system is powered by electricity. Even if the social conflict of deciding what constitutes a less racist design could be resolved easily, the tradeoffs between sustainable and resilient design adds yet another layer of complexity to the social structural and niche-regime conflicts discussed in the previous sections.

Resilience and sustainability goals also can come into conflict in planning for climate change. City, regional, and national governments throughout the world are producing not only climate mitigation plans but also climate adaptation plans. However, resources are limited, and choices arise between the two. Does the government invest in infrastructure to protect the city against floods, or does it invest in rooftop solar that would allow it to reduce its carbon footprint? These are not simply technical questions because constituencies will tend to line up behind the different options. Flood control may be an issue of life and death for some residents of a city, and if there are overlays of race and class with flood risk, then the supporters of climate mitigation may appear to be advocating a middle-class luxury.

A resilience perspective tends to disrupt the one-dimensional analyses of sustainable design. From a sustainability perspective, one can analyze building design changes, such as tradeoffs between weatherization and rooftop solar collectors, in a relationship between cost and benefit that shows how much of a reduction in greenhouse gases can be achieved with a certain level of investment and a certain technology. Such calculations often favor weatherization because it provides a better return of greenhouse gas mitigation per unit of expenditure. However, having access to a small amount of solar power may be sufficient to provide the needed electricity to keep a natural gas heating system operational in the event of a winter power outage, and thus at least some level of rooftop solar may be preferable from a resilience perspective (Hess 2013c,d). Even from the perspective of technical analyses of costs and benefits, the overlay of sustainability and resilience goals can disrupt standard ways of thinking and analyzing preferences.

Similar issues can disrupt sustainability thinking for other technological systems. Reliance on local, organic food offers potential sustainability benefits that go beyond the controversial "food miles" analysis of the carbon footprint of different types of food transportation and production. Among the benefits are enhanced feedback from customers to farmers and the denser social networks of urban and rural residents (Hess 2009a). But relying mostly on local food creates vulnerabilities in the event of local disasters such as a drought or flood, just as relying entirely on nonlocal food creates vulnerabilities to disruptions of the supply chain. A diversified system of food sources may not be the most sustainable option, but it provides resilience if one part of the food-supply system fails.

These design conflicts sit uncomfortably with a conventional sustainable-design orientation, because they could justify diversified portfolios of technologies in a technological system and therefore open the way for less sustainable system design choices. Having an electricity system highly dependent on hydropower in a region where there are concerns with short-term drought and long-term climate change may open the door for the decision to maintain some other forms of energy, such as nuclear or fossil fuels, as part of the grid mix. However, adding this layer of analysis could also mean looking more carefully at how new forms of renewable energy can be designed in ways that best promote system resilience. An example is using pumped water to store wind energy. Although the strategy is not very energy efficient, it links two systems, protects somewhat against droughts and floods, and provides some options if either the hydropower or wind power undergoes a temporary failure.

Conflicts between sustainability and resilience can also occur at the household level. In an extreme case, a household could power all of its electricity from solar panels with on-site storage, it could replace natural gas or oil heat with electricity, and it could power vehicles with plug-in electricity. This off-grid home may achieve kudos for its low-carbon transition, but it has reduced resilience in the event of a failure of its solar panels. By moving away from multiple and redundant systems, the household has increased its sustainability but also reduced its resilience.

Designing for resilience also presents its own conundrums because there are different forms of resilience. Examples of economic resilience include multiple income streams from more than one family member, high levels of savings and income, broad insurance coverage, good career networks, a solid resume, and transportation alternatives should a vehicle fail. But resilience can also involve a material form such as the ability to maintain technical functions like cooking and bathing in the event of long-term power outages. Consequently, even within the design criterion of resilience there are economic and material types that may be configured as tradeoffs.

Finally, the sustainability-resilience tradeoff varies by level of economic resources. In a comparison that I conducted of sustainability-resilience tradeoffs in a low-income and upper-income household, the lower-income household invested in future economic resilience by accepting reduced income temporarily while gaining education (Hess 2010b). The single-person household was also trading off higher rent for walkability, a move that increased both sustainability (lower carbon footprint) and resilience (lack of dependence on a vehicle to get to work). The person also reduced long-distance travel and purchased used goods, both of which saved money and were greener options. However, because of the conditions of renting and low income, the person did not invest in home energy savings or sustainable food options.

In contrast, an environmentally conscious, upper-middle-income household was purchasing organic food, green electricity, and energy-efficient vehicles and appliances. However, it considered recycled paper products, green furniture, organic clothing and bedding, hybrid-electric vehicles, and rooftop solar to be beyond its affordability limits. Furthermore, after a week-long power outage the household had invested in resilient technology for the home heating system, including a power-transfer switch for a generator and electric space heaters to back up the gas-powered boiler. It also was heavily insured. Thus, some expenditures were directed toward resilience rather than sustainability (Hess 2010b).

The comparison of the two households suggests that the sustainability-resilience relationship is heavily dependent on the resources available for investment in either. The relationship between sustainability and resilience becomes something like a production possibility frontier. If there are greater resources available, then the options for addressing both sustainability and resilience are enhanced. But the relationship need not always be configured as a guns-or-butter, zero-sum tradeoff (Hess 2013c,d). Returning to the example of urban transit systems discussed earlier, bus rapid transit may allow for a more flexible and adaptive transit system, because different types of transportation power can be used to power a diverse bus fleet (natural gas, diesel, electricity, hybrid power, and even hydrogen). If well designed, bus rapid transit might also mitigate some of the racially charged bus-rail tradeoffs that have occurred in some cities. Likewise, with respect to building design, the construction of green roofs in cities provides both sustainability benefits (air cleaning from the plants and reduced energy consumption because of the insulation of the building against cold and heat) and resilience benefits (capacity to reduce urban runoff, reduced demands on backup systems for heating and cooling, and reduction of the urban heat island effect). In general, energy and water efficiency projects can address both resilience and sustainability goals.

Thus, there are possibilities for bringing together sustainability and resilience considerations when designers begin with the double vision. The design choices might be modeled with complex algorithms that assign costs and benefits to different choices of sustainable, resilient, and hybrid designs. But in this book the focus is on the sociology of the sustainability-resilience tradeoff rather than on its economics. There are political constituencies that often have preferences for sustainability rather than resilience goals or vice versa, and there are inevitable conflicts over choices between investments in sustainability, resilience, or a combination of the two.

Conclusion

When one turns to the meaning leg of the structure, meaning, and agency triangle, a fruitful way to put SMS and STS in conversation is to expand and to develop the analysis of the design of material culture. Although the material culture approach that focuses on design conflicts may seem limited, it is especially important for the study of industrial transition movements. The enduring conflicts of social structure, such as racism in the United States, are often deeply interwoven into the design conflicts. The material culture of a society is both an expression of its values and a performance of its cultural repertoires. American cities have transportation systems that, even today, reproduce and modify the long-standing conflicts of race relations as they are secreted, like a snail's shell, into the built environment. Thus, the politics of the design of material culture should not be a mere peripheral enterprise in the analysis of the cultural dimensions of social movements. One needs only to look out the window onto a city street to see how much we are embedded in multiple technological systems that reflect, constrain, enable, and perform a wide range of social relationships.

But the analysis of design conflicts need not be limited to the classical SMS concerns of structural inequality. The alternative industrial movements also point to the niche-regime conflicts over the physical design of technologies and production processes (solar panels and sustainable farming), the financial support that enables them to scale up (third-party financing and packaged organic food products), and the regulatory standards that enable and constrain the capacity for scale shifts in the niche (net metering and organic food labels). Finally, I also draw attention to design conflicts in the nature-culture relationship over sustainability and resilience, which in turn can become aligned with social conflicts.

This approach does not exhaust the types of design conflicts that will appear in the study of the politics of industrial transitions. Instead, the goal is to outline a way of thinking about the problem of meaning and social movements at the intersections of SMS and STS that goes beyond conventional frame analysis or even the anchoring of frames in the analysis of narratives, cultural repertoires, or some other unit of cultural meaning. Throughout I have tried to move away from a first-order distinction of design conflicts (e.g., for or against women or the poor) to point to the ways in which the constant innovation of technology intersects with changing social relationships to produce layered meanings of design conflict. This view of the semiotics of mobilized publics and industrial transitions is consistent both with Bateson's metalogical approach to framing and with an approach to meaning and social movements that emphasizes the multivocality of cultural repertoires.

4   The Organizational Forms of Counterpublic Knowledge

This chapter focuses on the third side of the theory triangle: agency. To carry out their goals, people must mobilize, and they do so through organizations, which enable and limit their ability to achieve their goals. In the SMS literature these organizational forms are often called "mobilizing structures," whereas in STS the parallel discussion is of heterogeneous networks. After reviewing the two literatures, I will suggest a bridge that focuses on the organizational forms that emerge when counterpublics mobilize to transform industries and to get undone science done.

Mobilizing Structures

Resource mobilization theory drew attention both to the agency of activists in producing social movements and to the conditions under which the activists could achieve successful growth (McCarthy and Zald 1977). This perspective likened activists to entrepreneurs and suggested the value of an organizational approach to the analysis of social movements. In order to survive and prosper, social movement organizations must seek resources from the broader social environment, and they do so by exchanging action on a social change goal for the moral and political benefits that supporters enjoy. The exchanges with supporters, including donors and foundations, often involve negotiation, and the goals of social movements change in response to the negotiations. Movement organizations also change over time because of bureaucratization, and the goal of maintaining the survival of the organization can become more important than achieving the original social movement goals.

McAdam (1982) argued that "indigenous" organizational networks, such the African American churches in the civil rights movement, provide four crucial resources: members, a communication network, leadership, and an established reward system. Without strong networks anchored in preexisting organizations, activists are likely to sustain little more than short-term protest events. He also argued that in order to secure support, activists must also convince the members of the preexisting grassroots networks to dedicate resources to the social movement cause. Doing so involves constructing appropriate frames and narratives that are adjusted to a changing and changeable political opportunity structure. Subsequent work broadened the idea of indigenous networks by emphasizing the importance of networks of everyday life such as family and neighborhood ties, and it also drew attention to the networks that link social movement organizations (McCarthy 1996). The second issue was developed in research on social movements and coalitions (Van Dyke and McCammon 2010).

Subsequent research connected SMS with organization studies and some of the issues that emerge at the intersections of the two fields, such as the problem of organizational leadership (McAdam and Scott 2005). Negotiating both elite support and coalitions with other social movement organizations requires leadership skills such as the ability to define goals clearly and to build robust organizations that are adaptable to changing environments (Campbell 2005). Building coalitions often requires the skills of a "bridge broker," a leader who brings together disparate movements, such as the environmental and labor movement (Mayer 2008, 2009). A bridge broker must negotiate different configurations of interest and sometimes significant differences of habitus across class or other social structural divisions.

Putting together the factors of elite support, of preexisting grassroots networks and coalition networks, and of the need for leadership that can build and maintain coalitions, the literature suggests that the mobilizing structures of social movements involve crosscurrents that put contradictory pressures on movements and require adept leaders. On the one hand, the search for support with movement and community organizations can lead to a radicalizing tendency, which in turn can lead to divisions among the leadership and preexisting organizations. On the other hand, elite support can encourage leaders to become more moderate as their goals are incorporated into government policy and corporate strategy. Furthermore, when governments or corporations respond to advocacy and activism in support of access to basic goods, the funding for the delivery of the goods can flow through the social movement organizations. When the organizations receive funding for service provisioning, their goals can shift from activism to charity work and to community development. This pattern is prominent in a variety of access movements, especially in the fair-housing and anti-hunger movements (Hess 2007a). When both the radicalization and routinization patterns occur, the movements can face painful internal divisions over strategy. One outcome can be the splitting of a movement into an accommodationist wing, which utilizes institutionalized tactics and accepts modest reforms, and a radical flank, which seeks more disruptive tactics and more encompassing goals of structural change.

In summary, this literature draws attention to the various crosscurrents to which the organizations of social movements are subjected. These organizations need to acquire resources in order to grow and prosper, but doing so places them in a matrix of contradictory alliances with other actors and organizations. Social movement organizations need to find support among elites, both for access to funding and other resources, but they also need to build bridges to existing movements and grassroots organizations that can provide a source of support. Although the SMS literature does not highlight the role of scientists and inventors, the literature can be extended to them as additional points of alliance and support. To some degree, technical experts may be considered elements of the elites who might place moderating pressures on movements, but the experts themselves may be located in subordinate positions in the scientific, political, and industrial fields. In either case, opening up this dimension of social movements requires broadening the concept of mobilizing structures to include new forms that are specific to industrial transition movements.

Mobilization in the Scientific Field

The idea of a mobilizing structure within the scientific field has been well studied in the STS literature. Sociological work that developed from the idea of paradigm conflict (Kuhn 1970) recognized that challengers to dominant paradigms generally form networks, and often they encounter resistance from defenders of the established research programs (Collins 1983). The challenger-incumbent relationship may overlap with institutional position, where the challengers occupy subordinate positions in the research field, but the conflicts can also occur among two networks of well-positioned rivals. The outcome can be a major reorientation of research programs and the replacement of one network with another in the dominant position in the research field. However, the literature known as "specialty studies" also recognizes that sometimes the challengers will migrate out and form a new research field. (See, e.g., Mullins 1972.)

Thus, in the STS literature the primary mobilizing structure of scientific change is the network of scientists. The work on controversies showed that the networks of scientific change were heterogeneous in the sense of including people and their competing methods, theories, interpretations of data, and laboratory materials and instruments. Some of the work also pointed to the interfield dynamics of scientific controversies, which occurred when public policy controversies had important epistemic dimensions (Nelkin 1992, 1994) or when scientific controversies had policy implications (Collins 2004). This dimension of scientific change was developed more systematically in actor-network theory, which also expanded the idea of heterogeneity of networks to include its material dimensions. It is not necessary here to wade into the vexed philosophical implications of the claim of the "agency of things" (Collins and Yearley 1992; Yearley 2005). Rather, the general point is that the focus on heterogeneous networks of either the controversy type or the actor-network type brings to the study of industrial transition movements an important STS perspective of materiality, knowledge, and design that is largely missing in the SMS work on mobilizing structures.

In the study of how Pasteur managed to change both government and industry, Latour (1987) drew attention to the scientist's capacity to enroll allies by defining their interests to be in harmony with the new science of bacteriology and technology of anthrax vaccines. These allies included government agencies that provided research funding, public health officials who wished to reduce the threat of epidemics, and farmers who wanted to reduce the loss of livestock to disease. Latour's phrase "the pasteurization of France" suggests that when the scientific field generates technological innovation, the diffusion of the innovations can profoundly change not only the power relations between the scientific field and other social fields but also the relations among actors in the political and industrial fields. A society that recognizes the existence of microbes is different from one that does not. However, the change occurred within the context of an existing set of social and institutional structures; the laboratory's effects on society were made possible because it successfully aligned its research with the needs of powerful segments in society. Similar effects of research networks appeared in Callon's (1998, 2007) studies of economists, whom he portrayed as influencing the construction of markets. Subsequent studies pointed out that although scientific networks do influence other social fields, they often do so in ways that are consistent with elite interests even as they partially redefine these interests (Mirowski and Nik-Khah 2007; Mirowski and Sent 2008).

The study of scientists' construction of heterogeneous networks, both inside the scientific field and outside it, adds an important dimension that is missing from the main lines of SMS on mobilization and organizations, which has tended to leave out the material and epistemic dimensions of mobilizing structures. However, the STS approach also misses what McAdam (1982) called indigenous networks, that is, the actors and organizations in the subordinate positions of the social structure and the social fields. Neither SMS nor STS examines in any detail the organizational forms of mobilized counterpublics that are oriented toward industrial transition. Again, there is a good opportunity to think more synthetically about how these two fields might be brought together.

Types and Organizational Forms of Counterpublic Knowledge

Industrial transition movements and other types of counterpublic mobilization must articulate new goals for government policy and corporate strategy akin to the work of other social movements. However, they must also articulate new designs for the technologies, products, and infrastructures of the social world, and these new designs require new areas of research and expertise. I use the phrase "counterpublic knowledge" as a broad umbrella for the new forms of expertise, scientific research, and technological design that the industrial transition movements advocate and nurture. The idea of "counterpublic knowledge" is not new. In effect, this was Marx's central intellectual task when he developed an alternative science of political economy that was anchored in the goals of working-class social movements and was opposed to the "bourgeois" political economy of the day (Marx 2011). Perhaps the best-known analysis of counterpublic knowledge today is Brown's (2007) distinction between the dominant epidemiological paradigms, which are generally based on genetic and individual lifestyle factors, and public paradigms (Krimsky 2000). Public paradigms of scientific research emerge from social movements, community groups, and sympathetic scientists who wish to bring a more environmental and societal approach to research on disease causation and treatment. These oppositional frameworks often clash with both the dominant models of disease etiology and with the industrial interests that do not want to link disease causation to industrial pollutants.

Brown's approach to science and social movements informs the broader contrast that I will develop in this chapter between the sciences and knowledges of official publics, those of the counterpublics, and the syntheses and hybrids in between the two ideal types. To review, both construct knowledge and polices that are aligned with their definition of the public interest, which is why the terms official public and counterpublic are of some value. Scientists associated with incumbent industrial organizations and existing technological regimes generally position their work as in the public interest, as do their colleagues who share a similar orientation in government and industry. For example, in cancer research these mainstream scientists focus on genetics and lifestyle factors in cancer prevention and treatment, and there is little doubt that this knowledge is broadly beneficial and therefore in the public interest. Their research holds out the possibility of new, socially beneficial technologies that might prolong life if not provide a comprehensive cure for the disease.

Furthermore, the mainstream research community may also view as empirically and conceptually flawed the public paradigms or counterpublic knowledge. One example, as Brown has examined, is rejection of alternative approaches to disease etiology from the perspective of community-level and environmental variables. A related example is research on complementary and alternative medicine (CAM) approaches to cancer (Hess 1999, 2004a). In both cases, the mainstream researchers can argue not only that their research agenda is in the public interest but that the alternatives are not because they are empirically flawed. Even if the mainstream scientists do not reject completely the agendas of the counterpublic science, they may reject the value of public funding of such work because of the opportunity cost of decreased funding for other, superior research programs.

From the opposing perspective of the advocates of both environmental and CAM approaches to cancer, the dominant research agendas are deeply flawed and not serving the broad public interest. From the environmental perspective, the dominant perspectives exclude the potential for understanding how cancer etiology is shaped by the toxic brew of sub-stances that industrial society has produced. Likewise, the CAM approaches to treatment suggest the value of exploring gentler, less toxic, and more individualized approaches to therapy. These two alternatives can be linked via the emphasis of CAM approaches on detoxification as a therapeutic strategy. Both forms of counterpublic knowledge point to the role of indus-trial interests in blocking the advance of science and technology in the public interest, and they point to the undone science of the etiology of chemical exposure and of research on unpatented therapeutic options.

We do not yet have a good map of the forms of counterpublic knowl-edge. I found it helpful to distinguish between alternative and counter-vailing types (Hess 2014c). In the alternative type, there are fundamental disagreements over the priorities of a research field and the relationship between those priorities and the public interest, such as in the case of can-cer research just discussed. The policy conflict involves research funding priorities and the correction of the problem of undone science. There is fundamental disagreement among scientists about what kinds of research priorities best reflect the public interest, and reformers within a research field call for changes in research agendas that may be aligned with indus-trial niche technologies.

In the countervailing type, the clash of knowledges is less within the research field than between the scientific and the industrial fields. In the case of climate science, we do not find fundamental struggles within the research field over different agendas and their relationship to the public interest. Although there are some scientists who publicly deny the prob-lem of anthropogenic greenhouse gas emissions, they are generally not positioned as credentialed scientists within the research field. Instead, the problem is more with the epistemic rift that occurs between the scientific field and the industrial and political fields. Climate science suggests the need for policy interventions that are broadly consistent with the industrial opposition movements' goal to sunset fossil fuels and with the alternative industrial movements' support for low-carbon technologies. Likewise, the interventions are inconsistent with the business-as-usual scenarios of the fossil-fuel sector and with the merchants of doubt hired by the industry. In this case the entire research field becomes part of the countervailing powers to the fossil-fuel sector.

This typological division can assist with thinking through the concept of counterpublic knowledge and with bringing it more closely into contact with industrial transition movements, but it lacks the organizational focus of both the resource mobilization tradition in SMS and the network analyses of STS. In the remainder of this chapter, I build on both literatures by developing the analysis of the organizational forms that serve as vehicles of counterpublic knowledge. The literature has developed to the point that we can begin to conduct a general analysis of these mobilizing structures. The analysis that follows will focus on four groups of organizational forms. Scientific and intellectual movements involve efforts to build new theories, methods, and research problems, and they can involve alternative counterpublic dynamics. Organized scientist advocacy and activism is generally less focused on internal disputes in the scientific field and more focused on public policy; hence, it can map onto the type of countervailing counterpublic knowledge. The other two forms of mobilizing structures—citizen-science alliances and citizen science—tend to involve a mixture of the two broad types. After discussing the four organizational forms, I suggest some avenues forward for research on the systematic interactions among the types.

Scientific and Intellectual Movements (SIMs)

Scientific and intellectual movements emerge when scientists are dissatisfied with the trends of their research field and have a position of leadership that allows them to launch a reform movement (Frickel and Gross 2005). The reform movement takes places within the research field and has the goal of changing fundamental priorities for research problems, methods, and theoretical frameworks. Although Frickel and Gross do not rule out the possibility that SIMs can emerge from scientists located in the subordinate positions of a research field, they focus on movements that emerge from well-positioned insiders. Certainly many cases of intellectual reform in science have emerged from the innovations of scientists in dominant positions, and the studies of Mullins (1972) on the origins of molecular biology and of Ben-David and Collins (1966) on the origins of experimental psychology are examples of a pattern of innovation from high-status scientists who colonized lower-status fields to build new research programs.

Frickel and Gross also argued that standard SMS concepts can help to explain the success or failure of these scientific reform movements. For example, the leaders of a SIM must frame their cause in ways that resonate with others in the research field. To gain and retain recruits, a SIM must create an intellectual identity and a narrative of the SIM's history, which involves positioning it with respect to rival research programs if not other SIMs. The leaders of a SIM also develop mobilizing structures, such as having a cluster of people in university departments who can produce graduate students and who have adequate organizational means for the communication and diffusion of research. Mullins (1972) also emphasized the importance of developing organizations that could provide reproductive capacity, but as Frickel (2004) showed for the case of genetic toxicology, it is possible for a new research field to recruit via professional societies if it is an applied field that has good funding sources. With respect to the intellectual opportunity structure for a SIM, Frickel and Gross suggested that tight labor markets in one research field may lead to out-migration to other fields, as occurred with migration of physiologists into philosophy that led to the emergence of experimental psychology (Ben-David and Collins 1966). Likewise, a SIM will flourish when it provides followers with an opportunity to gain prestige. In summary, Frickel and Gross provided a balanced analysis of the triangle of meaning, agency, and structure that points to factors that might be less visible in STS approaches that focus on cognitive dimensions of paradigm change or on the strategic processes of enrollment of actors into networks.

One area in need of development in the analysis of SIMs and of networks of specialty formation is their connections with other social fields. The formation of a SIM or new scientific specialty is not necessarily linked to the broad political conflicts of official publics and counterpublics. This linkage is possible, and Frickel and Gross noted that SIMS "are influenced by direct or indirect pressures emanating from the broader cultural and political environment" (2005: 209). Frickel (2004) also showed how genetic toxicology emerged from the efforts of a network of relatively well-credentialed and well-positioned scientists whose work was related to the environmental movements of the day. In this sense, the SIM represented counterpublic knowledge within the scientific field because it attempted to address the undone science of the effects of lax chemical regulation. Thus, a SIM need not be merely an internal reform movement within the scientific field and a world apart from the political and industrial fields; instead, it can develop in interaction with the relations between incumbents and challengers in other social fields. Gross (2013) developed this point by arguing that differences in the political leaning of a social science research field may be partially an outcome of the history of multiple SIMs. These connections between intellectual changes in a research field and other social fields represent an important innovation for the broader STS literature on specialty formation and on controversies, and in the remainder of this section I will draw out and systematize some of the implications of this insight.

The connection between scientific controversies and intellectual reform within the scientific field and the broader political conflicts over constructions of public interest raises important questions for the analysis of SIMs. For the intellectual reform movements in the humanities, the connection with broader social conflicts is documented and also easily observed, such as in the topics of posters for lectures that can be found in university halls (Arthur 2009). Humanists revere a public audience and the role of public intellectuals, a valuation that connects them to social movements. For social scientists, the connection with external field politics is more complex and varies by the discipline's connection with the political and industrial fields. Gross (2013) suggested that sociology favors left-leaning SIMs and economics favors right-leaning ones, and he added that there are also feedback loops because the intellectual opportunity structure for left-leaning and right-leaning SIMs also varies across these two fields.

However, for the reform movements in the sciences, the connection with the political field can raise questions about the neutrality of the researchers and the scientific credibility of the SIM. This issue is especially important when scientific research has policy implications and when scientists participate in the political field. Thus, the advocates and leaders of SIMs may have to distance their reform efforts within the scientific field from the broader social conflicts, even if their SIM is in some ways responding to problems of undone science raised by social movements. When scientists are not successful at this boundary work (Gieryn 1983, 1994), then the conditions are ripe for the SIM to fail. Thus, the theory of SIMs requires attention to this interfield dynamic—the delicate balance of a relationship with broader social conflicts and social movements and the maintenance of credibility via political neutrality—as a factor that can contribute to the explanation of the success or failure of a SIM.

The eugenics movement is a good example of SIM that failed as a result of its relatively overt connections with broader political conflicts. Although eugenics had attained some scientific respectability and a place in university departments before World War II, it became widely discredited as a scientific enterprise after the holocaust. The rise of research in anthropology on cultural variation also discredited biological explanations of differences in human behavior. However, the general idea that genetic inheritance could affect differences in behavior among humans and other animals became the basis of a new research field that emerged during the 1950s and the 1960s. Panofsky (2014) showed how the founders of behavior genetics were careful to maintain distance between their field and researchers associated with eugenics. For example, they selected Theodosius Dobzhansky, an opponent of eugenics and racism, as the founding president of the Behavior Genetics Association. The first generation of behavior genetics researchers dissociated their research from the politicization associated with eugenic and racist thinking, and they offered a vision of a large research field that would be the common ground for scientists across the disciplines who were interested in the relationship between behavior and genetics.

However, in subsequent years behavior geneticists were drawn into the controversy that erupted when some researchers attempted to prove that racial differences in intelligence test scores had a significant genetic component. Rather than reject and attack the research on race and IQ, behavior geneticists attempted to provide the social and intellectual forum where the controversy could be vetted. In doing so their field became tainted by the controversy, and they failed to achieve their vision of creating a large interdisciplinary research field for a wide range of work on behavior and genetics. Increasingly research took place in a series of disciplines that often were not in communication with each other, and the original field of behavior genetics became smaller and increasingly focused on the genetics of human behavioral differences. Although behavior genetics retained a position in the university system in the United States, the position of the SIM was limited to a few departments and became increasingly concentrated in a small number of departments. The waning organizational base for this SIM suggests social isolation that coincided with the research field's intellectual isolation (Panofsky 2014).

The case of behavior genetics raises the interesting question of the conditions for the success or failure of a SIM. Frickel and Gross (2005) judiciously use the social theory triangle of opportunity structure, resources, and framing: scientists must provide a structure of opportunities for employment and prestige, gain control of departments that enable them to recruit students and to reproduce, and convince others of their frames and research programs. However, the fragmentation of behavior genetics and its failure to live up to the ambitions of its founders suggests that another factor may be quite important: a scientific reform movement (the S in SIM) must be perceived to be untainted by political ideology. The history of racist ideology that lay behind eugenics and the race and IQ controversy made the field tainted in the eyes of other scientists who worked on issues of inheritance and populations. In their eyes the field of behavior genetics, with its growing focus on human behavior and its willingness to provide a forum for the debate on race and IQ, was not properly neutral with respect to political conflicts (Panofsky 2014).

One could generalize from Panofsky's analysis to argue that a scientific reform movement, in contrast with an intellectual movement in the humanities, must be viewed as uncontaminated by any institutional logic outside the scientific field. This issue becomes especially acute when researchers pose the existence of an entity that is not known to natural science. Whereas the fundamental concepts of the race and IQ researchers were coherent with the broader fields of biology and neuroscience (e.g., genes, inheritance, behavior, and populations), in other cases SIMs proposed completely new concepts that raised deep consistency issues with other research fields. There are many examples in the health and psychology fields that draw on ideas from popular healing and spiritual traditions that are not accepted by the mainstream of the modern natural sciences. These ideas can include vitalistic forces such as the "chi" of acupuncture or the subluxations of chiropractic and the humors found in many of the Old World medical traditions. The general perspective on the relationship between these movements and the scientific field is that they are antagonistic; in other words, these reform movements in the health and religious fields provide explanatory models based on concepts that cannot be documented with scientific methods (Evans and Evans 2008). However, there is also a line of research that suggests that these movements can have a generative effect on the scientific field, albeit in somewhat indirect ways. For early modern science, the two main examples of this line of thinking are Merton (1970) on the positive effects of the Puritan religious movement on early modern science and Yates (1972) on the effects of Renaissance occultism on early modern scientists, including Newton.

Although one can document the generative effects of such religious ideas on the early modern scientific field, it is also the case that as the scientific field matured, it developed a "membrane" that filtered out ideas that were inconsistent with a broadly materialistic and mechanistic approach to the natural world. By the late eighteen century this repulsion of such ideas was fairly institutionalized. For example, a scientific committee rejected the claim of Franz Anton Mesmer that universal fluids could affect human health (Ellenberger 1970). In effect, the scientific field was posting a "keep out" sign to this health reform movement. By the late nineteenth century, similar ideas to those of Mesmer took the form of a SIM when the field of psychical research emerged in response to the transition of mesmerism into Spiritualism. The change occurred when some of the "mesmerized somnabules" became spirit mediums who claimed to produce otherworldly communications (Darnton 1968; Hess 1991). The psychical researchers were relatively well-credentialed members of the European and North American elites; they established peer-reviewed journals; and some of them, such as William James, had prestigious positions in the university system (Gauld 1968; Moore 1977). However, they never attained acceptance by the broader scientific community. Their focus on proving life after death, either through the analysis of mediums or through "spontaneous case" research on apparitions, remained heterodox. One might argue that if they had been able to produce an alternative industrial field that could generate profits from the phenomenon, such as a robust and profitable technology of psychic healing, they might have overcome some of the skepticism, but this translation of science into technology never occurred.

Interestingly, a similar fate befell the subsequent generation of parapsychologists, who turned away from the task of attempting to prove life after death and focused instead on the study of extrasensory perception and psychokinesis largely through laboratory experiments. However, their studies of "psi" phenomenon again relied on an entity that could not be measured, at least reliably, with standard laboratory instruments, and their work as a whole raised consistency problems that again failed to pass through the "metaphysics filter" of the scientific field. Like psychical researchers, parapsychologists failed to generate a marketable technology (although the military used psychics in a few remote viewing projects to try to locate hidden missile silos). Some parapsychologists have university positions today, and some graduate students have earned doctoral degrees under parapsychologists, but in general the field is maintained through a network of independent research institutes and foundations without support from government or industry.

One can explain the failure of psychical research and parapsychology as the result of an inability to mobilize crucial resources that would allow the reformers to attract and retain recruits. In other words, they were unable to attract the support of elites, at least the elites that mattered for credibility struggles within the scientific field, such as government and industry funders. However, the failure to mobilize successfully was at least partially a result of the lack of consistency between their fundamental orienting concepts and the mainstream of the scientific field. Like psychical research, the fundamental concepts of the field were unable to pass through the metaphysics filter of the scientific field, and they remained heterodox.

In contrast, a similar fate did not occur with meditation research, even though Eastern meditation practices were embedded in religious systems that recognized equally heterodox ideas such as reincarnation. Today, thousands of peer-reviewed studies of meditation have been published in the behavioral science and biomedical literatures, and there is widespread acceptance of the claim that meditation can be used to help treat disorders such as stress. (See, e.g., Goyal et al. 2014.) Some research measures neurophysiological correlates of meditation, whereas other research examines the effects of meditation on pain and disease outcomes. Together, the two types of research provide evidence for a measurable biological mechanism and for reliable clinical use when meditation is integrated with mainstream therapies or in some cases used as an alternative to them. However, the success of meditation as an alternative research field has also entailed leaving behind any metaphysical claims, such as the idea that advanced meditators can recall past lives or experience clairvoyance, and in this sense the history of the field is more similar to the transformation of mesmerism into hypnosis research than it is to behavior genetics, psychical research, or parapsychology. Conversely, when the religious component is reintroduced in the context of meditation research, controversy can erupt. For example, hundreds of neuroscientists signed a petition against a proposal to allow the Dalai Lama to speak at an annual research conference (Kaufman 2005).

The success of meditation research suggests that another important factor of the success or failure of a SIM from an interfield perspective is its connection to the industrial field: does the SIM produce technological innovations that can be of benefit to industry? One example of the importance of this factor is a discussion by Woodhouse and Breyman (2005) on two different versions of green chemistry, which they depicted as a "social movement" in the scientific and industrial fields. In one version the approach was to design chemicals in ways that could be metabolized and excreted easily by living organisms, but this approach involved profound knowledge of medicinal chemistry. Another version followed the traditional pathway of industrial chemistry and focused instead on making benign chemicals without taking into account their capacity to be metabolized. Woodhouse and Breyman argued that rather than shift the entire field of industry chemistry toward medicinal chemistry, which might have resulted in a much more environmentally benign chemical industry, the green chemistry movement followed the path of least resistance, which was consistent with the standard practices in industrial chemistry.

In summary, the connection between scientific reform movements and conflicts between challengers and incumbents in other social fields can pose problems for the acceptance of the new research field because the relative autonomy of the scientific field is predicated on maintaining at least the appearance of neutrality with respect to political and religious beliefs. The metaphor of a membrane on the scientific field suggests that when researchers appear to be importing political or religious ideas into the scientific field, their work undergoes scrutiny and the methodological barriers go up. In the cases of psychical research and parapsychology, the continued acceptance of religious or at least dualist ideas positioned the entire research field as heterodox, and it became socially isolated. Similar isolation also occurred for behavior genetics, not because its underlying scientific concepts were heterodox but because it became associated with political ideology.

The relationship between a SIM and the industrial field is more complicated. If the SIM has applications and potential financial benefits for industry, it may become channeled in directions that are consistent with industrial research frameworks and methods. As Woodhouse and Breyman (2005) suggest, a SIM may have different variants that are subject to differential selection pressures related to their applicability to industry. This insight would also apply to meditation research, which focuses mostly on mindfulness as the main type of meditation. These are important factors for the explanation of the success of SIMs especially when applied to the study of science, technology, and social movements.

In summary, as we move from the foundational essay by Frickel and Gross (2005) to the comparative analysis of SIMs, researchers probably will have to differentiate between the "S" and "I" sides. In the humanities and the social sciences the connections with social movements may be less contaminating than in the natural sciences. A SIM can be a vehicle for counterpublic knowledge, but this potential probably varies across the research fields. Some hypotheses emerge from the comparative approach sketched out here. The closer one gets to the humanities side of the SIM, the more open this relationship may be. On the science side, a SIM such as genetic toxicology or green chemistry can have a general relationship with the identification of undone science in an industrial transition movement, but the relationship is based on the definition of a priority for research. Within that connection, researchers then must establish conventional boundaries that define the methods and concepts as autonomous and neutral.

Organized Scientist Advocacy and Activism

Although SIMs can emerge in response to broader social movements and to changes in the political, medical, and religious fields, their goal is to reform a research field. In contrast, the second group of organizational forms of counterpublic knowledge involves scientists whose goal is to change public opinion and public policy. Although very different from SIMs, the same issues of balancing politics and credibility can be found.

Scientist advocacy and activism is best understood in contrast with the standard organizational forms that connect scientists with public policy: boundary organizations and scientific advisory panels (Guston 2001; Jasanoff 1990). These organizations provide communication between the scientific and political fields, and they mediate the scientists' research on risk with political responses. The organizations can also be sites of covert advocacy, when scientists have an opinion on political and policy issues but attempt to maintain political neutrality by providing advice on the range of solutions and on the best strategy for regulatory evaluation. So the advisory role of scientists can include the evaluation of different policy options, but even this task is usually framed as politically neutral advice.

When scientists find that these mechanisms of communication are broken, either because politicians view the scientific advice of expert panels to be biased or because the advice of these panels is ignored, scientists may find it desirable to be more publicly engaged in the policy issues of the day. One option is to go to existing civil society organizations and to ask them to address public interest issues that scientists think are important, such as nuclear weapons research. However, their ideas were not always welcome. Moore (1996) showed that the scientists whom she studied in the United States during the Vietnam War era met with resistance from social movement organizations such as the New University Conference and Students for a Democratic Society. The organizations did not welcome scientists' efforts to broaden their political agenda by including new science-related issues such as nuclear fallout and weapons research. Politically engaged scientists tend to bring their own sense of priorities that do not always mesh with those of the movements, and it is possible for movement organizations to reject the scientists' proposals. However, if the organizations were to accept the proposed partnership, then we would be in the terrain of the citizen-science alliance.

The second organizational pathway for scientist activism and advocacy is the professional organization. There is a literature on scientific professional associations, but it is not concerned with the problem of how the associations can become vehicles for political activism and policy advocacy, probably because this role is not commonplace. (See, e.g., Delicado et al. 2014.) Moore (1996) argued that in the United States professional organizations in the social sciences and humanities adapted to the demands from researcher-activists by establishing caucuses that addressed new research problems and policy positions. However, natural scientists encountered more resistance from their professional organizations, which became divided over the issue of developing resolutions on political issues such as opposition to the Vietnam War. Many scientists in the organizations rejected the proposals to adopt political stances because they wanted professional associations to be based on "the principle of promoting disciplines as purveyors of objectively produced products" (Moore 1996: 1608). The associations were concerned with the potential ramifications if the research field were to be perceived as lacking political neutrality. In turn, the more politically engaged scientists experienced frustrations with the limited role for advocacy work within these organizations.

The lack of opportunities with professional associations led to organizational innovation. Barry Commoner was motivated to form the Scientists'

Institute for Public Information when he became dissatisfied with the limitations of the Social Aspects of Science Committee of the American Association for the Advancement of Science; some of the radical physicists formed Science for the People in response to frustrations with their efforts to gain an anti-war statement from American Physical Society; and members of the faculty at the Massachusetts Institute of Technology formed the Union of Concerned Scientists in the context of debates over the university's role in defense research and the unwillingness of the faculty and administration to declare some forms of research off limits (Moore 1996, 2008). These alternative organizations—known as public interest science organizations (PISOs)—can emerge especially when professional associations or universities do not meet the needs of scientist reformers. Although the PISOs that Moore studied began with a focus on specific issues such as nuclear fallout and the Vietnam War, they evolved into general science advocacy organizations on a range of issues. Their strategies of public engagement varied from more activist approaches in Science for the People to providing information in the Scientists' Institute for Public Information.

By founding PISOs, scientists addressed some of the shortcomings of the professional organization as a mobilizing structure, but the PISOs still had to negotiate the terrain of neutrality and credibility. Because the public credibility of scientific research is based on the perception that scientific knowledge actively filters out religious and political beliefs, scientists who form PISOs can become more vulnerable to attacks that their work is politically interested. Moore (1996, 2008) argued that PISOs face a difficult balancing act of attempting to affect public opinion and policy makers while also maintaining credibility for their scientific claims and the appearance of using unbiased research. Even Science for the People, the most radical of the PISOs that she studied, focused on the misuses of science rather than on the broader issue of objectivity and bias of scientific knowledge. Moore argued that feminist scientists were an exception, at least at that time: they developed critiques of scientific objectivity that were much more connected with the sociology of scientific knowledge than the other PISOs, and the women's movement organizations were more open to including science-related issues on their agenda.

If one turns to other cases of scientist activism and advocacy, it is also possible to identify the mobilizing structures that Moore describes for her data set of the period 1945–1970 in the United States, but there are also some interesting differences. In the case of climate science denialism since 2000, scientists have experienced intellectual suppression and epistemic rift, and the industrial field has been polarized by a battle between the fossil-fuel regime organizations and the emerging niche organizations of the renewable energy industries. In this context, advisory bodies, professional organizations, and movement organizations have played a more significant role than they did during the Vietnam War era. For example, the National Academies of Science and the Intergovernmental Panel on Climate Change, as well as professional associations such as the American Geophysical Union, have been important mobilizing structures. By producing studies and press releases about the reality of climate change, the role of anthropogenic greenhouse gases, and the need for a policy response, they have provided an important countervailing source of credibility to the denialism that flows from the conservative think tanks through the media and political fields. Furthermore, the professional associations have in some cases gone beyond position statements to other interventions, such as honoring journalists who report accurately on the science and criticizing the government for its cutbacks on climate science research. In Canada in 2014 the suppression of scientists under the Harper administration led the Professional Institute of the Public Service of Canada, the union that represents scientists and other professional workers in the federal government's public service, to abandon its traditional role of political neutrality to campaign against the prime minister. The prime minister's war on science was one factor that led to the defeat of his party in the election.

Furthermore, unlike the frustrations that Moore identified for scientists' contacts with social movement organizations during the 1960s, in the case of climate science and policy the movement organizations have tended to embrace the work of climate scientists and their call for a rapid transition to low-carbon energy sources. In some cases scientists have been involved in protest events such as the stop coal campaign. The scientists' focus on carbon mitigation has also affected environmentalism by reconfiguring energy transition politics toward "low-carbon" energy rather than "renewable" energy. The most important effect has been the repositioning of nuclear technology from the strong opposition that environmentalists had during the 1970s to a more divided approach on the importance of nuclear energy in the generation mix.

PISOs have also played a role in combatting the disinformation about climate science that circulates in the media, and one of the PISOs that Moore studied, the Union of Concerned Scientists, has developed a program that combats climate science disinformation. However, the advent of the Internet has also changed the PISOs, and there are now "virtual PISOs" that operate as websites, such as Skeptical Science, and do not have much organization behind them. Although there is not yet a general theory of PISOs, the comparative perspective with climate science and denialism suggests that there are significant changes in PISOs over time.

The case of climate science and denialism also suggests a need to include other mobilizing structures in a periodic table of scientist activism and advocacy. The trade associations associated with the renewable energy industry provide public information about the value of renewable energy for the reduction of greenhouse gas emissions. We do not yet have research on how these organizations interact with scientists. Furthermore, informal networks of scientists have developed to respond to specific instances of climate denialism in the media (e.g., Trenberth 2012), and they have developed websites and blogs such as Real Climate. Finally, individual scientists have opted to become public figures who openly press for climate mitigation policies. (See, e.g., Hansen 2009.)

In the case of scientists who are combatting climate denialism and political inaction on greenhouse gas mitigation, one of the important battles has been over the level of government funding for climate-related research and for renewable energy research. Thus, the case of climate science and denialism suggests that there are two kinds of problems that scientist activism and advocacy can address: gaining a policy response to the established science about the risks of continued greenhouse gas emissions and gaining support for new research that can help inform a policy solution. The latter includes support for the analysis of potential risks and uncertainties associated with industrial technology and for the development of new research fields.

The comparison of science advocacy and activism during the 1960s with climate science and policy in the 2010s suggests that the professional associations may play different roles depending on the issue and the political opportunity structure. Professional associations and even advisory bodies are good at summarizing the science, identifying a policy problem, and communicating the problem to policy makers. They can play an important role when a situation of epistemic rift has emerged and when contrarian scientists are producing disinformation that affects public opinion and the positions of policy makers. In this situation international advisory bodies may be particularly effective because they are distanced from local and national political divisions and less easily tainted with claims of political bias. But where there is general policy inaction, the professional associations have less value, as Moore (1996) pointed out.

In this situation of general policy inaction, scientist advocates and activists may find other mobilizing structures to be more appropriate vehicles. These may include PISOs, but there are also civil society and social movement organizations, especially for environmental and health issues, that are willing to support the scientists' calls for policy action. Informal networks of mobilized scientists who are willing to become public figures on an issue may also be important, and the networks may congeal into a PISO over time. Where the politics of industrial transition include not only the sunsetting of particular industrial technologies but also the sunrising of alternative technologies, the alternative trade associations connected with the niche industries may be an important vehicle. As the alternative research fields develop, so might alternative research associations that advocate a reallocation of funding to the new research fields.

In summary, the study of mobilizing structures of scientist activists and advocates—like so much of the research on science, technology, and social movements—is still in its infancy. I have suggested a comparative approach that builds on Moore's foundational work. Additional vehicles of scientist advocacy and activism include informal networks of scientist advocates, alternative industry trade associations, and professional associations associated with alternative research fields. I have also suggested some ways in which research might be developed through a comparative analysis of types of goals of scientist activism-advocacy and the different roles for the mobilizing structures.

Citizen-Science Alliances

Scientists who wish to become public figures can do so through professional associations and PISOs, but they can also participate in citizen-science alliances. Brown defines the latter as "lay-professional collaborations in which citizens and scientists work together on issues identified by lay people" (2007: 33). He argued that such alliances challenge the dominant epidemiological paradigm, which often includes assurances of safety from regulatory agencies and industrial organizations when communities have raised doubts and concerns. Citizen-science alliances can be relatively short-term and informally organized, such as specific research projects in which scientists respond to the undone science needs of communities and social movements, or they can be more long-term and formally organized, such as the Silent Spring Institute, which brings together scientists and citizens in research projects (ibid.). The alliances can also include groups from other sectors, such as firefighters and furniture manufacturers in the case of environmental health activism directed at flame retardants (Cordner and Brown 2015).

There is a lack of comparative work on citizen-scientist alliances, but we would expect that significant differences would emerge across policy issues and across countries. In a comparative analysis of the environmental breast cancer movement in the United States and the anti-dam movement in Brazil, McCormick (2006, 2009) showed that the level of epistemic conflict was much lower for the anti-dam movement, but the political effectiveness of the citizen-science alliance was also lower. She argued that in Brazil the anti-dam groups have few opportunities to participate in the policy process other than via public hearings held by the federal government's environmental agency. However, when the anti-dam groups work with scientists, mostly from local universities, to some degree they are able to open up an otherwise scientized and closed policy process, and in some cases they are able to use scientists' expertise and participation effectively in their efforts to stop the construction of planned hydroelectric dams. Her study suggests the value of comparative studies of citizen-science alliances by pointing to variables such as the scientization of the policy process, opportunities for public participation, and the strength of alliances between citizen groups and scientists.

Citizen-scientist alliances can be initiated either by scientists or by citizen groups, and scientists may serve in a variety of roles, including advice, education, research, and even spokespersons for the citizen groups (McCormick 2009). But in general the focus of the citizen-science alliance is on the knowledge that scientists can provide, either as advisors or as researchers. In turn, research in the citizen-science alliance may take various forms: community surveys and the mapping of disease clusters, sometimes with advice from scientists; projects guided by scientists that are in response to the undone science needs of citizen groups and communities but that are not necessarily designed to include extensive citizen participation; and more intense collaborations of citizens and scientists in community-based participatory research. Some of these projects involve interdisciplinary research teams, a phenomenon that suggests research opportunities for understanding better the relationship between participatory research and interdisciplinary or transdisciplinary research (Hadorn et al. 2008).

As for the cases of SIMs, professional associations, and PISOs, scientists who join citizen-science alliances can face role conflict. By becoming involved in these alliances, scientists may lose credibility for their neutral advice-giving capacity in the political field. If the level of time commitment is high enough, then participation in a citizen-science alliance could also detract from the capacity to produce peer-reviewed research. Scientists may also suffer from intellectual suppression, including the loss of grants or litigation. Consequently, citizen groups may face difficulties when attempting to recruit scientists. One solution is to recruit retired scientists who have high levels of accumulated symbolic, cultural, and social capital but are no longer reliant on grant funding for their research (Downey 1988; Hess 1995). Another solution is for scientists to conduct their research and to provide assistance in a quieter and less visible manner. Frickel et al. (2015) noted that in response to these dilemmas, some scientists prefer to stay out of the limelight; hence, it is necessary to develop new methodologies to study the "shadow mobilizations" of scientists who are quietly providing expertise to movements and community organizations.

Scientists who do become involved with communities and citizen groups also have choices within the role of the counterpublic researcher. Allen (2003, 2004) compared two scientists who developed very different strategies for research that would help to alleviate the environmental injustice of low-income, African Americans and other ethnic minority groups living in Louisiana's chemical corridor known as "cancer alley." Patricia Williams, a university-based scientist, sought to conduct peer-reviewed research that would establish credible scientific evidence that addressed the problem of undone science. She maintained an independent role as a scientist and was not an active participant in a citizen-science alliance. She also came into conflict with the community members when they sought to gain access to her results as part of a class-action lawsuit. She resisted the request but was forced to turn over her data. In contrast, Wilma Subra, an independent scientist with her own firm, worked closely with the community and used her evidence of individual toxic exposure to gain media attention via the national television show "Sixty Minutes." Allen suggested that neither strategy is necessarily right or wrong but that they can succeed and fail in different ways. Williams' research was used to help support efforts to advance policy reforms that were eventually passed in the state legislature, and Subra was able to enact a boomerang effect by bringing the national spotlight onto the local environmental justice case.

Because low-income communities that are attempting to document hazards from industrial pollution generally lack the resources to hire scientists, they must rely on gaining pro bono support from scientists, who often have limited time available to help. However, some of the larger and better-established advocacy organizations have the resources to hire scientists. This is a special type of citizen-science alliance because the scientists become employees of the citizen organization or at least work for them on a paid basis. This kind of research, called "civil society research," is a counterpart to industrial research and development, and it can provide a mechanism to address the problem of undone science.

One example of civil society research is work sponsored by the large American environmental organizations. In an analysis of this type of research, I identified 202 research reports for the year 2006 (Hess 2009b). Only 18 percent of the reports were peer-reviewed scientific research, and most of that segment of the research was concentrated in a few organizations dedicated to conservation and preservation. The remaining reports fell into the following categories:

• Critical studies of the practices of large corporations and governments that pose severe environmental risk to tropical forests, wildlife refuges, and other ecologically sensitive areas. This work was based on original research, often including interviews and the analysis of documents.

• Analyses of the human effects on specific ecosystems, from climate change to the use of off-road vehicles. This research often cited the peer-reviewed literature.

• Review articles of existing scientific literature with a focus on its policy implications, of use to policy makers and the media. Some of this work could have been published as peer-reviewed review essays.

• Analyses of the economic and environmental impacts of proposed or existing public policies. Some of this research also could have been published as peer-reviewed policy analysis.

• Analyses of sustainable policies and environmental management practices, including evaluations of the progress or lack of progress of corporations and governments in achieving more sustainable alternatives (Hess 2009b).

In most cases, the intended audience of the research was the media, policy makers, and members of the organization. The primary goal was not published, peer-reviewed science that was valued and evaluated by the mechanisms of a research field such as citations and prizes. Rather, most of the civil society research in this sample, even when produced by persons who have a PhD or other scientific credentials, was closer to the products of think tanks and other policy shops. For this type of research, value is based on the extent of media coverage and on evidence that policy makers, members of the organization, and the broader public have paid some attention to it.

Although some organizations have the resources to hire scientists or fund research, they can face complex negotiations with their scientist partners. Clarke (1998) argued that, in exchange for access to high-quality research, movement leaders may have to redefine their priorities for research problems. In the case of the movement for birth control technologies, scientists initially rejected as crude and unscientific the advocates' preference for spermicides and diaphragms. Instead, the scientists redirected birth control research toward forms of contraception that might eventually flow from the basic research. Clarke showed that a "quid pro quo" emerged in which scientists engaged in peer-reviewed, basic research on reproductive endocrinology, and in some cases they accepted funding from advocates of birth control. In order to get the undone science done, advocates of birth control had to redefine what they meant by undone science by shifting their definition of birth control from spermicides and diaphragms to biologically based contraception. However, even with this change of goals, advocates of birth control found that in order to get applied research done for what eventually became the women's contraceptive pill, they had to recruit scientists on the fringes of academia and in industry, and they had to provide them with financial support. Thus, the second prong of the strategy involved civil society research because the advocacy organizations funded the crucial translational work that created the new reproductive technology. "It was not until well into the 1960s," Clarke noted, "that 'population' funding from foundations and the federal government filtered into academia on a scale massive enough to involve basic reproductive scientists in research related, both directly and indirectly, to endocrinological contraception." (1998: 195)

Similar negotiations occur in one of the primary modes of citizen-science alliance research: community-based research projects. There is general agreement in the literature on community-based research that both scientific research and public policy are improved when the research projects involve consultation with the involved communities. Often the community members can point out gaps and shortcomings in the official knowledge and bring complex new factors into the analytical framework. Corburn (2005) noted that the alliance of local knowledge with scientific research can also help researchers to avoid treating all sites in similar ways rather than attending to local variability, the heterogeneity of populations, and local lifestyle factors.

Despite the advantages, community-based research also poses significant challenges for both communities and researchers. This type of research can lead to peer-reviewed publications, but the goal may be difficult to achieve when the community's definition of a research problem is not in alignment with what the prominent researchers in a field consider to be an interesting problem. In this case, the value of the research as a source of symbolic capital within the research field is likely to be low. Negotiations between scientists and community members over the research questions and methods will occur, and the research projects of community-based research can emerge as boundary objects that enable scientists to gain peer-reviewed publications while also allowing community members to gain quality research that addresses their questions and can be used in political advocacy (Brown 2007). Nevertheless, these negotiations of problem selection may pull researchers away from topics at the center of the research field. Even if they publish peer-reviewed research, it may be in lower-tiered journals that are identified as venues for less prestigious applied research. Scientists must also grapple with the different uses for their research, including the goal of community groups to use research for "data judo" on official reports (Morello-Frosh et al. 2009). Thus, community-based research requires thoughtful, reflexive evaluation of the process and the goals of the research (Brown et al. 2012).

Institutionalized forms of community-based research pose a different set of challenges. In some universities there are centers that work with community groups and adopt research projects that the groups have defined as important. In Europe, science shops provide research for community groups that come to universities with their undone science needs, and faculty supervisors recruit students who wish to work on the projects. The first wave of science shops emerged during a time when faculty and students were more willing to invest their resources in pro bono research projects (Leydesdorf and Ward 2005). Although science shops have diffused to universities throughout Europe, they have been vulnerable to the enterprising trends of the contemporary university and to budgetary cutbacks (Wachelder 2003). Some have been closed, and others have had to adopt more entrepreneurial forms supported by the search for external research funding. Nevertheless, some science shops continue to play a role of brokering community needs with graduate student research projects.

In summary, there is a wide variety of ways that citizen-science alliances can be configured: partnerships that emerge between scientists and mobilized citizen groups, the direct employment of scientists in civil society research, negotiations of research and funding that Clarke describes in the quid pro quo, community-based research, and science shops. In all of these cases, researchers face the risk of producing results that run counter to what the movements or communities want. For example, Vitamin C and other high-dose nutritional supplements may turn out not to be an effective treatment of solid tumors, contrary to the perspectives of alternative medicine advocacy groups, and the presumed risks of new smart meters may turn out to be much lower than some community groups believe. As Yearley (1992) argued, this tension produces an irreducible ambivalence in the relationship between scientists and the citizen group because the latter may not always get what they want from scientific research. Again the state of the literature is still in its infancy, and it will probably take some time before researchers identify the conditions under which these citizen-science alliances work well for both scientists and citizens.

Lay Knowledge and Citizen Science

The fourth main organizational form of counterpublic knowledge, citizen science, is based on research by laypersons. There are various types of lay knowledge, including knowledge associated with a nonscience occupation, with the habitus of a location in the social structure (e.g., by class, race, ethnicity, or gender), and with a community or a geographically restricted environment (local knowledge). Although lay knowledge is empirically based, it is not scientific knowledge. Scientists may accept or reject lay knowledge, and they may also get involved in a controversy over what parts of lay knowledge claims are true and what parts are false. Like the political and metaphysics filters discussed above, there is another filtration effect whereby a research field appraises lay knowledge claims from the perspective of the field's concepts and methods. However, it would be misleading to describe lay knowledge only as belief, because often lay knowledge is based on well-tested expertise, such as occupational and geographical knowledge, that is absent in the scientific field and unknown to scientific researchers. This point emerges in some of the STS studies of scientific and lay knowledge, such as Wynne's (1996) work on the sheepherders of the Sellafield area, whose combination of occupational and local knowledge could have benefited scientists as they developed their plans of remediation for radiation exposure.

In the context of industrial transition movements, lay knowledge can become the basis for the formation of a mobilized counterpublic. It may emerge as the result of an inverted cogito by which laypersons come to doubt the official assurance of safety or efficacy. In other words, they are thinking "I am sick; therefore, I doubt" or "I can smell the pollution in the air; therefore, I doubt" (Hess 2007a: 56). These cogitos cast doubt on official knowledge from industry and government agencies that claim that the laypersons are imaging their illnesses or other problems. The doubts arise especially in communities that suffer from toxic exposure, but they also appear in patients who have come to doubt the efficacy and safety of conventional therapies (Hess 2004b). Clearly, laypersons do not have enough advanced educational training to evaluate scientific knowledge in the way that experts do. In the terminology of Collins and Evans (2007), they generally lack both participatory expertise (the ability to produce scientific knowledge) and interactional expertise (the ability to propose research topics and to evaluate research methods and findings). However, laypersons are still able to evaluate the general credibility of experts, and Wynne (1996) noted that in some ways their understanding of the social construction of expertise is quite sophisticated and similar to the approaches adopted in the sociology of scientific knowledge. To evaluate the credibility of experts, laypersons look at consistency across expert statements, a history of accuracy or inaccuracy, and indications of interest or disinterest. When laypersons experience personal loss and suffering, when the experts lack credibility, and when no scientists have entered the picture with community-based research projects, then conditions ripen for the transformation of lay knowledge into citizen science.

Communities and other lay organizations do not necessarily respond to this situation by producing citizen science. Environmental justice struggles can begin with the lay cogito, but the communities can jump to demanding policy changes such as the closure of a polluting chemical plant or a bus barn without seeking additional documentation and research. However, the alleged polluters often argue that the claims of toxic assault lack scientific rigor, and they may argue that they have complied with government regulations. Regulators may also weigh in on the issue and say that their standards have been met. Their rejection of laypersons' experiences tends to create an epistemic conflict, where laypeople doubt the credibility of the official experts because of the mismatch of personal experience and the assurances of safety.

An epistemic standoff of this type will tend to transform lay knowledge into the quest for research to resolve their problem of undone science. Laypersons may then go to local universities, nonprofit organizations, or government agencies and call for new research to document their claims of toxic harm. Citizen-science alliances may form if a scientist or group of students responds to the call for help. But in some cases a community takes its local knowledge and formalizes it via citizen science, which transforms lay knowledge into the more rationalized and systematized collection of data. Brown and Mikkelson (1990; see also Brown 1992) explored popular epidemiology as one type of citizen science exemplified by the cases of Love Canal, New York, and Woburn, Massachusetts, where members of communities exposed to toxic substances documented the health effects of exposure to toxic chemicals from industrial waste.

I follow several of my colleagues in using the term "citizen science" to refer to research by laypersons who are attempting to formalize lay knowledge by developing data sets. The data sets can come from measurements from instruments that are accessible to laypersons, from the collection of interview data and testimonials, from photography and film, and from mapping of exposures and illnesses. Citizen science can involve countersurveillance, especially of polluters, but, as Monahan (2010) has explained, the concept of countersurveillance is broader and includes other kinds of activities. A potentially confusing use of the term "citizen science" occurs when researchers use it to describe volunteer work to help scientists gather data for research projects. Although the term "citizen science" is sometimes used for this category of lay research (see, e.g., Dickinson et al. 2012), Moore (2006) suggests that we use the term "amateur science" for conceptual clarity. I agree that it is useful to distinguish these two types of lay research: citizen science is a politically motivated form of lay research that aims to develop data in response to undone science, and amateur science is research by nonexperts who complement or assist scientists in their data-gathering projects. There are vast networks of amateur scientists associated with many research fields, including astronomy, paleontology, and many different areas of study of natural environments and animals (Greenwood 2007; Halffman and van Hemert 2010; Mims 1999). As a type, amateur science is not involved in the politics of industrial transitions, and it does not have a social change goal.

However, as Kinchy et al. (2014) showed, in practice amateur science and citizen science may occur together. In a study of volunteer water monitoring, her team found that organizations had at least three objectives: policing streams to gain the attention of regulators, gathering information that can be used to educate the public about conservation, and assisting scientists in data-gathering efforts. Whereas the first goal is an example of citizen science and the third approximates amateur science, the second goal lies somewhere in between. Furthermore, although it is possible to distinguish organizations using the categories of amateur and citizen science, both goals can also appear within a single organization, and the goals can change within and among organizations over time. For example, her team found that the development of hydraulic fracturing technologies has increased the interest in the policing goal.

There are several different types of citizen science. Arguably the best-known form of citizen science involves community-based attempts to remediate risks to pollution exposure. In the case of pollution from manufacturing facilities, members of a community begin with their lay knowledge of the effects of pollution. Usually they can detect exposure by smelling it in the air or by seeing stains on their buildings and cars, and they also know about the range of local diseases that appear to be linked to toxic exposure. The development of "bucket brigades" (citizen groups that monitor ambient air quality near toxic emissions sources to document violations of air quality standards) is one of the better-known examples of the translation of lay knowledge into mobilized citizen science. With inexpensive bucket technologies that capture air samples, citizens can transform their lay and local knowledge about air pollution into something more measurable and replicable. Ottinger (2010) found that a community is able to use these technologies to document spikes of airborne pollutants over a short time period that corresponds to the exposures that community members experience with their senses. In some cases the information can spur a company or a government regulator to conduct its own studies.

Another example of citizen science involves participatory mapping. Unlike direct citizen research on toxic exposure, participatory mapping can produce new types of knowledge, and it can help to educate communities about the range and variation of exposure and risk. In India opponents of a proposed dam in the state of Pune worked with nongovernmental organizations to develop two alternative proposals based on mapping the reduced negative effects of the alternative proposals on households. Although the government rejected the alternative proposals, it agreed to reduce the level of the surface of the water for the proposed dam in order to reduce the number of homes submerged. Phadke (2008) argued that the improved outcome for the villagers rested on two factors: mobilized opposition to the dam, which the government could not ignore, and the construction of a credible alternative based on a combination of citizen science and technical expertise.

In another example of citizen science as participatory mapping, McCormick (2012) showed how the Louisiana Bucket Brigade went on to develop a new form of participatory mapping after the 2010 Deepwater Horizon oil spill. The brigade partnered with an open-source, online mapping system to create a citizen-driven database of information on the effects of the oil spill. The citizen-driven database was also different from the official, government investigation, which had a more restricted methodology and set of research questions. McCormick argued that the crowdsourcing model represents the next step in community-based citizen science that allows it to shift toward a larger scale of aggregation of local knowledge than is typically found in the community-based model of lay mapping of unassessed risks and exposures. This approach to citizen science also produces a new kind of knowledge that is complementary to research generated by the regulatory agencies.

Another type of citizen science involves the formalization of local and indigenous knowledge as part of a mobilization to change policy. Leach and Fairhead (2002) described how government-based research in Trinidad assigned the cause of mammalian depletion to overhunting. In contrast, the hunters' organization argued that the depletion of mammalian populations was due to habitat destruction caused by marijuana growers and poachers. The hunters' organization used their local knowledge to develop methods for measuring the decline of the size of animal territories. Importantly, the leaders of the hunters' organization were well educated, and one had a science degree and could interact with the conservation biologists on their own terms. Thus, the advocacy organization served as a bridge between the knowledge of lay hunters and the research by wildlife management and conservation experts.

Although the literature on citizen science is still limited, research on this topic may eventually provide insights into the effectiveness of different kinds of citizen science. For example, it might show the effects of direct measurement strategies such as the bucket brigades versus mapping strategies, and it could assess the extent to which Internet-based crowdsourcing improves the chances of gaining remediation for toxically assaulted communities.

Interactions of Organizational Forms

Having now outlined four organizational forms for counterpublic knowledge—SIMs, scientist organizations, citizen-science alliances, and citizen science—the question emerges of how these different types interact with each other and with official research communities of industrial, government, and academic scientists.

The first level of interaction occurs when one form of knowledge spurs another form into action. For example, one goal of the bucket brigades was to use the lay research to gain attention from experts who might conduct additional, confirmatory studies. In effect, it became a demonstration of undone science and a call for expert researchers to complete it. However, Ottinger (2010) noted that when regulatory agencies responded with research they still preferred their own summa canisters. There is a politically and technically important difference between the two research methods and technologies: the regulators' devices focused on twenty-four-hour averages that could miss chemical spikes that the citizens' bucket technology was able to document. Thus, the bucket measurements had an instigating effect, but the regulators responded by passing the citizen-based knowledge through a methods filter that required revalidation with their own instruments and methods. The regulators were skeptical of the bucket methodology, and some of the comparisons with the standard canister method confirmed their perception that the citizen methodology was less accurate (Ottinger 2010, 2013).

Although citizen science can help to gain attention, it was difficult to get regulatory and industrial scientists to change their methods of evaluation. However, Ottinger (2013) also noted that the technologies of measurement themselves are changing, and with technological innovation there may also be changes in government regulatory standards that respond to some of the community's concerns. Furthermore, regulatory agencies may also arrive at opposing conclusions. In Woburn state and federal environmental scientists documented some exposure, but the US Centers for Disease Control and Prevention and the US Department of Public Health rejected the lay study for failing to document a link between exposure and health outcomes (Brown and Mikkelson 1990, Brown 1992).

The effectiveness of citizen science in bringing about both more research and some remediation also depends greatly on the local political opportunity structure. In Louisiana there is a long history of government corruption and acquiescence to the chemical industry. Ottinger (2013) argued that the lack of government support for citizen science has contributed to a tendency for citizens to solve their differences with corporations directly in a neoliberal mode of private governance. She showed how one corporation successfully divided a fenceline community and worked out a resolution with a portion of the community. The corporation later sold its facility to a larger company that had a stronger corporate responsibility ethic and administrative structure. The larger company then worked out a partnership with the community to resolve the pollution issues, but the community's more critical activists were also sidelined in the process.

Allen (2014) showed that the political opportunity structure is quite different in Italy's chemical corridor of Porto Marghera. A retired chemical worker, Gabriele Bortolozzo, drew on support from local medical students and collected data on chemical exposure and diseases in the region. He published his work in the labor-environmental journal *Medicina Democratica*, where he documented the history of chemical exposure, mortality rates, and broader environmental damage. He also helped to recruit scientists, who began their own research on the pollution, and he presented his work to the district attorney for Venice, who then assembled a team of experts to support the prosecution of the chemical companies. On appeal, the superior court convicted five executives and managers of manslaughter and other crimes. Allen argued that citizen science was particularly effective in this case partly because of the independence of the Italian judiciary and the way in which the roles of prosecutor and judge are blended. Unlike the Louisiana courts, the Italian courts were more willing to accept citizen science as evidence.

An important factor in the relationship among citizen science, industrial science, and regulatory science is the role of research conducted by scientists located in independent institutes or in universities. In the Woburn case the citizen science helped to spur interest from the Harvard School of Public Health, whose scientists designed a study with stronger methodological controls than the citizen science but that nonetheless documented health effects related to chemical exposure. A subsequent reanalysis of data by the US Department of Public Health confirmed the relationship between childhood leukemia and maternal consumption of water from contaminated wells (Brown 2003). Thus, citizen science can help to trigger a response from independent, university-based scientists that can become the basis of citizen-science alliance. Conversely, where laypersons do not establish a solid citizen-scientist alliance, such as in the case of Gulf War veterans who demanded recognition for their symptoms that did not reduce the etiology to stress-related causes, their capacity to influence the dominant epidemiological paradigm is much weaker (Brown et al. 2000).

What would a general model of the interactions among these different types of official and counterpublic knowledge look like? A processual approach would begin with the rationalization or formalization of lay knowledge via the development of citizen science. Bucket brigades and similar types of data gathering by laypersons then face revalidation through official methods and thus are passed through a methods filter, whereas the mapping approaches tend to produce a parallel knowledge base to that of the regulators. In either case, the first stage of citizen science can lead to the formation of citizen-science alliances that produce new research that addresses the undone science. The scientists can assist the citizens through community-based research, or they can develop their own research projects that begin with the lay knowledge but independently investigate the claims of the citizen science. The scientists who become involved in the citizen-scientist alliances may themselves have long-standing connections with social movements via participation in PISOs or social movement organizations, and they may see the specific citizen-science alliance as part of a broader strategy of epistemic and political change. Social movement and civil society organizations may also become involved by providing resources for more research and by generating civil society research.

An important juncture in the process is the response of the industrial scientists and the government regulators to the citizen science and citizen-science alliance: Do they remain convergent on the hypothesis of little or no risk, or do they become divided? If the government scientists agree that there is some documented risk that requires a change, then the opportunity structure is much more open for the citizen groups and social movements to gain some remediation. If the government and industry scientists are not divided, then there could be a controversy between the citizen-science alliance, which documents a problem and the need to remediate it, and the scientists who are funded by industry and whose results are supported by regulators. The controversy could then slide into suppression of the academic and independent scientists and the closing of the opportunity structure.

Thus, the analysis of the organizational forms of counterpublic knowledge can be integrated via a processual model of the interactions among the different types of knowledge. However, other patterns of interaction also occur, and this first approximation of a processual model is unlikely to be adequate. Epstein (1995, 1996) developed one important complication when he drew attention to the fluidity of the categories of analysis. He showed that AIDS activists first sought more rapid drug approval and targeted the US Food and Drug Administration, and at this stage they were not involved in questioning research priorities. However, activists soon shifted to the goal of improving drug development and of altering research priorities. When they made the shift, they also started to pay more attention to the politics of research and to the priorities of the National Institutes of Health. To be more effective, some of the leaders of the AIDS movement acquired impressive knowledge of biomedical research. Although the AIDS activists whom Epstein studied were not engaged in citizen science in the sense of lay-based research, they acquired what Collins and Evans (2007) later described as interactional expertise. Once the activists had mastered this level of expertise, they found that researchers were inclined to take their arguments seriously, and government administrators granted them access to scientific review boards. Thus, there is a need for a second-order processual model that also tracks the shifting position of actors across the types.

Conclusion

Research on the mobilizing structures of counterpublic knowledge takes us some distance from the view of scientific research as a black-boxed prop that is just one more resource that movements may mobilize. When studying the complex relations between experts and movements, it is important to remember that scientists are people, not passive resources. Even when they conduct research in response to the calls from civil society to address undone science, they do not always end up supporting the epistemic claims of their community or social movement partners. Research often involves surprises, and the data do not always cooperate with the counterpublic goals. Scientists also have to negotiate the expense of doing what may be unfunded research, the possible loss of symbolic capital from letting their community or movement partners guide the choice of research problems, and the role conflicts that can occur when scientists become publicly engaged in related policy issues.

Scientists can also be instigators when they recruit civil society, community, and social movement organizations to help advance their proposals for change. They may seek the support of allies in struggles over the reconstruction of agendas in the scientific field, and some scientists also have long-standing commitments to social movements. In turn, activists and advocates who work with scientists have to negotiate the problems of expense, timing, methods, and other issues that occur with their involvement in the politics of science. Despite the complexities, counterpublic knowledge is made, and both the SMS and STS literatures can be advanced by examining in a more systematic way how this knowledge is made and negotiated.

The organizational approach developed here takes us some distance from the approach of SMS, which focuses on mobilizing support from donors, grassroots networks, and other movements. But it also shifts the model of scientific change some distance from heterogeneous networks of STS, which mobilize to change a paradigm, to resolve a controversy, or to found a new research field. Instead, researchers working at the boundaries of SMS and STS are mapping out new organizational forms. As I have indicated throughout the chapter, the study of the organizational forms of counterpublic knowledge is still very much in its infancy, and the research field has only begun to reach the stage of comparative studies of different types of organizational forms. We know little about the conditions under which these mobilizing structures arise, flourish, and have effects consistent with their goals. Only disciplined comparative research can address these issues.

We also know little about how these different modes of counterpublic knowledge interact. The processual model that I outlined is one possibility, but Epstein (1996) suggested that there is a need to show how the actors change their skills and goals as a result of the interaction, and the discussion of other organizational forms in this chapter suggests additional complications for a general model of interaction. For example, scientists may become more aware of lay perspectives and incorporate them into their research programs, including via community-based research or even via a SIM. But scientists may also become activists and take up the policy issues in their scientific associations and PISOs. Likewise, activist and advocacy organizations that have resources may hire scientists to produce civil society research, thereby recruiting scientists and influencing them to change their research programs. At the same time, laypersons may become more educated and acquire interactional expertise. In some cases, they may even develop the professional credentials needed to become scientific researchers. Thus, we need an approach that tracks not only the interactions of the different types of counterpublic knowledge and science but also the changes that are occurring among actors as these different forms of knowledge and advocacy interact.

5   Institutional Change, Industrial Transitions, and Regime Resistance Politics

The goal of an industrial transition movement appears to be straightforward: to change an industry in a fundamental way. However, the definition of a fundamental change is complicated. It may include the structure of organizations and their decision-making processes; the design of technologies, products, and production processes; and the values and research programs that guide decisions and innovation strategies. The paradigmatic example is a movement to transform an industry to make it more "sustainable" by, for example, reducing the greenhouse gas emissions and pollution from electrical power plants. Often an industrial transition movement finds that its aspirations of change, such as decarbonizing electricity production, fall far short of realization.

In the previous three chapters I developed the framework for explaining the capacity of an industrial transition movement to mobilize support successfully. In this chapter I focus more on the processes by which movements overcome the pervasive problem of incumbents' resistance to change. To address this issue, I draw on two background literatures: the SMS side focuses on the institutional literature on industrial change and social movements, and the STS side begins with the transition studies literature on the same topic. I show some ways in which the two literatures converge on the types and processes of change. But within this broad topic of the processes of industrial change, I focus especially on the important but not yet fully explored topic of regime resistance, that is, the study of how industrial incumbents block fundamental transitions. Then, I present some of my more recent research on the strategies of challengers to overcome regime resistance.

Institutional Theory and Institutional Logics

The idea of an industrial transition entails a fundamental change in the underlying institutional structure of an industry or industrial sector. One prominent and relevant framework for examining this problem in institutional theory is the analysis of "institutional logics." Friedland and Alford (1991) drew on the work of anthropologists to argue that each of the main institutions or social fields of society—state, economy, religion, family, science, media, arts, and so on—has a unique institutional logic or "set of material practices and symbolic constructions" (248). From this perspective the term "institutional logic" is similar to that of a cultural system (e.g., religion as a cultural system, ideology as a cultural system) (Geertz 1973).

The use of the culture concept allows students of industrial and other types of institutional change to include Weberian questions of meaning in their analyses. However, one of the pitfalls of this approach, as in other forms of cultural analysis, is that it can emphasize shared cultural categories and values, as occurs in the analysis of holistic cultural patterns (Benedict 1934) or of unified cultural systems (Geertz 1973). Such approaches can overemphasize the irenic quality of culture and underplay conflict. Friedland and Alford recognized this limitation, as they indicated in the following passage:

> The meaning and relevance of symbols may be contested, even as they are shared. Individuals, groups, and organizations struggle to change social relations both within and between institutions. As they do so, they produce new truths, new models by which to understand themselves and their societies, as well as new forms of behavior and material practices. (1991: 254)

Within institutional theory, an influential example of the analysis of conflicting institutional logics is DiMaggio's (1991) analysis of the curatorial and public education models in the art museum field. (See also Fligstein 1990.) STS researchers have also studied conflicts between a market logic and basic science logic that characterizes the institutional politics of modern universities. (See, e.g., Berman 2012; Kleinman and Vallas 2001.)

The analysis of changing, contrasting, and conflicting institutional logics was part of a general shift in institutional theory from the problem of reproduction and institutionalization to that of institutional change. For example, in an analysis of change in a regional US health-care system, Scott et al. (2000) highlighted the conflict between dominant and secondary logics as a way of interpreting the process of industrial transition. Their approach also linked changes in systems of meaning to changes in organizational forms and power relations among actors.

The analysis of institutional logics does not require that institutional change involves a complete replacement of a dominant logic by a secondary or challenger logic. Often the older institutional logic does not disappear, and opportunities for creativity and synthesis among institutional logics occur. These relationships of synthesis and conflict take place in a field structure where there may be challenges from actors in subordinate positions, including social movements, to those in dominant positions. Thus, the SMS perspective on how incumbents respond to movements and how movements change their goals in response to incumbents is relevant for understanding the change of institutional logics.

One example where the role of social movements in relationship to changing institutional logics is visible is in the transition of water supply systems. Fuenfschilling and Truffer (2014) examined regional water supply systems in Australia and utilized the concept of institutional logics to explore systematic tensions within the water supply system. Specifically, they argued that there was an established and formerly dominant "hydraulic logic" characterized by three main aspects: values that favored economic growth, an infrastructure of centralized supply and delivery, and engineers as the dominant actors. This institutional logic was partially displaced after reforms in 1994 that supported two alternative logics. The "water market logic" was based on the goal of privatization, organizational consolidation of formerly small-scale utilities, the construction of water markets for trading between rural and urban consumers, and a profitability and efficiency culture led by economists and consultants. The "water sensitive" logic was based on a goal of developing decentralized water recycling technologies and water conservation, an infrastructure and policy framework that supports water conservation, and new government organizations supported by community and environmental organizations. Thus, the two emergent logics have connections with movements: a professional reform movement, which emphasizes the transformation of public utilities by importing economic models that support market development, and the environmental movement, which emphasizes conservation. Fuenfschilling and Truffer argued that "traditionally very institutionalized actors such as governments and utilities are trying to incorporate the new demands where possible but also show a considerable amount of concern, resistance, or even ignorance towards certain topics" (2014: 784).

We have extended this framework in our research on the transitions of the water supply regime in US cities (Hess, Wold, et al. 2016). We developed a somewhat different typology of institutional logics that is more closely connected with metropolitan politics and urban social theory. Water supply politics in American cities are governed largely by a growth logic that is connected with urban growth coalitions and favors the expansion of water supply sources through long-distance importation and the construction of new reservoirs and pipelines. Engineers are important actors as the builders of the infrastructure, but the dominant actors are political and industrial elites that back an institutional logic that prioritizes finding new water sources. The goal of a continuing effort to build more infrastructure to increase water supply can in turn lead to mobilizations against the projects from different constituencies. We also identified the following institutional logics:

• a rural preservation logic based on movements that oppose changes in the landscape and favor traditional uses of surface and groundwater systems
• an urban consumer logic (often connected to low-income urban political constituencies) that in some cases involves mobilizations of angry consumers who reject the high costs of Promethean investments
• an environmentalist logic that favors conservation policies over energy-intensive and environmentally destructive water importation.

The outcome of the conflicts among the logics is a transition in the water supply infrastructure, usually toward a more diversified portfolio of sources that includes aquifer recharging, desalination, recycling, and conservation (Hornberger et al. 2015; Hess, Wold, et al. 2016).

Another example of the role of movements in the changes of institutional logics involves the emergence of recycling in the waste-management industry after 1970 in the United States. Lounsbury (2005) argued that recycling activists promoted an institutional logic that was based on training of at-risk populations and a vision of a more sustainable and just society. Organizationally, this wave of recycling was located in nonprofit drop-off centers and made use of volunteer labor. However, the incumbent organizations of the waste management industry adopted and transformed recycling into a technological system based on curbside pickup, sorting facilities with poor labor practices, and a strong concern with profits (Weinberg et al. 2000). The activist institutional logic then continued in new organizational forms and social change projects. Lounsbury found that activists shifted into opposition to waste-to-energy incinerators, a change that linked the recycling movement to the emergent environmental justice movement. Furthermore, as I have shown, some recycling advocates also shifted into founding reuse centers and supporting zero-waste activism (Hess 2007a, 2009a).

Other research on social movements, industrial change, and institutional logics draws attention to the combinatorial and synthetic relationships among different institutional logics. In an analysis of the preference of the Progressive political movement for rationalized, bureaucratic organizations from 1890 to 1928, Haveman et al. (2007) studied the effects of the political movement on the transition of thrift organizations from a mutual, short-term association to a bureaucratized savings structure that had various hybrid forms. Likewise, in a study of the regulation of fire insurance in the United States between 1900 and 1937, Schneiberg and Soule (2005) described alternative regulatory frameworks advocated by industry, social movements, policy makers, and other actors. They suggested that the different institutional logics were subjected to recombination and that is it necessary to analyze the relative success of different institutional logics from a multilevel perspective that includes national government conflicts, interstate relationships such as diffusion, and state-level political dynamics. Schneiberg (2007) also argued that even unsuccessful movements leave behind organizational innovations and practices that are of value to future generations of industrial innovators and social change activists.

The analysis of conflicts and syntheses among institutional logics leads to the conclusion that industries can go through periods of heavy contestation and relative quiescence or "settlement." Schneiberg and Lounsbury argued that research on social movements and institutions supports "a view of institutions as settlements of political struggles over the character of fields fueled by the mobilization of challengers around competing projects and logics" (2008: 655). They further argued that by including movements in the analysis of institutional change, attention shifts away from "'cooler' imageries of paths as based mainly in diffusion, taken-for-granted practices, theorization, and normative endorsement by professions or states" (ibid.: 653). The "cooler" dimensions are still relevant, but the analytical

framework combines them with the "warmer" dimension of social movement contestation, which leads to the formation of new institutional logics
and to organizational innovation.

So far most of this research develops theory in the sense of analytical categories that can guide research on single cases or industries. However, some
of the research is also beginning to develop hypotheses about the general
causal conditions under which different types of institutional change occur.
On this point, Rao and Kenny (2008) developed a typology of four main
types of changes and associated conditions:

• Where proposals are incompatible but no champion has enough power
to impose an outcome, settlements tend to be fragmented and precarious.
• Where the proposals are compatible and power is dispersed, settlements
tend to emerge as a patchwork, but they remain precarious.
• Where proposals are incompatible and one party has the power to impose
a settlement, the settlement is the result of an imposition by the dominant
actor.
• Where proposals are compatible and one party has the power to impose a
settlement, the settlement tends to be integrated.

In summary, the analysis of institutional logics makes it possible to
analyze both the power struggles among actors in a social field and the
constructions of meanings that they produce as they engage each other. A
small but insightful literature has pointed to the role that social movements
play in articulating and enacting alternative institutional logics that may
replace or recombine with the dominant logics of an industrial field. Thus,
the combination of social movement and institutional perspectives provides a good basis for understanding the long-term transition of an industrial system that is the goal of an industrial transition movement. However,
attention to the material dimension, including the design conflicts, is missing, and again there is room for integration of SMS and STS perspectives.

Transition Studies and Social Movements

The second theory tradition that is relevant for the study of how movements affect industrial change is based on transition studies, a research
field that developed from innovation studies and STS research on large

technological systems. A large technological (or technical) system is a heterogeneous ensemble with three main types of features:

• natural resources, which include the raw materials of industrial processes, the use of nature as a sink for industrial wastes, and the interaction of landscapes and infrastructures
• a sociotechnical system, which includes the organizations, laws, practices, infrastructures, products, and consumers
• a cultural system, which includes the cognitive categories and values that orient discourse and practice

Large technological systems are generally associated with broad industrial sectors such as electricity, transportation, buildings, biomedicine, chemicals, and food. Thus, there are clear parallels with institutional theory, such as the attention that both give to industry-level change over time and to the role of cultural meanings in those changes. The crucial difference is that the transition studies approach also draws into the analytical framework the important role of infrastructures, products, and practices, and it draws attention to the relationship between institutions and the natural environment.

A transition in a large technological system involves substantially different technologies, infrastructures, raw materials, and waste in addition to changes in organizations, laws, consumer practices, and cultural systems. Hughes (1983, 1987) developed one of the foundational approaches to the study of industrial transitions in his work on the development of the electricity grid. This approach focused on a multidecade change in one industrial sector, and it also analyzed the changes as a procession of phases. Hughes argued that large technological systems often begin with the innovations of inventors and entrepreneurs, but as they grow and expand, the systems undergo bureaucratization and a shift in control to managers. His analysis of large technological systems also drew attention to the material dimensions of the system, such as the tendency toward lock-in after the organizations had built expensive infrastructure. Thus, one dividend of the material orientation of transition studies is immediately evident. The resistance of incumbents to change is not necessarily based on protection of profits, and indeed they can have solid reasons of public benefit associated with maintaining system stability, environmental adaptation, and resilience.

Other research on transitions examined causes that affect transition trajectories. Transitions can take place within the private sector as the result of technological innovation and marketplace competition; however, exogenous factors can also drive transitions. Summerton (1994) argued that an important exogenous cause of system change is interconnection with parallel systems (e.g., between different gauges of railroad) and the related problem of bridging system boundaries (e.g., between railroad systems and other transportation systems). Other researchers—among them Coutard (1999) and La Porte (1991)—drew attention to the role of government policy and the intentional steering of technological change. Even where there is an important entrepreneurial dimension, such as in the case of the rise of automotive manufacturing companies that displaced horse-powered transportation, the transition requires a network of changes in regulatory practices (e.g., traffic laws), infrastructure (roads and gasoline stations), and consumer practices (e.g., safety rules and practices; see Geels 2005). These changes generally require substantial government intervention, even if government policy is occurring along with market-driven change.

As with institutional change in general, the transitions of large technological systems are contentious processes. Although Hughes mentioned the efforts of the gaslight companies to block the electricity transition, his phase model of transitions did not highlight conflict. To address this issue, Rip and Kemp (1998) and Geels (2002) developed the analysis of the conflict between the niche and industrial regime. In the broader language of SMS and strategic action fields, the relationship might be translated as a challenger-incumbent dynamic within an industrial field; however, the two relationships are not always identical. The niche is the site of radical innovation, and it is located organizationally in "'protected spaces' such as R&D [research and development] laboratories, subsidized demonstration projects, or small market niches" (Geels 2011: 27). The niche may take the form of small, entrepreneurial companies that have developed potentially disruptive technologies that are a threat to large corporations, and in this case the niche-regime relationship and the challenger-incumbent relationship are congruent. However, the niche may emerge within large incumbent organizations that may nurture the niche technology until it is market ready, then release it on the market in order to gain marketplace advantages over other incumbents. When a technology is stabilized, the incumbent organizations share a sociotechnical regime (Geels 2011: 27; Nelson and

Winter 1982). I use "regime" as the general designation for a particular configuration of a large technological system.

There is a third category in the multilevel approach: the landscape, which consists of "deep structural trends" and includes background conditioning factors such as "oil prices, economic growth, wars, emigration, broad political coalitions, cultural and normative values, environmental problems" (Geels 2002: 1260). This is a residual category that is not particularly satisfying from a field or institutional perspective because it mixes together many disparate sociological categories. However, against the backdrop of the STS theories of technological change, the landscape concept has the advantage of moving the analysis well beyond the limitations of microsociological and mesosociological frameworks associated with the social construction of technology and actor-network theories. Likewise, in the context of innovation studies it has the advantage of injecting historical and sociological perspectives into a field that was dominated by frameworks such as evolutionary economics. In short, the primary value of the concept of the landscape is in the context of the limitations of STS and innovation theories of technological change.

Of the many causal factors that affect transitions, some of the case studies in the literature on industrial transitions indicate that social movements and professional reform movements can be important. (See, e.g., Geels 2005.) In general, the diverse mobilizations of environmentalists have played a primary role in advocating the transition of multiple industrial systems toward sustainable alternatives. However, as was discussed in chapter 3, other movements have also attempted to modify large technological systems to address inequalities of design related to structural inequality. An example of a study in the transitions literature that examines social movement mobilization is an analysis of efforts to bring about more humane animal husbandry for hogs and pigs in the Netherlands. Elzen et al. (2011) compared the successful outcome of animal rights advocates' support for group housing for sows with the unsuccessful outcome of their goal of obtaining more humane ways of fattening pigs. Consistent with the traditional triad of SMS explanatory factors, Elzen et al. bring together an analysis of a favorable regulatory attitude from the government (in turn related to the exogenous shock of the swine flu epistemic), framing in the form of normative contestation, and social movement mobilization. However, they argue that together the three factors are not sufficient to explain the differential outcome and that the alternative technology and markets must also be ready.

Elzen et al. provide an example of how transition studies can complement both social movement theory and institutional analysis by integrating the material or technological innovation dimension into the framework. They also argue that in the case of group housing for sows there was a brief period during which the different causal streams became aligned and change occurred. However, in the case of pigsties for fattening, the technology was not developed when the political opportunity structure opened. Against the broad background of SMS, their study goes a long way toward addressing the call of Jones et al. (2013) for a greater attention to material factors in the analysis of institutional change. Elzen et al. also showed how attention to those factors can help to provide a sharper explanation of the conditions for success of industrial transition movements.

Although much of the literature on transitions is based on the case study method, Geels and Schot (2007) have taken a step toward theoretical integration by developing a comparative analysis that identifies four basic patterns of industrial transition using the concept of "landscape pressure." In this context the term refers to general policy guidance that in turn may reflect a wide range of political pressures that include but are not limited to social movement mobilizations. They develop the following four hypotheses about relationships among the different levels:

• Where the landscape pressure is moderate and niches are not well developed, the regime will undertake modifications gradually and largely on its own terms (transformation type). An example is the gradual transition of the European sanitation system from open sewers to septic tanks and a sanitary sewer system.
• Where the niches are better developed and symbiotic, the regime will incorporate the niches but with existing actors still largely in place (reconfiguration type). An example discussed previously is the incorporation of organic food into the industrial food system.
• Where there is high landscape pressure for change but niches are not well developed, the regime will become destabilized, but it will restabilize when one of the niches develops into the new regime (dealignment and realignment type). An example is the collapse of animal-powered urban transportation in the United States and the subsequent rise of multiple modes

of mechanical transportation that gradually developed into dominance by automotive vehicles.

• Where there is high landscape pressure and a sufficiently developed niche, the regime will adopt the new technologies (substitution type). The example given is the transition from sailing ships to steamships.

This approach suggests three main variables that affect the potential for a scale shift in the niche toward integration with or displacement of the regime. First, there is the degree or extent of landscape pressure, which can include economic or environmental crises, consumer acceptance, and social movement mobilization. Second, there is the readiness of the niche technology for a scale shift in terms of its technical functionality and economic affordability. Third, there is the degree to which the niche technology is complementary to the existing regime or disruptive to it. Thus, the original conception of a niche as inherently disruptive to a regime is rejected in favor of a more nuanced view of the degree to which a niche is disruptive.

Like the typology of Rao and Kenny (2008), the typology of Geels and Schot laudably moves theory away from descriptive categories toward general explanatory hypotheses about the conditions and outcomes of transitions. The approach of Rao and Kenny draws attention to the power of incumbents to control the proposals of challengers, a variable that is consistent with the degree of landscape pressure in the analysis of Geels and Schot. Likewise, Rao and Kenny's idea of the compatibility of proposals is similar to Geels and Schot's emphasis on the extent to which the niche technology is complementary or alternative. But Geels and Schot's approach also draws attention to readiness, which involves the relationship between technological design and markets. This issue, like the general focus on materiality and design in the STS literature, brings a new perspective to institutional theory.

Regime Resistance

The two background literatures (institutional logics and industrial transitions) are mostly parallel intellectual universes with striking similarities and complementary strengths. On the institutional theory side, it is valuable to understand the institutional logics at play and their relationships to organizations in an institutional field; on the transitions theory side, it is also valuable to take into account the readiness of a niche technology to scale up and the design conflicts between niches and regimes. However, for the advocates and activists of the industrial transition movements, there is still something missing from both approaches to industrial change. These mobilized counterpublics often face strong resistance to proposed changes from the regime actors. Resistance is especially evident where counterpublics advocate rapid, government-driven changes of the large technological systems to address the problem of environmental sustainability. The alternative technologies of organic food, green chemistry, renewable energy, and so on do not always fit well with the existing regime, and the incumbent organizations often engage in their own mobilizations to block reform efforts. The next step in a synthesis of institutional and transition theories of industrial change should address the research problem of how change occurs under these important circumstances of incompatibility. If social theory and empirical research can shed some light on this issue, there would also be significant practical dividends.

The topic of regime resistance has emerged in the institutional literature as a problem of failed institutionalization. (See, e.g., Davis and Anderson 2008.) Likewise, in the transitions literature there is increasing attention to problems of power and regime resistance, especially in the context of the slow pace of sustainability transitions (Geels 2014; Kern and Smith 2008; Meadowcroft 2011; Verbong and Geels 2007). However, analysis of regime resistance and of the pathways for overcoming them is still in its infancy. In the remainder of this chapter, I will suggest some ways in which this important topic can be developed.

In the case of sustainability transitions, there is a high level of variation in regime resistance by country. In China and in other newly industrializing countries, advocates of a sustainability transition face problems of growing demand for energy, food, and other products; the intertwining of state and industry; and the lack of political freedoms that can open opportunities for mobilization. However, when the government decides to make a change, industry is not able to resist the change as it can in less authoritarian countries, where there are more open opportunities for direct and indirect industrial influence on government. In Europe, the relative autonomy of the political field from the industrial field, in combination with a political culture that favors a more interventionist state, has also led to a higher level of cooperation between state and industry than in the United

States, Canada, and Australia. In the latter three countries, the problem of regime resistance to sustainability transitions is especially acute, and it is very prominent in the policy field of transitions from dependence on fossil fuels. The remainder of this chapter will focus on the work that I have been doing on regime resistance to an energy transition in the United States. I will argue that the twin perspectives of institutional logics and transition studies have some value for addressing this issue but that again one must develop new concepts that emerge from the empirical material. Before discussing how challengers can overcome regime resistance, I will provide some background on the fossil-fuel sector, the utilities, and energy policy in the United States in order to demonstrate how the opportunity structure for an industrial transition to low-carbon energy is relatively closed in this country.

Regime Resistance and the Energy Transition in the United States

In the United States, as in many other countries, the electricity, transportation, and building sectors are heavily reliant on fossil fuels. This reliance results in the need to decarbonize energy sources and the need to reduce pollution from energy. There are various terms for the transition. The term "clean energy" can include more energy-efficient and less polluting forms of fossil fuels, the replacement of coal with natural gas, and the continued growth of nuclear energy; "low-carbon" energy can include fossil fuels but mainly when linked to carbon sequestration technologies, and it also includes nuclear energy; and "green" energy often means renewable energy and energy efficiency (REEE). In practice these categories tend to be mixed, as political alliances evolve and fade for specific issues. I will focus here on the transition understood as decarbonization that involves a scaling up of REEE.

A transition to low-carbon energy sources presents a significant challenge to incumbent firms in the petroleum, natural gas, coal, and utility industries, not to mention to the manufacturers of vehicles. Sustainability transitions in these sectors pose significant risk to the incumbent organizations even as they pose opportunities for innovators located either in entrepreneurial organizations or in incumbent firms that see opportunities for a better market share. Because the political field in the United States is open to industrial influence, there are also opportunities for incumbents to block proposals for policy reform. Transition coalitions of environmentalists, some unions, clean and green companies, and other actors have been effective in some cases, but generally only in state governments controlled by the Democratic Party. Regime actors have formed a coalition with the Republican Party and political conservatives, and to date this coalition has been highly effective in blocking efforts to deepen support for energy transition policies.

Both the framework of institutional logics and that of industrial transitions provide some general guidance for thinking about regime resistance to energy transition policies. First, there is a basic problem of incompatibility—that is, a fundamental design conflict—between the ideal configuration of the large technological system advocated by the challengers and that advocated by the incumbents. There may be ways in which fossil-fuel technologies could be adapted to a low-carbon electricity and transportation system, such as by implementing carbon capture and storage technologies for electricity generation. But such adaptation is expensive, and the technology is unproven at full scale. Thus, industrial regime organizations view the challenge as a threat. For the oil, gas, and coal industries, the long-term transition poses the prospect of sunsetting, and for the utilities the convergence of energy storage technology with low-cost solar energy could mean an end to the electricity grid as we know it. Second, there is the problem of inequality of political power: the transition coalitions lack resources in the field of campaign finance, and in the United States they have mostly failed to mobilize a politically powerful grassroots social movement.

With respect to campaign finance, it is necessary to consider a few more details of how the regime coalitions work in the American system. Most industries donate more to Republicans than to Democrats, with exceptions for lawyers and for the communications and electronics sector, but the fossil-fuel sector donates very generously to Republicans. For example, in some campaign cycles about 80 percent of the oil-and-gas industry's donations were to Republicans, the industry was ranked ninth among eighty industries in the level of donations to federal political candidates, and the fossil-fuel sector has also increased spending in support of hydraulic fracturing for natural gas (Citizens for Responsibility and Ethics in Congress 2013; Center for Responsive Politics 2016e). The utilities have a more balanced pattern of donations, but on the average they also give more to Republicans than to Democrats.

A few details will provide a sense of the financial power of the energy regime organizations. During the 2012 election cycle (the last presidential cycle for which full information was available), the oil-and-gas industry donated $77 million in federal elections, and the coal industry donated $16 million. Of the donations to candidates, 90 percent were to Republicans (Center for Responsive Politics 2013b). These figures do not include the increasing levels of "dark money" associated with independent spending, and they do not track spending in state and local elections. In contrast, the "alternative energy and production services" sector gave only $3 million, 58 percent of it to Democrats, and environmental organizations gave $16 million, 90 percent of it to Democrats (Center for Responsive Politics 2013b, 2013c). Thus, the alternative energy and environmental organizations donated at one-fifth the level of the fossil-fuel sector.

One might think that the lopsided donations would translate into measurable political influence, but it is difficult to gauge the political outcomes of the spending on specific bills or on other policy outcomes. One reason is that many Congressional votes are based on party affiliation, and when researchers control for political party, other effects tend to disappear. A meta-analysis of 40 studies for the general literature on campaign contributions found that in 75 percent of the cases the effects of contributions on votes were either insignificant or in the opposite direction than predicted (Ansolabehere and Snyder 2003). However, some meta-analyses suggest that donations are associated with voting outcomes (Stratmann 2002, 2005), as does some subsequent research (see, e.g., Peoples 2010). A cautious conclusion is that donations help to gain access but do not guarantee outcomes, and that their effectiveness varies by industry and issue (Clawson et al. 1992).

With respect to the issue of legislation that affects the possibility of energy transition policies, there is some evidence of a relationship between levels of contributions and voting record, but again caution is warranted in interpreting the results. Studies by watchdog groups provide suggestive data but do not provide multivariate controls, and because the voting record of legislators is also closely linked to party affiliation, causal attributions are difficult to make. For example, the Center for Responsive Politics examined the relationship between donations from the fossil-fuel sector and votes on a "selection of eight major bills concerning preferential treatment for the oil, gas, and coal industries" (Oil Change International

2013a,b). Although Republicans tended to receive more donations from the fossil-fuel sector and to vote at a higher rate in favor of the bills, votes also tended to align with party affiliation. In the House of Representatives, 124 members received over $75,000 each in donations from the fossil-fuel sector, and all but 13 of those members were Republicans. The Democrats included nine who supported laws favorable to fossil fuels at a rate of 50 percent or higher and only four at rate below 12 percent. Nineteen Democrats received less than $10,000 in contributions, and they were nearly all in the 0 percent category of support for legislation favoring the fossil-fuel sector. The analysis suggests that donations from the fossil-fuel sector go to both Republicans and Democrats, but at a much higher rate to Republicans. When Democrats receive support, it is because they are either committee members or supporters of the fossil-fuel sector.

Similar patterns occur at the level of state governments, where utility influence is especially important. The American Legislative Exchange Council has worked to develop model legislation in support of a wide range of conservative causes, among them the reversal of REEE legislation. An estimated one-fourth of all state legislators were members of that conservative organization (American Legislative Exchange Council 2016). The efforts by ALEC and the utilities to convince state legislatures to reverse state laws that support net metering and renewable portfolio standards have been successful in several states (American Legislative Exchange Council 2106; Galluci 2013). Although utility influence is clearly important for energy transition policies in state governments, the size of the fossil-fuel sector in a state is also negatively associated with the level of development of its REEE policies (Coley and Hess 2012; Vasseur 2014).

Mobilization of utility companies and of fossil-fuel companies became especially pronounced after 2008, when Barack Obama was elected president. Congressional Democrats attempted to pass a bill that would have created a national renewable portfolio standard for electricity and a national cap-and-trade program for greenhouse gas emissions (Clean Energy Jobs and America Power Act, S. 1733 of 2010). However, the bill was defeated in 2010, and at the federal level there was little opportunity for major legislative reform during the remainder of Obama's eight-year presidency. Likewise, Republican opposition to REEE policy also increased in state legislatures after 2010. For the utilities there is also concern with the rise of distributed solar energy and its potential threat to the model of centralized power generation, and they have actively sought to weaken policies in support of distributed solar generation (Hess 2016).

In short, the opportunity structure for a low-carbon energy transition has been closed in the United States so far in the twenty-first century, with the exception of a few states controlled by the Democratic Party. The fossil-fuel sector has strengthened its coalition with political conservatives and made opposition to energy transition policies a litmus test for Republican candidates in state and federal elections. The utilities are especially active in state governments, where they have successfully stalled momentum toward higher levels of renewable energy portfolio standards and other important policies. Where Democrats control governments, mostly in the Northeastern and Pacific Coast states, the transition policies have continued to advance, but in many states the opportunity structures are relatively closed. The fossil-fuel sector and utilities have not embraced energy transition as a long-term corporate strategy, and climate-change denialism is widespread among elected officials the Republican Party.

Finding Cracks in the Wall of a Closed Opportunity Structure

The closed political opportunity structure for energy transition policies in the United States may be at odds with the situation in many other countries, but it is of great importance because of the influence of the US on global politics and because of the importance of achieving global reductions in greenhouse gases. But beyond the political and environmental importance, the closed political opportunity structure is also of great interest theoretically because it provides a good example of a situation that all industrial transition movements face: regime resistance. In the case of a blocked opportunity structure for transition policies and a relatively weak transition coalition, is it possible to develop an analysis of the strategies that are available to the transition coalitions to overcome their weak position? To paraphrase Scott (1987), what are the "weapons of the niche" that can be mobilized to overcome regime resistance? In the remainder of the chapter, I advance the literature on regime resistance by analyzing how transition coalitions can operate within a relatively closed political opportunity structure. In doing so, I discuss three strategies that have emerged from our empirical research on regime resistance in the United States:

• With respect to the political and industrial opportunity structure, there are important divisions among powerful industrial groups, whereby some industrial groups can provide countervailing power to the fossil-fuel sector.
• With respect to the systems of meaning, there are ways in which the dominant political ideology of neoliberalism can be turned toward policies that favor energy transitions, a process described as "ideological judo."
• With respect to mobilizing structures in the form of alliances with other constituencies, there are ways to configure energy transition policies as serving multiple uses if considerations of "dual use" design are taken into account.

Although these approaches will not solve the challenge of unequal political power, they do point to some cracks in the wall of a relatively closed opportunity structure.

Countervailing Industrial Power

In the SMS literature on outcomes, a useful approach for examining the causes of movement success and failure is analysis of political mediation (Amenta et al. 2010; King 2008). To gain successes that are essential for maintaining support from adherents and donors, advocates and activists must build coalitions with powerful political and industrial groups. Conversely, political leaders have good reasons to form coalitions, because social movement support may give them credibility with their constituents. Likewise, one industry or one firm (or even networks within a firm) may see competitive advantages in pursuing a strategy that is aligned with the goals of a social movement. The political mediation approach suggests that the divisions within political and industrial elites are important to a movement's success, and this approach is broadly consistent with the emphasis of early resource mobilization theory, which also emphasized the importance to gain support from elites.

In the context of the blocked opportunity structure for energy transition policies in the United States, I have argued that transition coalitions have an untapped potential to develop ties with countervailing industrial power (Hess 2013a, 2014b). The concept can be traced to efforts in Western societies to build constitutional forms of governance that empowered some institutions to serve as a counterweight to the overwhelming power of the church or the state (Gordon 2009). In a context closer to my use, Galbraith (1952) studied responses to a situation in which a group of corporations achieves a dominant market position and is able to use its market power to take profits at the expense of other economic actors. Galbraith's examples of countervailing power include unions, farmers' cooperatives (both for selling and purchasing goods), chain stores, and retail cooperatives. Disadvantaged groups mobilize in the economic field to form these new organizations, but they can also mobilize in the political field to obtain regulatory advantages. Although Galbraith did not focus on political countervailing power, he noted that "a very large part of all modern political activity consists in efforts to capture the power of the state in support of, or in resistance to, some exercise of power" (1983: 74).

In the context of energy transitions, social movements and associated entrepreneurial enterprises exercise some countervailing political power, but they have a limited capacity to influence the political field because of the greater resources of the incumbent organizations. In a political field in which large corporations exercise strong influence on issues that they deem central to their viability and their profits, there is a need to expand the idea of countervailing power to include a form that Galbraith did not study: the role of alliances between transition coalitions, including niche organizations, and large corporations in neighboring industries. Previous research (Bauer et al. 1963; McFarland 2004) has recognized divisions within the business elite and the potential for those divisions to lead to political conflict, so this is not an entirely new topic. Such divisions may be on the rise historically because divisions in the business elite are growing as measured by the fracturing of corporate network ties (Mizruchi 2013).

A good example of countervailing industrial power involves the transition politics for the utility industry. American electric utilities are concerned with preserving a regime based on an institutional logic of centralized production and distribution anchored in stable baseload generation. Although stable baseload generation can include low-carbon sources, such as hydropower and nuclear energy, in most regions of the US it has traditionally meant coal and natural gas. The utilities are wary of the problems of intermittency, storage, and load management associated with both centralized and distributed renewable energy. The utilities have been willing to shift away from coal, but the shift has been to natural gas, which fits with the general logic of centralized, stable, baseload distribution. The utilities also have tremendous political power to affect regulatory policies, and the alternative institutional logic that is grounded in environmental concerns with greenhouse gases has weak political constituencies. As noted above, the transition coalitions generally are not able to influence the political system except in states where there is Democratic Party control of both the legislature and the governorship.

Countervailing industrial power can introduce a third institutional logic based on the idea of a smart grid that is driven by innovations from the technology sector. This third institutional logic transforms the terms of the conflict between grid stability and environmental benefit to a conflict between twentieth-century technologies and the new smart grid. This third institutional logic is consistent with the environmentalist logic, but the focus is on building a different sort of large technological system—one that has room for small-scale distributed generation, intermittent energy sources, microgrids, energy storage, demand management, smart meters, and the coordination of a much wider portfolio of energy sources (Stephens et al. 2015). Some states are moving ahead with policies that support this fundamental transition of the electricity grid.

The third institutional logic is consistent with that of the information technology sector, and there is some evidence that the sector has provided countervailing industrial power to the utilities and fossil-fuel sector. As was discussed in chapter 2, large financial and technology companies have invested in third-party ownership and in other financial products that have led to a high growth rate for rooftop solarization. In addition to countervailing economic power, the same industries sometimes also become involved in the political system through donations, thereby exercising countervailing political power. Some wealthy industrialists have supported a transition to low-carbon and green technology, even though the wealthy in general tend to be more conservative than the electorate, including on environmental issues (Page et al. 2013). For example, in 2010 Bill Gates (Microsoft), Jeff Immelt (General Electric), and John Doerr (Kleiner, Perkins, Caufield, and Byers)—two corporate leaders from the communication and electronics sector and one from a Silicon Valley investment firm—formed the American Energy Innovation Council to advocate a national agenda oriented toward green technology, and some of their recommendations were implemented as policy during Obama's first term. Rather than portray the low-carbon energy transition in the terms of an environmentalist logic, they focused on technological innovation, global competitiveness, and the advantages of grid modernization.

The leadership from some segments of the industrial elite on sustainability transition policy, especially industrialists associated with the technology and venture capital industries, suggests that the alignment of the niche industry (REEE companies) with a powerful countervailing industry is one strategy for overcoming the political weakness of the transition coalition. Although it is difficult to show countervailing political power via the analysis of general campaign donations, it is evident in the study of states' ballot initiatives (Hess 2014b). A good example that shows that donors associated with the technology sector will mobilize to provide political countervailing power can be found in the 2010 California ballot initiative called Proposition 23. The ballot proposition, which was funded almost entirely by three oil-and-gas companies, sought to delay the implementation of AB 32, the state's law that set in motion the process for the cap-and-trade program for greenhouse gas regulation. Supporters of the global warming law claimed that the ballot measure was as an assault on California's green politics by oil-and-gas firms from Texas, and implicitly the ballot battle represented a "war" between two large and powerful states, one relatively progressive and the other much more conservative. A coalition of community organizations, environmentalists, the clean-technology sector, and unions formed to oppose the proposition. To reach diverse constituencies, they also framed the ballot measure as contributing to dirty air, an issue that in California has been linked to environmental justice struggles such as the clean bus controversy discussed previously. Crucially, in addition to astute framing, the coalition raised three times more funds than the fossil-fuel sector raised, and the proposition failed (that is, the transition coalition defeated the fossil-fuel-sector coalition). Many of the large donations came from wealthy individuals associated with the communications and electronics sector either directly or through their investments (National Institute for Money in State Politics 2016a). In this significant battle with the fossil-fuel sector, the state's technology and communication sectors came to the side of the REEE industry and environmentalists. Top individual contributors to the effort to defeat the oil-and-gas proposition (that is, contributors other than environmental organizations, which also received support from the sector) included Thomas Steyer (investment firm with strong holdings in the technology sector), John and Ann Doerr (Silicon Valley investment), Vinod Khosla (Silicon Valley investment), Gordon Moore (Intel), James Cameron (film), Robert Fisher (The Gap), Bill Gates (Microsoft), Claire Perry (Getty family), John Morgridge (Cisco), Julian Robertson (hedge funds), Wendy Schmidt (Google), Susan Packard Orr (Hewlett-Packard), and Lauren Powell Jobs (Apple) (National Institute for Money in State Politics 2016a).

I have identified similar patterns of support from donors who made their fortunes in the communications, electronics, and finance sectors for other state ballot initiatives that support green-transition policies (Hess 2014b). Furthermore, there is some evidence for institutionalization of these donor preferences. The Green Tech Action Fund, a nonprofit organization that has support from wealthy donors associated with Silicon Valley, has played a role in some of these initiatives. Between its founding in 2008 and 2013, the fund spent over $35 million and contributed to the Blue-Green Alliance (the leading labor-environmental coalition) and to various environmental organizations involved in political campaigns (Center for Responsive Politics 2016d). It is not clear how much of the spending went into political communications, but the broader point is that there is an institutionalized connection between the countervailing industrial power and the political field. Again, funding is easier to track for state ballot initiatives: the organization supported the "No on 23" campaign in California, and it was also a major donor to a 2012 ballot campaign in Michigan that would have increased the state's renewable portfolio standard (National Institute for Money in State Politics 2016a,b). The sources of funding for the Green Tech Action Fund include a network of foundations that leads back to individuals and companies in the information technology industry and in related investment companies (Bartosiewicz and Miley 2013; Pignataro 2010). These funding connections have received attention among political conservatives, who borrow a page from progressives' exposés of the Koch brothers and of donors from the fossil-fuel sector to argue that there is a "billionaires' club" supporting the environmental left (US Senate 2014).

Countervailing economic and political power may be particularly important in the United States, which has permissive campaign finance laws and high levels of donations from corporations and wealthy donors. The influential role of progressive Silicon Valley donors may also be relatively unique to this country. However, at this point we do not have comparative research that can assess the effects of countervailing industrial power in other countries. In the next chapter, I will return to the issue and show that the concept can be applied to another industrial conflict within the United States.

Ideological Judo

Because in the United States the fossil-fuel sector and utilities have generally built coalitions with political conservatives and the Republican Party, opposition to energy transition policies has become embedded in broader ideological conflicts. Conservatives tend to reject energy transition policies as unnecessary interference in the economy, and they are especially repelled by policy instruments that involve mandates and taxes. Within these limitations, it is possible to reconfigure green energy policies to be more compatible with conservative ideology. Before showing how this "ideological judo" works, it is necessary to say a little more about how I will use the term "ideology."

In the Marxist tradition (see, e.g., Althusser 1984), ideology is closely associated with class interests. That approach is valuable to the extent that it links the concept to structural inequality, but it tends to instrumentalize ideology, fails to capture the wide diversity of expressions of ideology beyond the standard right-left polarizations, and underplays the partial autonomy of ideologies in the political field. However, the alternative culturalist tradition (see, e.g., Geertz 1973) suffers from opposite shortcomings. That approach has the advantage of paying attention to the symbolic complexity of ideology as a cultural system; however, there is a tendency for the analysis to underplay conflict among ideologies, changes over time, and connections to social structure and to field positions that are brought out in Marxist and other conflict sociologies. Field and institutional sociologies offer a middle ground that provide connections between intellectual and social positions but also recognize the partial autonomy of action in the political field. Thus, I will use the term "ideologies" in this more specific sense as the competing institutional logics of the political field. In other words, ideologies are broad systems of meaning that are defined oppositionally and provide models of and for action in the political field.

The primary ideological division in advanced industrial democracies is generally between liberalism and conservatism. Although in constitutional governments one could say that everyone is a liberal in the broad, historical sense of general agreement on the need to limit government's power over other social fields, there is considerable disagreement over the degree to which government intervention is valuable and necessary. In the United States the tension between forms of liberal ideology is described as tension between liberal (or progressive) and conservative (or neoliberal) ideologies.

The terminology is unfortunate in the international context because in the US the liberals are the left party, whereas in other countries they are often the right party. The tension between liberals and conservatives is reflected both between parties and within wings of the same party; however, there are also important areas of agreement, especially the tendency for American liberals and conservatives alike to support trade liberalization. Historically, liberal ideology was ascendant in the United States until 1980, but since then a conservative or neoliberal logic has infused both parties. Even when liberal reforms take place, they often use market-oriented policy instruments (e.g., health-care exchanges, cap-and-trade regimes, solar energy credits) that suggest the recombinant dynamics among these institutional logics that occur as political compromises are forged.

The structure of ideology in the American political field is transected by a second ideological divide over government support for the private sector. This division is not polarized by the issue of the ideal level of government intervention in the economy but instead by the issue of what type of business the government should nurture and support (Hess 2012a). The dominant logic supports public spending in favor of the development of high-tech industry, and it is evident in federal research-and-development policies and in state governments' economic development programs. This high-tech developmentalist logic is oriented toward competitiveness in the global economy, the production of intellectual property rights, and the construction of innovation clusters. In contrast, the subordinate logic draws on the country's history of populist and progressive social movements to support the small-business sector and to support control over regional economies by local governments (e.g., local public ownership of water and electricity utilities). I refer to this tension as a "developmentalist" polarity between a mainstream, global form and a populist, localist form that is resurgent in some communities in which independent business associations have mobilized (Hess 2009a). But the general point is that the institutional logic of the political field in the United States has this cross-cutting developmentalist polarity that overlays the more recognizable right-left polarization. This cross-cutting polarity of ideologies can be useful for the practice of ideological judo.

In summary, the political field today favors neoliberal and mainstream developmentalist ideologies. This dominance of conservative, innovation-oriented institutional logics over progressive-liberal and localist alternatives is relatively stable, but the stability is maintained through ongoing mobilizations of incumbent actors. Corporate benefactors and wealthy donors shape the ideological preferences of the political field not only through lobbying and political donations but also through the creation of a broad organizational field that influences government. The organizational field includes think tanks, public relations firms, and the other accoutrements of hegemony that Barley (2010) describes as the corralling of a government.

Like the concept of countervailing power, the concept of ideological judo begins with the closed political opportunity structure for energy transitions. Thus, advocates and activists who support policy reforms that run counter to the desires of the dominant institutional logics of the political field must translate their proposals into terms that can gain political traction. One option is to define energy transition policies as government interventions in the economy that are aligned with liberal ideology and anathema to conservative ideology. However, in the United States this has only been a viable political strategy in a limited number of state governments, and in general there are always times and places where conservative hegemony is strong. Thus, I argue that a second "weapon of the niche" is to take the force of the dominant ideologies and redirect it away from its close connection with regime stasis. I refer to this strategy as "ideological judo," basing that term loosely on the idea of redirecting the force of one's opponent to one's advantage. (Also see Morello-Frosh et al. 2009 on the related idea of "data judo.")

As Klein (2014) has argued, in a certain sense climate mitigation policy (like other environmental policies) is difficult to square with conservative political ideology. Market mechanisms are not adequate for addressing the degree of intervention that is needed to mitigate the problem of greenhouse gases in a climatologically and ecologically relevant time frame, and the same is true for a wide range of other environmentally related externalities. In short, government intervention is needed. Although the fossil-fuel sector has pumped money into its alliance with political conservatives to close the opportunity structure, at some level Klein is correct to say that "the right is right" in the sense that the policy conflict is ideological. If one accepts the science and the verdict that change must occur more rapidly than market mechanisms would allow, then climate mitigation is a case of market failure, and there is a need for government intervention. Nevertheless, I depart from Klein on the question of whether there is an opportunity to craft policy in ways that are more palatable to political conservatives.

In the United States energy transition policy has become polarized politically, especially during the presidency of Barack Obama. For Republicans, the promise to create 5 million green jobs also implied potentially creating 5 million more Democratic voters. The issue of green jobs and green energy is only one of many that have fallen victim to Congressional polarization and gridlock. However, at the level of state government the policy landscape is different. One might conclude that only in states in which the Democratic Party holds legislative majorities does energy transition legislation have any chance of passing, but in fact the situation is more complicated (Hess et al. 2015; Hess, Mai, and Brown 2016).

In some states where Republicans control the legislatures, there were signs that these legislatures provided ongoing support for some types of REEE policy even after the election of Barack Obama. Using a variety of data sets that we developed—votes by individual legislators in a single session of a state government, semistructured interviews with state legislators of both parties, and longitudinal and cross-sectional records of passed and unpassed bills—my colleagues and I were able to show relationships between type of REEE technology and policy and levels of cross-party support. We did this by linking laws and policies to ideologies operationalized as bill characteristics or frames, thus building on a distinction in the SMS literature between ideologies and frames (Benford and Snow 2000: 613; Snow and Benford 2000).

We showed that laws that support REEE policy and involve mandates on the economy, business burdens, taxes, the creation of government commissions, and so on will harm the chances of bipartisan support, whereas laws that support REEE but do so via more conservative policy instruments— such as reducing wasteful spending by the government, providing consumers and businesses with tax credits and choices, and reducing regulations that make it difficult to develop renewable energy—will improve the odds of bipartisan support. In our data set, support for net metering, solar tax credits, government building efficiency requirements, and measures to reduce permitting burdens for REEE was relatively high across party divisions. Support for property-assessed clean energy bills, which allow homeowners and businesses to access funds from government bond issues to finance REEE building improvements, was more mixed. Although this was a market-enabling measure, our interviewees indicated that there was some ideological opposition based on concerns about the role of government. Banks also opposed the measure and argued that it was an improper extension of the role of government into the economy, but this opposition could be overcome when business owners testified about how the improvements were helping them to avoid unnecessary costs. Likewise, in some states the heating and air conditioning industry supported PACE legislation, as did small businesses, thereby providing countervailing industrial power to the banks. In other words, the conservative ideological argument of the banks was countered by a local developmentalist argument from countervailing industries.

We also used qualitative interviews to investigate how legislators evaluate different types of policies. Not surprisingly, mandates such as carbon emissions regulations and renewable portfolio standards are often nonstarters among conservatives. For example, a Democratic legislator from South Carolina commented: "Not in South Carolina. We're far off from California; that's another country." A Republican legislator from Utah voiced similar concerns: "When it seems like government is dictating something to a business, that is a negative here. If you do it by tax credit, or make it optional, that is okay, but mandates don't play well up here." (Hess, Mai, and Brown 2016) However, we also found that the same conservatives were more open to other types of energy transition policy proposals that were consistent with conservative ideology. For example, green building standards for government buildings (as opposed to those for the private sector) can be accommodated to a conservative concern with cutting wasteful government spending. Conservatives also support tax credits for renewable energy. A Republican legislator in the liberal state of Massachusetts commented: "Anything you can do to cut taxes, even tax credits, will bring a smile to the Republican caucus, and even for a lot of Democrats." Likewise, a Democrat legislator in Florida developed a bill that prohibited local governments from increasing property taxes after a building owner installs solar panels, and the Republican-controlled legislature passed the pro-green, anti-tax measure (Hess, Mai, and Brown 2016).

The strategy of ideological judo has its limitations because it favors modest reforms such as government building efficiency standards, solar tax credits, and the reduction of regulatory hurdles for REEE. More comprehensive policy reforms that can lead to a scale shift in support for a niche industry, such as a renewable portfolio standard or carbon regulation, remain caught in the crossfire of political polarization. Nevertheless, we showed that it is important to take the category of REEE policy out of a black box and examine the varieties and flavors of different subcategories of policy. Methodologically, this approach is consistent with the design conflicts approach that I have outlined in chapter 3 above. The different types of policy support, in some cases associated with different types of REEE technologies, have ideological valences that we can document with both quantitative analysis and with qualitative interviews that show how the legislators draw on ideology to evaluate the policy proposals. Thus, this approach provides another example of a crack in the wall of the closed opportunity structure.

Policy Translation

The third weapon of the niche involves redefining a policy as addressing a different problem that may be more amenable to political compromise. Although one might describe the strategy as reframing, the institutional logics perspective can be helpful because this strategy involves repositioning a policy proposal as part of a different institutional logic. In turn, the translation also enables coalitions to be built across diverse constituencies and interests. For environmental and sustainability policies, three primary alternative institutional logics are those of health care, disaster relief, and economic development.

One long-standing avenue of policy translation for environmental policy is to redefine environmental policy as health policy. Where air quality is a matter of great public concern, there is support for addressing the problem from a public health perspective even when there is a lack of support for addressing it from an environmental perspective. Even in very conservative states such as Utah, air quality issues have led to environmental reforms. In another example, a powerful industry lobby has successfully blocked reform of the Toxic Substances Control Act and supported the rapid growth of nanotechnology without concomitant evaluation of environmental, health, and safety implications (Hess 2010a). However, in cases that involve prominent health concerns for specific chemicals, such as phthalates in children's toys or the effects of ozone depletion on skin cancer, advocates have successfully redefined the issue and have gained broad bipartisan support for policy action.

Another type of policy translation is to search for ways to overcome the sustainability-resilience conflict by building mitigation efforts into climate adaptation programs. A disaster generally requires an immediate response, then a long period of rebuilding. After a major disaster, it may be possible to tap public support for investments in adaptation technologies such as infrastructure hardening. The previous discussion of design conflicts showed how a zero-sum relationship can develop between mitigation and adaptation goals; however, careful thinking about the two goals can lead to creative design solutions that address adaptation while also mitigating greenhouse gas emissions or other environmental problems. This approach to climate policy as concurrently adaptation and mitigation can lead to reprioritizing interventions so that both goals are met simultaneously.

The third area of policy translation for environmental issues involves shifting the attention to job creation and economic development. The strategy often is consistent with attempts to parry neoliberal ideology by reframing an environmental policy in developmentalist terms. Recent experience in the United States shows that the strategy can sometimes be effective. For example, during the 2008 presidential candidate election, when Obama promised to create green jobs, he was translating a policy initiative from a liberal ideology (government intervention in the economy for an energy transition) into an institutional logic of mainstream developmentalism. That attempt to define energy transition legislation as about job creation and business development lasted for a short while; then conservatives reframed green jobs as industrial policy and an unnecessary government interference in the market. Liberals protested that such views were hypocritical because conservatives looked the other way with respect to the subsidies for the fossil-fuel sector and nuclear energy, but the lines had been drawn.

Although the attempt to utilize a developmentalist logic to defend green jobs policy has not been especially successful at the federal level, the picture shifts somewhat when one looks at the state governments, where industrial policy remains relatively healthy and is much more bipartisan. Much of the energy transition legislation in the state governments during the period 2000–2010 was framed in terms of job creation and business development, and our analysis of state laws during this period indicated that many significant REEE laws passed with bipartisan support and with the support of Republican governors. The term "industrial policy" is rarely used at the state and local levels, and the term "economic development" is used instead. However, the implementation of economic development policy is often de facto industrial policy because it involves an inventory of a state's leading industrial clusters and the development of plans that target existing industrial strengths. Often the regional strengths in green or clean industries involve the use of local natural resources, connections with universities, and synergies with existing industries such as agriculture (biofuels) and the manufacturing supply chain (wind turbine manufacturing).

Even after the mobilization against energy transition policies from the Republican right and the fossil-fuel sector, we found that state governments tended to provide continued support for their clean-technology industries (Hess and Mai 2015). Support for a sectoral strategy of economic development does not divide sharply along partisan lines, as one might expect from conservative rhetoric in the federal government about the Obama administration's green industrial policy. Some conservatives criticize a sectoral strategy of economic development (essentially an industrial policy by another name) because it puts governments in the role of picking winners and losers rather than leaving that determination to markets. However, in the practical world of economic development programs in state governments, these ideological concerns are trumped by the pressures to develop a state economy's existing strengths and to support existing industrial constituencies of both management and labor. Thus, we found that many Republican governors included their state's clean-technology sector in the list of prioritized industrial clusters, especially in states where the fossil-fuel sector was not a major industry.

In summary, there are various ways to translate energy transition policies into policies associated with another institutional logic: a response to a health problem, a positive dividend from a thoughtfully designed project of resilient infrastructure or disaster response, or an attempt to create jobs and develop businesses. These strategies are not immune from contestation and ideological crossfire, but they also provide another mechanism by which advocates of transition policies can build coalitions and support where they might not otherwise have the capacity to influence policy outcomes.

Conclusion

In this chapter I used the case of the failed sustainability transition in the energy sector in the United States as an empirical basis for developing the social theory of industrial transitions. A successful outcome for energy transition coalitions in this policy field would be the decarbonization of the electricity, transportation, and building industries. Note that some activists and advocates also combine this technologically focused outcome with social outcomes such as environmental justice or greater local economic ownership. However, as an ideal type the industrial transition movements are concerned with the change in the configuration of the large technological system.

I argued that the analysis of industrial change and social movements can benefit from bringing together two literatures, institutional logics and transitions, to focus on the research problem of regime resistance. Unless the transition coalitions are highly organized and well supported, they lack the capacity to influence the government to implement crucial energy transition policies. This problem is particularly acute in the United States, where the political system is relatively open to influence from the business lobby and from political spending. The result is a powerful political regime coalition that has formed between political conservatives and donors from the fossil-fuel sector and utilities. The polarization became especially acute when Obama was elected, and the transition coalitions were not able to bring about major policy reforms except in state governments controlled by the Democratic Party. Gridlock in Congress forced the president to pursue carbon mitigation policy through executive branch powers, a strategy that led to even more strident opposition from conservatives and to litigation.

Although the focus in this chapter was on the United States, the problem of regime resistance and policy stasis is certainly not limited to this country. At the global level there has been limited progress on climate action because of the perceived costs of a low-carbon energy transition and the prioritization of economic growth over decarbonization. Comparative studies of transition stasis and reform will still be necessary. In our venture into this area, we found that for a data set of Asian countries the strength of a country's fossil-fuel sector, the health of its democratic institutions, and its per capita income were associated with more developed green energy policies such as renewable portfolio standards (Hess and Mai 2014).

Because of the importance of transitioning the global economy to a more sustainable technological basis, especially for greenhouse gas emissions, there is a pressing need for research that seeks to understand how to open closed opportunity structures. This chapter outlines three strategies. First, by building alliances with powerful regime organizations in neighboring industries, it is possible to pursue a well-recognized strategy in SMS that involves alliances with segments of the elites. In this case, the strategy shifted the terms of the conflict of institutional logics from one between the benefits of regime stasis (grid stability, low costs) and the environmental necessity for change (mitigation of greenhouse gas emissions) to one between an older, centralized, and out-of-date model of the grid and a more technologically sophisticated smart grid that was more integrated into the computer, electronics, and finance industries.

The second strategy for transition coalitions working in politically closed structures is to redefine action in terms of the dominant ideology in the political field. In this chapter I follow Klein (2014), who argued that conservatives are right in the sense that the mitigation of environmental problems requires substantial government intervention in the economy. However, I argue that where conservative ideologies and parties are dominant, it is possible to develop some policies that are consistent with conservative ideology but that also support an energy transition. My approach of ideological judo also involves opening the black box of energy transition policies and technologies in order to select ones that have a greater chance of conformity with conservative ideology. The effectiveness of this approach can be analyzed quantitatively, as we have done in our research on bill passage, and it appears to be limited to incremental policies rather than landmark political shifts (Hess et al. 2015; Hess, Mai, and Brown 2016).

The third weapon of the niche is similar, but it redefines a policy by recasting it in the terms of a different institutional logic, such as by making a greenhouse gas mitigation policy a health, environmental adaptation, or economic development policy. This strategy can also enable new coalitions to be built. Like the second approach, this strategy has limitations because not all energy transition policies can be recast in this way.

The study of regime resistance politics and the weapons of the niche does not lead to simple solutions to the problem of overcoming policy stasis when the incumbent organizations of an industrial regime have mobilized to oppose transition policies. Certainly, other factors may also help to open a blocked political opportunity structure. For example, in the field theory of Fligstein and McAdam (2012), one important factor can be an exogenous shock, such as an economic or natural disaster. Certainly a hurricane or drought can open political opportunities, but the shocks are themselves subjected to clashing interpretations that requires quite a bit of work to translate the event into policy. There are no easy solutions to the problem of overcoming regime resistance, but I have suggested that it is possible to develop a systematic analysis of potentially successful strategies.

6   Contemporary Change: Liberalization and Epistemic Modernization

Although the study of industrial transition movements is not central to either SMS or STS, there is good reason to believe that it will become more important. As the technological complexity of the modern world and the pace of innovation have increased, the politics of expertise and design have become more central to the study of contentious politics. Likewise, the role of mobilized publics will probably become increasingly important in the study of the public understanding of science and technology. Although there were epistemic and design conflicts in other times, these issues have become more salient in a world of nuclear energy, greenhouse gas emissions, genetically modified foods, and chemical pollution. However, this historical claim raises a general theoretical problem. It may be intuitively clear that there are broad changes in the historical landscape that will make the study of industrial transition movements increasingly important to both SMS and STS, but how does one theorize these changes from the perspective of a more systematic historical sociology of contemporary change?

The Historical Sociology of Contemporary Social Movements

One starting point in the SMS literature for a historical sociology of contemporary social movements is European work on "new social movements." The concept draws attention to the shift from the capital-labor conflict of industrial society to social conflicts associated with feminism, ethnic and racial justice, and environmentalism that became more prominent after World War II (Melucci 1980; Touraine 1992). The approach also draws attention to diversification of the target of mobilization from governments to nonstate actors and even to consumption and everyday life. However, there is considerable disagreement about the utility of the concept of new social movements. There have been struggles over gender and ethnic justice for more than a century, and previous generations of social movements sometimes developed countercultural lifestyles. Thus, critics have argued that the novelty of the concept of "new" social movements is difficult to defend (Pichardo 1997).

A better approach is to start with changes in society, then to examine how they are related to changes in social movements. Adopting this strategy, Tilly argued that the development of industrial capitalism, urbanization, and the mass media affected the scope, scale, goals, and organizations of social movements (Tilly 1978; Tilly et al. 1975). Social movements have become broader in temporal scope and geographical scale, more proactive than reactive, and based more on formal social movement organizations than on informal solidary groups and communities. This approach does not suffer from the problems of new social movement theory because it does not assign a particular type of social movement to a particular historical period. However, the approach is cast against the broad time frame of Western modernity understood as the transition to legal universalism, religious pluralism, and industrial capitalism, and it does not address the problem of contemporary historical change. How might this approach be formulated more specifically for the problem of changes that began with the global order established after World War II and that deepened with the diffusion of neoliberal policies during the 1980s and the 1990s?

A good starting point for this more specific question of the historical sociology of social movements is to begin with liberalization. The term is used in diverse ways, and in this context I will use it in two main ways. At the global level, liberalization refers to the reduction of barriers to trade and investment among countries. Although in theory the change is beneficial to all countries, there is considerable evidence that it benefits workers in and owners of globally oriented businesses, especially in the advanced industrialized countries (Chang 2008). Liberalization in this sense can be dated to the Breton Woods institutions of the post-World War II global order and their further institutionalization with the formation of the World Trade Organization in 1995. In the developed countries, global liberalization was generally a consensual policy across moderate left and right parties, and until the 1980s these countries tended to allow the newly industrializing countries to maintain protectionist policies such as import-substituting industrialization.

In contrast, liberalization in the second sense refers to neoliberaliza-
tion, which is understood here as reducing government commitments to
intervention in the private sector to redistribute wealth and to correct market failures such as externalities. This type of liberalization has been more
politically polarizing. Since the 1970s large corporations have mobilized to
shape government policy in a liberalizing direction and to move the political center away from the socialist and progressive ideologies of the twentieth century. (See, e.g., Harvey 2005; Peck and Tickell 2002, 2007.) The
capacity of large corporations to move well-paying unionized jobs to other
countries led to a weaker bargaining position for the unions, and with their
demise the left parties and progressive ideologies lost power in the United
States and in some other developed countries. As conservative parties and
political leaders became more ascendant, there was a broader shift in the
institutional logic of the political field toward the valuation of individual
self-responsibility, entrepreneurship, and innovation that was reflected in
the confluence of conservatism and high-tech developmentalism. As this
shift in institutional logics occurred, governments lost their taste for impos-
ing burdensome regulations and taxes on footloose corporations, which
could move well-paying jobs to another country, and they instead focused
on how to develop and protect industrial clusters that could attract innovation, jobs, and corporations in a competitive global economy.

With these changes the opportunity structure for industrial regulation
tended to close down, with great variation across the major world regions
and countries. As this liberalizing trend deepened, social movements
diversified their target of action toward directly targeting corporations
and toward private governance strategies. Furthermore, the proliferation
of new, supranational institutions of governance also tended to erode the
power of national and local governments to steer their economies, and
activists tended to shift scale toward transnational action and international
governance organizations. (See, e.g., Della Porta and Tarrow 2004.) But they
also shifted the scale downward to movements that protected local communities, rebuilt their economies, and experimented with new economy
organizations, all of which responded to questions of community power in
a liberalizing global order (Hess 2009a).

The changes also led to the growth of countermovements that were
aligned with industrial incumbent organizations and conservative political
coalitions, such as the climate denialism movement (Brulle 2014; Meyer

and Staggenborg 1996, 2008). Some countermovements also articulated futures associated with a premodern social order, such as religious states that suppressed civil society and the media and isolationist parties that promised to protect the working class against immigration and competition from foreign producers. In the United States, countermovements tended to be politically conservative, but in other countries, such as France, isolationist movements tended to reconnect with redistributive politics of left ideologies.

Thus, social movements became both opposing forces to liberalization trends and vehicles of those trends. They followed changes of power out from the nation-state toward sites of nonstate, supranational, and local governance. The movements themselves tended to broaden from protest toward the politics of everyday life, including the choices of consumption such as green lifestyles, and into private-sector vehicles of reform. Finally, the field of social movements became complicated by the rise of countermovements that in some cases were aligned with neoliberal globalization.

It is in this nexus of changes that a historical sociology of the contemporary must situate the industrial transition movements. Rather than argue that they represent a new type of social movement or a flavor of new social movement, it is better to follow Tilly's strategy and situate their goals, targets, and repertoires of action in these changes of the global politics and economy of the late twentieth and early twenty-first centuries. The industrial transition movements become especially important in the context of weakened governments that are not able to develop robust democratic politics to steer industrial innovation in ways that are broadly beneficial across the social pyramid. But they must maneuver in this new terrain of private governance and countermovements.

Liberalization and the Scientific Field

A parallel literature in STS has mapped out the liberalization of institutional logics in the scientific field. Scientific research has long served the needs of state and industry (see, e.g., Hessen 1971; Noble 1977), and the idea that universities once conducted only pure or basic research is not accurate historically (Daniels 1967; Mulkay 1976). However, since the 1970s the importance of translational research that serves economic competitiveness goals has increased and has had a transformative effect on the university. The emphasis of governments on global competitiveness and the importance of research to an innovation economy have repositioned the university as an engine of economic development and a center of regional industrial clusters.

One effect of the changes is that research fields that are more closely aligned with the priorities of the global innovation economy—such as information sciences, molecular biology, and nanotechnology—have gained prestige and resources (Berman 2012). Scientists in research universities have learned to build diversified research portfolios that include goals of both high citation yields from publications and royalties from patents. Valuations of pure and applied research also have changed as younger cohorts of researchers have learned to invest in both the producer pole (research of value mainly to other researchers) and the consumer pole (research of value to external corporate and government funders) of their research fields. In doing so, they have learned to move investments across the two poles through strategic allocations of their diversified research portfolios (Albert and McGuire 2014).

However, changes in the valuation of research and in career strategies are not the only example of the effects of globalized liberalization on the university. There are also significant changes in the governance of universities (Slaughter and Leslie 1997; Slaughter and Rhodes 2004). The old models that linked faculty to institutions for lifetime appointments, where they participated heavily in academic governance and often moved into administrative positions as their careers developed, have shifted to models in which faculty move across universities and between academic and industrial positions. Scientists, institutes, and departments have become more entrepreneurial, and the central administration provides rewards to the actors who are in alignment with entrepreneurial goals, especially when those goals are cleverly combined with the accumulation of both financial and symbolic capital. The older institutional logic of collegial self-governance has not disappeared, but it is subsumed in a transformed governance structure that is in alignment with the competitiveness needs of state and industry. These transformations are accelerated by directives from university governing boards, which include corporate leaders who wish to bring business efficiency and models of corporate governance to academia.

In an influential analysis of the changing institutional logics of the scientific field, Kleinman and Vallas (2001; see also Vallas and Kleinman

2008) argued that both academic and industrial research have undergone similar changes. They demonstrated that the science-based logic, associated with university-based research and publication for a research community, and the commercial logic, associated with industrial research and development, are found in both types of organizations. They cautioned against an analytical strategy that focuses on how the commercial logic replaces the traditional science logic in universities. Instead, their analysis of "asymmetrical convergence" demonstrated how the institutional logics coexist and recombine in both academic and industrial science. Scientists working in industrial research and development laboratories have increasing access to the benefits of academic life. They have more choices in research problems, in the capacity to present research at conferences, and in the ability to publish in peer-reviewed journals and to participate in government-funded sponsored research projects. In other words, control over industrial research has loosened to the extent that some scientists find life in this setting to be as fulfilling and in some ways better than in the academic setting. In contrast, scientists who work in universities have found themselves increasingly subjected to demands for greater productivity, reporting, and extramural funding, and they have experienced the evisceration of faculty governance.

Thus, Kleinman and Vallas argued, there is a convergence between academic and industrial science, but it is asymmetrical because of the dominance of the market-oriented logic in both settings. Berman (2014) also analyzed the shift in institutional logics from what she terms a science logic to a market logic, and she argued that the primary drivers of the change were large industrial corporations with substantial research-and-development operations. These corporations supported policy changes in favor of a shift to research oriented toward competitiveness and innovation, which policy makers favored because of growing concerns with global competitiveness.

In summary, the relationship between liberalization and the scientific field involves a shift in institutional logics so that the scientific field becomes more congruent with the industrial field. There is now more monitoring of scientists and academic researchers in general, both within the "audit culture" of the university (Strathern 2000) and by industry. Both government and industry funders select for higher levels of funding the research fields most aligned with the needs of the innovation economy. As research programs and research fields become recalibrated to the innovation economy, the opportunity structure for finding scientists who are able and willing to take on pro bono research that confronts the interests of industry has weakened. However, the private sector is not monolithically geared toward regime reproduction. In fact, disruptive innovation is often a major goal if it can put one corporation out ahead of its competitors or if it can launch a start-up company into a solid market position. In some cases this entrepreneurial logic can become aligned with the industrial transition movements, especially the alternative industrial movements. So if the general direction of liberalization is to weaken the opportunity structure for the industrial transition movements, there are also countervailing currents generated by the historical changes of liberalization.

Liberalization and Reflexive Modernization

This review suggests that the trend of global liberalization and the rise of neoliberal institutional logics in the political and scientific fields provides a good starting point for the historical sociology of contemporary industrial transition movements. However, this approach by itself is inadequate because it represents only one side of the historical sociology of the contemporary. It is necessary to balance the liberalization framework by tacking in another direction that focuses on the countertrend of reregulation that is summarized with Beck's term "reflexive modernization" (1992, 1999, 2000). My approach to this dynamic relationship between liberalization and reflexive modernization is intended to be continuous with Polanyi's analysis (1944) of the double movement of the expansion of markets and the attempts to build social protections for those affected by the change. He used the term "countermovement" for the social protection side, but I will use the term "countertrend" instead because the term "countermovement" has a specific sense in the SMS context related to social movements that emerge in response to other social movements.

As Beck argued, one of the motivations for the institutionalization of policies that would advance reflexive modernization is to protect the public against risk. Risks are generated by many sources, but salient among the sources are the technological innovations of industrial capitalism such as nuclear energy or greenhouse gas emissions. Risks can also include the potential for systemic instability posed by an increasingly complex, liberalized global order, such as the economic instability associated with the global financial crisis of 2009–2012. Although concern with controlling risks motivates the countertrend to liberalization, it does not automatically translate into action because risks must first be made meaningful and actionable. As Irwin notes, "The 'risk society' is not about physical or ecological risks alone but rather the way that citizens feel themselves 'at risk' from social and technological development" (1995: 47). In this sense, the recognition of risks is refracted by the institutional logics of the political field. Where conservative ideologies are dominant, leaders may reject policy responses to risk management because there is a sense that markets should handle the adaptive response.

The use of the term "risk" has drawn much criticism, and it is worth pausing for a moment so that this perspective on contemporary historical sociology is not overstated. Douglas (1992) suggested that in the political field the concept of danger would do as well, Ravetz (2005) argued that issues of safety and danger are not reducible to risk, and Yearley (2011) noted that for the politics of air pollution the favored idiom is harm rather than risk. These criticisms suggest the need to ensure that discussions of risk are opened up to include a family of concerns such as safety, danger, and harm in the context of uncertainty. Other critical analyses of risk suggest the need to steer public debate to broad questions of social desirability or lack of desirability of a technology (Fischer 2005; Winner 1986; Wynne 2005). The criticisms also draw attention to how a closed opportunity structure for decision making—especially a process characterized by scientization and lack of public participation—can place the focus of regulation on narrow downstream effects rather than on broad upstream design choices.

Another limitation with the focus on the concept of risk, however flexibly it is defined, is that the greater problem in contemporary societies is ignorance in the sense of an unknown unknown that is only knowable after a surprise (Gross 2010; Hoffmann-Riem and Wynne 2002; Wynne 2005). Although the accumulation of capital, the rationalization of institutions, and the progressive preponderance of organic solidarity continue to characterize contemporary historical change, the processes identified in classical historical sociologies of modernity have become involuted and self-contradictory. Capital accumulation leads to technological innovations that sometimes involve nasty surprises, societal differentiation creates unforeseen problems of coordination, and the rationalization of institutions must now include the invention of new modes of governance of societal complexity that confronts the unknowable. As Gross notes (2010: 54), this is "a shift that scientists, policymakers, and the public have begun to acknowledge—that potentially harmful consequences cannot be established reliably by further research since they fall into the domain of ignorance." Gross suggests a concrete strategy for confronting this problem, an approach that is missing in Beck's analysis: political experimentation that adapts as surprises become manifest. This approach is consistent with an open-ended design process and with the strategy of intelligent trial-and-error in policy studies. (See, e.g., Lindblom and Woodhouse 1992.) From this perspective, reflexive modernization requires devising institutions that can contribute to the long-term sustainability of life within ecological limits and to resilience in the face of surprises, many of which are produced by transgressions of those limits.

Just as Beck's concept of "risk society" invites criticisms for both narrowness and vagueness, the phrase "reflexive modernization" requires similar inspection. The phrase may be unfortunate because in some quarters it has connotations with modernization in the sense of the development projects of wealthy, Western countries in less developed regions of the world and therefore with Western imperialism and neocolonialism. But most readers of Beck are sophisticated enough to understand that modernity or modernization are not everywhere the same and that his use of the term is more to indicate an engagement with modernity as a central problem of social theory. They also understand that the emergence of reflexive modernization as a descriptor for coping with risks and ignorance does not imply that new policies and institutions will necessarily emerge or that they will be successful. Sharp conflicts usually erupt over differing assessments of what the problems are and the level of resources that will have to be allocated in order to address them. But when governments, corporations, and other organizations respond to these concerns, they may modify their policies and practices in ways that are consistent with what Beck called reflexive modernization.

Unfortunately, organizations and individuals often fail to heed warnings from scientists and social movements about risk, and they may fail miserably, as the global response to climate change suggests. To this point, Beck may have underestimated the continuous challenges posed by the constant innovation of technologies and the increasing level of destruction of our contemporary industrial and postindustrial global society (Schnaiberg and

Gould 1994). Although policies and government agencies can be identified that correspond with the reflexive modernization of the political field, the concerns of local communities, civil society organizations, social movements, and other counterpublics are often not addressed well or at all in these policies. Thus, reflexive modernization should be viewed not as an inexorable process of historical change but as contested and historically contingent.

Thinking about reflexive modernization as historically contingent requires pairing it in a Polanyian relationship with liberalization. But the relationship is not simply oppositional, especially in the era of neoliberal ascendency. One result of this dynamic historical process is that when new protections are enacted in the current order, they often take the form of market-based interventions in markets, such as the development of the cap-and-trade system for greenhouse gas regulations. Thus, unlike in the first-order double movement that Polanyi describes, in this second-order double movement even the countertrend toward protection tends to be inflected by marketization.

Lave (2014) provides an example of this dance of liberalization and reflexivity in her analysis of stream mitigation banking in the United States. The approach to environmental policy began as a government-sponsored program that allowed developers to accumulate credits before the implementation of a development project. Much like carbon markets, these credits allowed for developers to compensate for the damage to streams in one location by providing for the regeneration of streams in other locations. Thus, even at its outset, this policy of environmental mitigation was defined in the liberalized frameworks of market development. After 2000 stream mitigation banking became an industry in which credits could be bought and sold, and the industry then lobbied Congress to establish guidelines that could facilitate standardized packaging of the credits. If one thinks of the government intervention for environmental purposes to protect streams as a form of reflexive modernization, then in this case it takes a highly liberalized form.

But there is another turn to this dynamic of liberalization and reflexivity. The creation of new markets appeared to inflect the policy instruments of reflexive modernization with liberalization, but it also tended to create new actors in emergent industries that could support the industrial transition movements. For example, the use of market-based policy instruments of

carbon credits and trading enrolled the financial sector in the project of climate change mitigation and created a potentially powerful countervailing
industrial power, just as the use of market-based mechanisms for solarization (such as markets for renewable energy credits and for distributed solar
energy) encouraged the financial sector to enter the solar industry.

Liberalization and Epistemic Modernization

This dynamic interplay of liberalization and reflexive modernization can
provide a broad lens for thinking through the more specific changes associated with the industrial transition movements. But to do so well, it is necessary to extend the idea of reflexive modernization toward the politics of
expertise and design, and I have used the term "epistemic modernization"
as descriptor for this extension (Hess 2007a). A countertrend in the scientific field to academic capitalism and asymmetrical convergence, epistemic
modernization is the process by which scientific research becomes opened
up to the agendas and concerns of the counterpublics. In the political field,
it can include the use of public engagement mechanisms that open the
opportunity structure for counterpublics.

In the scientific field, two mechanisms of epistemic modernization
are the diversification of the social composition of science and the institutionalized integration of lay knowledge. The globalization of the world
economy and the political gains associated with the universalizing social
movements have led to the diversification of the social composition of science. The change includes both between-country diversity as a result of
internationalization and within-country diversity as a result of the opening
up of the scientific field to women, ethnic and religious minorities, and
other previously excluded groups. These changes often affect the content
of scientific knowledge, including the prioritization of research problems
and the reconceptualization of theory-method packages used to advance
knowledge in a field. The mechanism of the change in the sociology of
scientific knowledge can involve the habitus of scientists who bring new
perspectives and questions to research fields. This pathway to change can
result in the growth of standpoint epistemologies and the strengthening of
the objectivity of research fields when the new entrants reveal biases that
may not have been previously visible (Harding 2008, 2015). The diversification of the scientific field can also lead to changes in research agendas

to respond to new concerns, such as the health problems of historically excluded groups (Epstein 1996).

One of the best early studies of the effects of the diversification of the social composition of a research field on the field's problem areas and methods is Haraway's *Primate Visions*, which portrays changes in the research field of primatology that occurred when its social composition changed. The change included the internationalization of the field and the growth of research communities of primatologists outside the West. For example, in India and Japan primatologists introduced new problem areas (e.g., human-monkey interactions in India) based in part on conditions of access to animal populations and in part on the cultural lenses that Indian primatologists brought with them. Likewise, when women entered the field in substantial numbers, there were significant changes in fundamental theories (e.g., the reevaluation of the man-the-hunter thesis) and in methods. However, as Haraway argued, the changes were not always in a direction easily predicted by gender stereotypes. In other words, the women primatologists did not usher in a wave of empathetic and ethnographic approaches; rather, their feminism became manifest in a wide variety of methodological changes.

The second mechanism of epistemic modernization involves the institutionalized integration of lay knowledge. During the colonial era scientific research teams appropriated indigenous knowledge systems and codified local knowledges into cosmopolitan sciences. This "primitive accumulation" of knowledge became less important in established research fields, but it continued to be evident especially in the social sciences. For example, ethnographic and focus group methods in particular remain vehicles by which lay knowledge enters into the social sciences to inform general knowledge about nature and society. As natural science research has increasingly shifted to transdisciplinary teams that include social scientists, especially in the health and environmental sciences, these perspectives also percolate in the natural sciences. Likewise, in the engineering and technology fields, the growth of user-centered design allows inventors to consider new perspectives that might not have been considered when design is undertaken only by groups of engineers and industrial designers.

The development of community-based participatory research, participatory action research, participatory design, and related research methods take the additional step of opening up the research process and the selection of research problems to new perspectives. As was discussed in chapter

4, these forms of research can become a mobilizing structure utilized by citizen-scientist alliances to develop research in support of a policy position. But from the perspective of historical sociology, they are examples of the transformation of the permeability of the scientific field that enables scientific research to follow new leads that draw on the perspectives of laypersons and counterpublics. However, this transformation is limited and incomplete. The invention of participatory research and user-centered design does not necessarily make science more reflexive, and it can also be configured in ways that marginalize community partners (Eubanks 2011). Despite the potential shortcomings with respect to marginalized groups and the problem of career risks to researchers, participatory research is growing in popularity. When the Surgeon General of the United States declared that "community-based participatory research (CBPR) has become the preferred model for conducting research in communities" (Benjamin 2013), there was a historic indication that this form of epistemic modernization has become institutionalized, at least in some of the community-based health research fields in the US.

Although the epistemic modernization of the scientific field can open the intellectual opportunity structure to the perspectives of counterpublics, it does not necessarily entail this development. Both the diversification of the social composition of science and the development of participatory methods can occur without contact with mobilized counterpublics. Rather, these processes of historical change open an opportunity structure that may be otherwise closing down because of liberalization trends. The diversification of the social composition of science creates an opening for counterpublic perspectives to enter into the scientific field when new entrants have a history of participation in social movements and have retained the experience in their habitus. Likewise, the institutionalization of lay participation in research and policy can create openings for counterpublic perspectives to become visible to researchers when those perspectives are shared by members of a community that is collaborating with scientists in a research project.

In the broad historical dynamic of the trend toward liberalization and asymmetrical convergence and the countertrends of reflexive and epistemic modernization, science and technology have become increasingly important, but at the same time they have become more politicized. Even when scientists attempt to maintain political neutrality, they are not safe from the possibility of intellectual suppression and epistemic rift. Thus, there is a tendency toward the "unbinding" of the authority to speak in the name of science from the credentialed experts in a specific research field (Moore 2008).

The Movement for CAM Cancer Therapies

An example of the dynamic relationship of liberalization and epistemic modernization can be found in the alternative industrial movement that calls for increased access to and research on complementary and alternative medicine (CAM) approaches to cancer. This movement involves networks of scientific researchers, especially in the area of nutritional research on the treatment and prevention of cancer; clinicians who make CAM therapies available to patients; and patient advocacy organizations, which advocate a transition in the industrial regime of surgery, radiation, and chemotherapy. The terms "complementary" and "alternative" refer to the relationship of the therapy to conventional cancer treatment; the same therapy may be complementary if it is used alongside conventional treatment, usually in an adjuvant mode, or alternative if it is used instead of conventional treatment. Strict regulation of medical therapies in many countries often places alternative therapies in an ambiguous legal position and creates risks of prosecution for the physician who offers them to patients. However, there is enough variation across countries that an international traffic of wealthy and desperate patients has emerged, especially for CAM-oriented clinics in Germany and Mexico.

The field of CAM approaches to cancer treatment is diverse, and it includes some of the herbal and dietary remedies of ancient and non-Western healing traditions (Hess 1999, 2004a). Some of these approaches may be bolstered by nutritional research that demonstrates the role of pharmacologically active properties, but the approaches can also be based on concepts such as subtle energies and humoral balance that would not pass through the metaphysics membrane of the mainstream research fields. In this sense, a portion of the CAM cancer field faces the boundary issues discussed above in the analysis of SIMs. However, the CAM cancer therapy field also includes products that have been developed within the framework of modern medical science, including bacterial vaccines, immunological therapies, and combinations of high-dose nutritional supplements sometimes described as "orthomolecular" medicine. Thus, the scientific credibility and professional standing of the clinicians and researchers who support CAM cancer therapy is highly variable. At one extreme are well-credentialed researchers who have produced scientific publications to support their research, such as Linus Pauling on vitamin C (Cameron and Pauling 1978) and Virginia Livingston on autogenous vaccines (Livingston and Alexander-Jackson 1965); at the other extreme are lay practitioners and some cases that would best be described as fraud. I will focus here on the highly credentialed end of the spectrum.

In addition to clinicians and researchers, the alternative industrial movement in support of CAM cancer therapies includes patient advocates. In the United States, patient-based organizations in Southern California played an important role in linking American and Canadian patients to the network of CAM cancer clinics and hospitals in Tijuana, Mexico. Several of the clinics and hospitals began with specialties associated with laetrile (a food-based, nontoxic chemotherapy) or with the dietary therapy of Max Gerson, but often they diversified to include a wide range of conventional and unconventional therapies. The German cancer clinics also provide access to CAM treatments for the global cosmopolitan elite. In the US the laetrile movement was built partially on the mobilizing structure of the John Birch Society, a very conservative political group with 30,000 members. The John Birch Society became involved when one of its members, a physician named John Richardson, was prosecuted for prescribing laetrile (Culbert 1974; Markle and Peterson 1980). However, in my ethnographic research on the CAM cancer therapy movement in the US during the 1990s, it was clear that patient advocacy groups and clinicians held a wide range of political views. The prominent direction was a tendency toward a libertarian view of the federal government and stigmatization of the Food and Drug Administration, which was believed to suppress CAM therapies at the behest of the pharmaceutical industry. More generally, the reform movement sought the liberalization of the regulatory regime (less regulation) as one means for advancing its goals. We might think that mobilized publics would always be against the deregulation of industry, but this is not the case where there is an alternative industrial movement whose products are being prevented from market access by regulatory policy that favors the incumbents.

Liberalization   The liberalization of the therapeutic field involved significant changes in regulatory law. A watershed change in the United States was
the Dietary Supplements and Health Education Act of 1994, which classified nutritional supplements as food and allowed manufacturers to make
limited health claims. Under the new regulations manufacturers of supplements could mention structure and function effects (e.g., a specific nutritional supplement supports prostate or breast health) in their labeling and
advertising, but they could not make disease treatment claims, which would
cause supplements to be reclassified as drugs and would require expensive
clinical trials (Bass 2011). The nutritional supplements industry considered
this law a substantial boost, and often I encountered great concern among
the CAM and nutritional supplements industry advocates that the pharmaceutical industry would like to weaken the liberalized supplements regime.
Thus, the supplements industry has been vigilant over attempts to weaken
the law in Congress or via international standards such as the Codex Ali-
mentarius, which are set by the World Health Organization and the Food
and Agriculture Organization. In this sense the supplements industry has
exercised countervailing power to the pharmaceutical industry in support
of a liberalized regulatory regime. For example, the Alliance for Natural
Health USA (2010, 2011) ran a "Stop Censoring Medical Science" campaign
that included a proposal for additional changes in advertising rules favorable to CAM. The industry's protections of supplement liberalization allow
greater freedom for clinicians and researchers to develop CAM therapies,
and they grant greater access to high-dose supplements for patients.

The second aspect of the liberalization of the therapeutic field occurred
when some conventional oncologists and large cancer treatment centers began to offer complementary medicine services such as nutritional
counseling and mind–body therapies. A new market emerged for cancer
patients who wished to pursue integrated treatments of conventional and
CAM therapies. Beginning in 1998, the Center for Mind-Body Medicine at
George Washington University and the National Cancer Institute began
to sponsor conferences on "comprehensive cancer care," which publicized
the new approach of evidence-based integrated medicine. But these trends
toward integrated treatment also coincided with the use of CAM therapies in the complementary mode; the older model of alternative cancer
therapies that might replace conventional chemotherapies was replaced by
the model of integrative medicine. These changes are consistent with the

general "incorporation and transformation" process that I described for the alternative industrial movements.

Although liberalization in this context involved mixed benefits for the CAM cancer therapy movement (its integration but also its complementarization), the broader processes of global trade liberalization were not always as beneficial. For example, the North American Free Trade Agreement (NAFTA) led to greater regulatory scrutiny in Mexico of the CAM cancer clinics in Tijuana, and the availability of the complementary side of CAM cancer treatments in US hospitals also weakened demand for the full range of therapies available in the Mexican clinics and hospitals. One of the outcomes of the trade agreement was that the NAFTA governments formed the Mexico–United States–Canada Health Fraud Work Group (abbreviated MUCH) to investigate fraud in health care, and beginning in 2001 the Mexican government closed some of the CAM clinics (Moss 2005, 2011). But the drug wars and crime also reduced the once-thriving medical tourism industry, which like the tourist industry in general to Tijuana, has declined substantially.

Epistemic Modernization Just as the analysis suggests crosscurrents by which liberalization benefited and restricted this alternative industrial movement, so similar complexities can be found with the processes of epistemic modernization. Patient advocates sought research funding for CAM cancer therapies from Congress, and their efforts led the government's Office of Technology Assessment (1990) to produce an investigation into possible research bias against CAM cancer therapies. The report documented existing evidence and became a source of contention over CAM cancer therapies (Hess 1999). However, the report played a role in justifying the creation in 1991 of the Office of Alternative Medicine of the National Institutes of Health, which in 1998 became the National Center for Complementary and Alternative Medicine (NCCAM).

The creation of NCCAM represented an advance for the epistemic status of CAM cancer therapies because in theory the whole CAM field would no longer be rejected pro forma. Rather, it would be subjected to evidence-based evaluation that could guide consumer choices, medical practice, and regulatory policy. At the same time the CAM professions were enhancing their credentials, especially in fields such as naturopathy, which was gaining ground as a medical specialty that required four years of graduate-level training. In some states the degree of "ND" was accompanied by a scope of practice similar to that of the MD (medical doctor). Advocates and CAM professionals also served on the NCCAM advisory board.

However, the hope represented by the institutionalization of CAM research and CAM professional education was not fully realized. Even though cancer was a focus of attention during the years that led up to the founding of the Officer of Alternative Medicine, only 9 percent of the 147 completed studies listed by NCCAM during the ten-year period after 2001 were for cancer (Hess 2015a). Most of these studies were on prevention, subclinical efficacy, or behavior. Thus, by 2011, little more was known about the clinical efficacy of most CAM cancer therapies than had been known two decades earlier, when the Office of Alternative Medicine was founded. The one major exception was a study of a therapy for pancreatic cancer that used enzymes and nutritional supplements. The therapy was developed by Nicholas Gonzalez, a medical doctor who had been trained in some of the best medical institutions in the country and who had substantial cultural and social capital. The therapy was well known in the CAM cancer treatment world, and versions of it have been used since the early twentieth century. The breakthrough of the NIH-funded study allowed a head-to-head test of the enzyme therapy with the conventional chemotherapy cocktail, and Gonzalez was to be included in the study design. I remember well the high expectations and hopes that the CAM cancer community had for this new direction of research. However, in 2009 Gonzalez found out that the study had been published in the *Journal of Clinical Oncology* (Chabot et al. 2009) without his knowledge, and he initiated complaints and an investigation into possible bias. Thus, the one study that many in the CAM cancer community hoped would be the breakthrough that allowed CAM treatments to gain a fair evaluation via a government-funded clinical trial ended in a breakdown of trust (Gonzalez 2009, 2012).

This breakdown of trust echoed previous examinations of CAM cancer therapies by conventional medical centers, such as the epic conflict between Linus Pauling and the Mayo Clinic (Moss 1996; Richards 1981). Gonzalez died in 2015 without having fulfilled his dream of gaining mainstream acceptance for the enzyme therapy for pancreatic cancer. Thus, the change in the cancer research and treatment field—the institutionalization of research for CAM therapies—that led to an expectation of the beginning of a new era was not realized. The example suggests that the potential for the epistemic modernization of the cancer research and treatment field is limited even for well-positioned reformers with high levels of capital.

Summary   The case of CAM cancer therapies provides an example of the complicated dynamic of liberalization and epistemic modernization for an alternative industrial movement. One general and perhaps counterintuitive implication of the case is that the liberalization process can be favorable to the industrial transition movements under some circumstances. This insight would probably not be as obvious if one were to focus entirely on environmentally oriented industrial transition movements. Liberalization of the therapeutic field has benefited the nutraceutical industry and made it easier for doctors, hospitals, and CAM providers to prescribe nutritional supplements in the treatment of chronic disease. However, there are also proposals to reregulate the industry, and there are ongoing conflicts between the nutritional supplements industry and the pharmaceutical industry about the degree of regulatory liberalization that is desirable. Nevertheless, the case of CAM cancer therapies shows that in a highly regulated industry, the regime is protected by a regulatory structure, and thus liberalization does not always benefit the industrial regime.

With respect to epistemic modernization, the case suggests that an alternative industrial movement was able to institutionalize funding for the alternative research field. The nutraceutical industry also provides some direct funding for the evaluation of supplements. A translation process was set in place whereby the lay knowledge of patients and the occupational knowledge of CAM providers could be vetted with scientific research on subclinical mechanisms and clinical effectiveness. However, the evidence for epistemic modernization through the incorporation of CAM research into the government's funding agenda is balanced by the fact that the funded research has tended to avoid the highly contentious issues of evaluating the clinical efficacy of alternative cancer therapies. Instead, the focus has been on CAM therapies for other diseases and, for cancer, on studies of prevention, behavioral interventions, and subclinical mechanisms. Even within the new field of government-sponsored evaluations of CAM, there is a reproduction of undone science that was a central concern of the coalition that supported the creation of the government organization in the first place. The one, highly visible study of an alternative modality ended in a bitter dispute between the CAM physician and the mainstream researchers, and the controversy suggests that there are still very strong limits on the epistemic modernization process for this industrial transition movement.

Conclusion

In this chapter I have suggested an approach to the historical sociology of contemporary science, technology, and social movements that does not begin with an attempt to delineate a particular type of social movement (e.g., "new" social movements) as the starting point for the historical socio-logical project. Instead, I have suggested the value of using the dynamic relationship of liberalization and reflexive modernization. From there it is possible to identify more specific processes of the liberalization and reflex-ive modernization of the regulatory and scientific fields. Although I have drawn on Polanyi (1944), I have suggested that there are differences because the countertrend of reflexive modernization itself is sometimes inflected by market-oriented institutional logics.

A methodological caution is in order: in developing a historical sociolog-ical approach to science, technology, and mobilized publics, the broad ref-erence concepts of liberalization and reflexive modernization, or the more specific formulations of asymmetrical convergence and epistemic modern-ization, are not causal explanatory factors. The goal is not to treat them as independent variables that explain the success or failure of a particular industrial transition movement. Although I have utilized causal, explana-tory approaches elsewhere in this volume, in this case the concepts serve more as an interpretive lens to enable a historical and ethnographic analy-sis of a changing industrial and political field. The concepts allow specific field-level changes to be interpreted in a broader theoretical framework that describes contemporary historical change.

The example from the CAM cancer therapy movement also suggests that liberalization is not necessarily an unfavorable process for the industrial transition movement, nor is epistemic modernization always a favorable process. For the alternative industrial movement in support of CAM cancer therapies, there are potentially beneficial effects from regulatory liberaliza-tion. Likewise, even when government policy has firmly institutionalized some aspects of epistemic modernization, such as the creation of a national center to evaluate CAM therapies, the institutionalization is limited because it is biased against the alternative end of the spectrum of CAM therapies. Indeed, through the creation of integrated cancer care, CAM therapies have been repositioned (the "A" or alternative approach is deleted in favor of the "C" or complementary approach), and in some ways the therapeutic regime organizations have coopted the CAM therapies. The case provides a methodological caution for the use of historical sociological methods in SMS and STS. My general argument is that the way forward for such methods is first to use a dynamic approach similar to that of Polanyi and second to examine the complex ways in which this dynamic plays out in historical cases.

Conclusion

The study of science, technology, and social movements could develop as a syncretism of concepts from the fields of SMS and STS, but I have argued that the research field requires its own conceptual toolkit that builds on and modifies the frameworks of the existing fields. To this end, I have suggested various bridges that synthesize the empirical research and conceptual developments of the two fields into a more coherent whole.

The concept of the mobilized public is a good place to begin such an effort. Far from representing a rejection of the concept of a social movement, the idea of a mobilized public suggests continuity with a trend in SMS toward a broader scope of study. There is no need to reject the concept of a social movement in the sense of a group of long-term campaigns that involve multiple organizations, a combination of disruptive and institutionalized repertoires of action, and the goal of fundamental changes in the policies and practices of states and other institutions. But I have broadened the scope toward the idea of a counterpublic, which includes mobilizations for public interest benefit by networks of scientists, business organizations, community groups, and civil society organizations. Furthermore, the idea of the mobilized public also includes the symmetrical problem of how elites form advocacy coalitions to mobilize in support of an existing regime and its approach to public interest.

On the side of STS, the idea of a "mobilized public" broadens the already existing "public turn" from the analysis of the lay individual public. As with the concept of the social movement, I have not advocated rejecting the idea of the lay individual public. Instead, I have used that idea throughout the book, and I have argued in favor of expanding the analysis of expertise and publics to include mobilized publics.

My focus in this book has been on the industrial transition movement as one type of mobilized counterpublic. As with most concepts, a contrast is useful to bring it into relief, and I think of the industrial transition movement as distinct from the universalizing movements that have tended to be the main focus of SMS. Movements that attempt to defend human rights in various forms—movements for democracy, of working people, of gays and lesbians, of women, of oppressed ethnic and religious groups, and so on—have been the mainstay of SMS, but I have suggested that there is a need to recognize another type of social movement and to think systematically about it. I have pursued a typological approach for the study of industrial transition movements. The mobilized counterpublics may seek an end to an existing technological system or even a whole industry (the industrial opposition movements), but they can also advocate new and alternative industries, technologies, and products (alternative industrial movements). The movements also intersect with the universalizing movements when they raise issues of social justice by demanding access to basic goods and services (industrial access movements) or by developing alternative organizational forms that are anchored in democratic aspirations (industrial restructuring movements). In this book I have focused on the first two categories, but elsewhere I have examined the other two in more detail (Hess 2007a, 2009a). The four types of movements also draw attention to different types of undone science and generate different levels of epistemic conflict (highest in the industrial opposition movements). The industrial regime can respond to the industrial transition movements by embracing them and by altering the proposed alternative designs to make them compatible with the existing technological regime, but in general the movements propose such fundamentally different patterns of technology, organization, and distribution that there is often a more complex response.

For the task of explaining the conditions of emergence and success of industrial transition movements, I have used the basic social theory triangle of structure, meaning, and agency (sometimes also called the "three I's" of institutions, ideology, and interests). However, working at the intersection of SMS and STS also provides opportunities for formulating new concepts associated with the triangle. For example, I contribute to the process already underway of broadening the concept of the political opportunity structure by examining its epistemic dimension. I have drawn on the work of researchers in the political sociology of science to analyze two pairs of processes by which the political opportunity structure can be deemed more or less open to change. I have identified some patterns, as well as problems for future research, about the conditions under which these processes become prominent or fade and how they affect the capacity of mobilized publics to achieve their goals.

The second main change is to build on trends moving "beyond framing" in the SMS literature by connecting those discussions with the politics of design in the STS literature. I have suggested the importance of reorienting the analysis of meaning toward material culture and its design conflicts, a shift that is especially necessary for the study of industrial transition movements but could have broader implications for SMS, which tends to treat material culture and technology as black-boxed props for movement actors. Three main areas of design conflicts are explored, again in an open-ended way that does not preclude others from advancing their own approaches: conflicts based in social structure and drawing on the literature on technology design and gender, labor, and race; those based in the challenger-incumbent conflicts of the industrial field, such as the rise of solar energy and organic agriculture; and those based on the broad environmental tension associated with conflict between adaptation and mitigation. The goal is to advance the analysis of meaning from a language-based orientation to one that makes material culture and the politics of design much more central.

With respect to the agency dimension of the social theory triangle, I have argued that new organizational forms have emerged as mobilized counterpublics attempt to bring about social change. There is already a base of research on the mobilizing structures of elites (see, e.g., Barley 2010; McCright and Dunlap 2010) and on those for social movements (see, e.g., McAdam et al. 1996). I have expanded on this literature by analyzing the organizing forms of "counterpublic knowledge," which provide ways to get undone science done and to develop new research that is often in opposition to the official versions of knowledge offered by industry and sometimes also by government regulators. The work of various scholars suggests that there is a range of fundamental mobilizing structures: scientific and intellectual movements, scientist activism and advocacy that include scientific associations and public interest science organizations, citizen-science alliances with their collaborative projects often based in participatory methods, and the projects of lay citizen science. I have suggested some ways forward on studying the interactions of these mobilizing structures.

With respect to the problem of studying the process of industrial transformation, I have argued that there are opportunities to synthesize institutional and transition studies. An important topic that these perspectives identify is the failure to generate change, and researchers who study industrial transitions, especially sustainability transitions, have drawn attention to the problem of stasis and regime resistance. In some countries and for some policy arenas there is political consensus about the need to change, and the resulting social science problem is mainly one of effective management of transitions, but the hardening of regime resistance to sustainability transitions requires a different kind of analysis that attends much more closely to power, politics, and strategic action. I have argued that the next step in the literature is to move from the analysis of why and how regime resistance occurs to the analysis of the "weapons of the niche" that can be used to overcome powerful regime organizations. I have suggested three strategies being used by transition coalitions: countervailing industrial power, ideological judo, and policy translation. Although the focus is on sustainability transitions, there are many other types of industrial transitions that could be studied, including ones associated with the structural inequalities of the design conflicts.

Finally, I have contributed to the historical sociology of science, technology, and social movements. I have argued that the study of counterpublics and industrial transitions is not a passing fad but a response to pervasive historical changes that have made politics more attentive to risks, technological design choices, and the need to have political guidance of the transitions of technological systems. I have argued against approaches in SMS that situate the historical sociology of contemporary social movements in the description of a new type of social movement; a better strategy begins with the dynamic historical interaction of liberalization and reflexive modernization, then seeks to understand how this double movement affects mobilized publics in general. The liberalization of regulatory policy usually, but not always, favors transition stasis and the incumbent organizations of an industrial regime. The countertrend of reflexive modernization is continuous with the Polanyian protective movements, but I also have argued that in the contemporary period (which I treat as mostly from the 1980s to the present) the countertrend is itself inflected with liberalizing tendencies. This double movement can be applied to regulatory policy and to changes in the scientific field, and I have developed a case study based on my research on complementary and alternative cancer care to show how the analysis might be applied to an alternative industrial movement.

The field of science, technology, and mobilized publics is still in its infancy, and it is difficult to predict how it will develop. At this point much of the work is still anchored in the historical or ethnographic case study, and there is a need for more systematic comparative and quantitative studies. The chapters in this book have opened up several types of comparative projects:

• To date there is very little systematic comparative work on the different types of industrial transition movements, their outcomes, and their variability across countries.

• There is potential to unpack the different elements of the opportunity structure, design conflicts, and organizational forms to develop comparative analysis of the conditions under which these elements emerge and recede. For example, to date we have little in the way of systematic comparative research on scientization, public participation, types of design conflicts, SIMs, PISOs, and citizen-science alliances.

• An important question, especially for the study of sustainability transitions, is the problem of regime resistance. More research is needed on how industrial regime organizations resist transitions and how that resistance is overcome.

• There is an opportunity to develop systematic analyses of the double movement of liberalization and reflexive modernization across countries and across policy fields.

There is also a general need for integrated theory that includes the development of causal models of the conditions under which types appear and fade. Achieving this goal requires moving toward comparative and quantitative analysis. Although the rich historical and ethnographic studies that populate the field can offer insights, often by drawing attention to new phenomena that were not anticipated, there is also a place for work that draws together the mountain of case studies, organizes them, and sorts out general patterns. Most of the researchers in this field are oriented toward qualitative methods, and although we may find some large-N quantitative studies in the future, I expect that this work will proceed along the lines of small-*N* comparisons. Comparison can be across cases of a type, such as cases of scientization, but it should also include comparisons across space and time, including comparisons across countries and world regions. Much of the work that I have discussed in this book focuses primarily on the United States and secondarily on Europe. I am acutely aware of the differences in social and institutional structures across countries and the need for cross-cultural comparison and transnational analysis. Research comparing colony collapse disorder among bees in France and the United States (Suryanarayanan and Kleinman 2014), health and environmental movements in the US and in Brazil (McCormick 2009), and the movement against genetically modified food in Canada and Mexico (Kinchy 2012) show that deep insights can emerge from comparative work.

The other future direction for the field is to attend to policy implications. In SMS the main practical implication of the research is to produce awareness of the patterns and effects of mobilization. Research on mobilization processes and strategies can provide ideas for activists and advocates about how to improve their strategies and how to avoid pitfalls such as splintering and cooptation. Perhaps one of the most pervasive of such ideas is the concept of framing, which is now widely used in popular culture. In the extension to the study of science, technology, and social movements, the persons benefiting from the research include not only advocates and activists but also scientists and the innovators and entrepreneurs associated with the alternative industrial movements.

The main policy implication of STS research on the public understanding of science has been somewhat different from that of SMS because STS research can inform governments about the scientific advisory process and public participation. One of the central ideas is to advocate more democratic accountability in decision making via processes that incorporate public commentary and participation and that expand decision-making criteria away from formal evaluation of safety and risk. To the extent that governments have experimented with deliberative and participatory mechanisms, the STS literature has also responded with cautionary studies of the limitations of such mechanisms and the potential for them to be used as a legitimizing cover for decision-making processes that occur elsewhere. Furthermore, the mechanisms can also serve to delegitimize the counterpublics that formulate an alternative public interest because the "public" has already been consulted through the participatory mechanisms. One implication of the approach developed here is that shifting the focus of the public from the lay individual opinion public to the mobilized public may make it possible to develop more robust types of participatory mechanisms. For example, instead of a consensus conference based on lay consultation and a resulting consensus report produced by the group, it may be better to have dissensus conferences that publicize both official public and counterpublic views of the public interest. As in debates among political candidates, there is a political calculation to the advantages and disadvantages of such debates, and it may be necessary to have such dissensus conferences funded by private foundations.

The other implication is to develop strategies and structures for getting undone science done by enhancing civil society research, citizen-science alliances, and pro bono options for researchers. However, research that benefits the mobilized counterpublics is not always aligned with the goals of success in university settings. Thus, the development of research that is attuned to the needs of counterpublics ultimately requires reforms of the reward structure of the scientific field (Woodhouse et al. 2002). Achieving such a fundamental change is likely to be difficult because the reward system favors teaching, research, and administration. Having "community service" included in a broader definition of service and supporting connections between this work and teaching and research would help to modify the reward system. But we also need studies of scientists and social scientists who do pro bono work, such as serving as part of a citizen-science alliance, to understand how they negotiate this work within the reward system.

Another policy implication emerges from studying the power of industrial regime organizations and their capacity to resist or absorb challengers. The transformation of our industrial systems is of paramount importance not only for the survival of the planet and other species but also for human health, privacy, justice, and security. These industrial systems are embedded in political economies of market and state capitalism that concentrate wealth and power in the hands of elites. Although the industrial transition movements can achieve effects within the structure of modern industrial societies, there is a need for deeper changes in the relations of structural inequality that have long been the focus of the universalizing social movements. Research at the intersections of SMS and STS can contribute to understanding effective strategies for gaining the political will to support industrial transitions.

In summary, the study of science, technology, and mobilized publics is still a relatively small research field, but it is likely to grow and become more influential because of the importance of the politics of technology in modern industrial societies and because of the continued failure of governments and industry to respond to problems of risk and public concern. As a research field it offers new opportunities for researchers in both SMS and STS to rethink basic conceptual frameworks and priorities for research questions. It also provides some hope that social science research can remain relevant to the pervasive problems of our time.

Appendix: Additional Reading

This book represents a summing up and reappraisal of various research projects that I have completed during a thirty-year career. Although the demands and opportunities of sponsored research tend to push one's work in multiple directions, I have consistently worked on the theme of science, technology, and mobilized publics for most of my career. Some readers may find it valuable to follow up on the ideas in this book by selecting from a more detailed bibliographic review of my contributions to this nexus of STS and SMS.

Undone Science and Industrial Transition Movements

I first introduced the concept of undone science in "Science Studies and Activism" (Woodhouse et al. 2002). Likewise, my first analyses of industrial transition movements were of the organic food movement (2004c) and "technology- and product-oriented movements" (2005). That line of work came together in *Alternative Pathways in Science and Industry* (2007a), in which I developed the four types of industrial transition movements and the analysis of the patterns of long-term cooptation and change. Although I discussed undone science in *Alternative Pathways*, the topic was not well integrated into the analysis of industrial transition movements. I did more work on undone science in an essay on civil society organizations and nanotechnology (2010a) and on what I termed "civil society research" (2009b), and I worked with Scott Frickel to develop a panel of conference papers on undone science into a co-authored single essay (Frickel et al. 2010). In an essay in the *Routledge International Handbook of Ignorance Studies* (2015c), I developed a more integrated analysis that connected undone science with the four types of industrial transition movements and that became the basis for chapter 1 of this book.

Epistemic Dimension of the Political Opportunity Structure

With respect to repression, I co-authored a paper on backfire, repression, and social movements (Hess and Martin 2006), and I developed the idea of epistemic rift when writing about the politics of climate denialism in the United States (2014c). On the issue of public participation, Lamprou and I developed analyses of nanotechnology policy in the United States and in the European Union (Hess 2010a; Lamprou 2010; Lamprou and Hess 2016). We focused on the role of civil society organizations as mobilized publics, and we discussed some of the strategies that they used to open a relatively closed political opportunity structure.

With regard to the politics of precaution, Jonathan Coley and I analyzed how a movement to allow consumers to opt out of smart meters draws on precautionary politics because of a range of concerns that include health, privacy, and security (Hess and Coley 2014; Hess 2014a). This is a particularly controversial issue because many experts believe that the claims of health effects from wireless smart meters are expressions of the public misunderstanding of science and that a precautionary policy response is unfounded. In these two articles we examined how claims of health risk may also be a means for expressing dissatisfaction with the failure of policy makers to regulate such technological changes via a democratic process and the failure to provide protections for privacy and security.

Design Conflicts

Chapter 3 summarizes some of my work on design conflicts in the transit system, including the study of the greening of diesel buses (2007c). I also analyzed design conflicts regarding food, electricity, and transportation in my book on localist movements (2009a). After writing broadly about the topic, I focused on conflicts in the solar industry, including the changes from grassroots innovation to corporate-controlled distributed solar energy (2013a) and disputes over distributed solar versus centralized solar that crystallized in the policy struggles over net metering (2016). Although I have not written extensively about alternative food movements, I conducted some interviews with leaders of community gardens (posted on my website as interviews and summarized in Hess 2009a), and I analyzed the history of the organic food movement (Hess 2004c). I also explored the design conflict between sustainability and resilience at the household level (2010b) and at the level of technological system design (2013c,d).

Organizational Forms of Counterpublic Knowledge

My primary publication in this area is "To Tell the Truth" (2011c), which related the idea of a scientific counterpublic to subordinate positions in both the political and scientific fields. When I turned to the case of climate science and denialism, I recognized that some scientific counterpublics represent high levels of consensus in the scientific field and that there was a need to distinguish types of counterpublic knowledge (2014c). The main work on organizational forms has been undertaken by other scholars; my contribution to the literature consists of work on alternative research fields, which connects with work on SIMs. The main examples are controversies over complementary and alternative medicine and religion-science issues (1991, 1997, 1999, 2004a,b, 2006). I also worked on civil society research, which I have argued is a type of citizen-science alliance (2009b).

Institutional Logics, Ideology, and Regime Resistance Politics

I have been working with a team of colleagues at Vanderbilt University to develop a synthesis of institutional logics and transition studies in the politics of water supply and water conservation in American cities (Hess, Wold, et al. 2016; Hornberger et al. 2015). My colleagues and I also have studied divisions in ideology in the political field and their relationship to technology regulation, with a focus on renewable energy and energy efficiency (Coley and Hess 2012; Hess 2011b, 2012b; Hess, Mai, and Brown 2016). In my books on localism and green jobs (2009a, 2012a), I argued that the conservative-liberal ideological continuum was transected by developmentalism and localism. I am especially interested in how design distinctions can map onto distinctions of ideology.

On finding cracks in the wall of a closed opportunity structure, I developed the idea of countervailing industrial power in research on the scaling up of solar energy, which in the United States was driven partly by the high levels of interest and investment from large technology and financial companies (2013a, 2016). I then investigated how countervailing industrial power can also play a role in the campaign finance system by potentially balancing the high levels of spending in the United States by the fossil fuel sector. I was able to demonstrate this effect for spending on state ballot initiatives (2014b), but we found it difficult to demonstrate an effect on aggregate measures in Congress using League of Conservation Voter scores because of problems of endogeneity in the multivariate analysis.

With respect to ideological judo, my colleagues and I found that when energy transition policies involve tax cuts or credits for renewable energy, support of consumer choice, reductions in bureaucratic regulations, and decreases in government spending via energy efficiency, the policies are able to gain a higher level of support across parties (Hess, Coley, et al. 2015; Hess, Mai, and Brown 2016). We documented these effects both with quantitative analysis and with qualitative interviews with state legislators about their preferences for different types of green energy laws in relationship to ideology.

With respect to the idea of "dual use" approaches to policy, I worked on designs that that take into account both adaptation and mitigation. (See, e.g., Hess 2013c,d.) Mai and I also showed that at the state level developmentalist goals tended to trump the neoliberal reluctance to support industrial policy even in states with conservative governors and legislatures (Hess and Mai 2015).

Liberalization and Epistemic Modernization

The fundamental approach that my colleagues and I used for the problem of the historical sociology of contemporary change for social movements, science, and technology is explained in a co-authored essay in *Theory and Society* (Moore et al. 2011). I also developed the argument that the transition from Mertonian functionalism to microsocial negotiation in the sociology of science involved changes in research topic that were consistent with the broader political shift away from social liberalism to neoliberalism (2013b). The discussion of the relationship between liberalization and epistemic modernization for the case of CAM cancer therapies began in my essay on "medical modernization" (2004b) and was developed in my essay

"Beyond Scientific Consensus" (2015a). I also argued that localist movements are a reaction to the challenges posed to small businesses and communities by neoliberal globalization (2009a). In the book *Good Green Jobs in a Global Economy* I argued that developmentalist ideology in the United States, which was dominant politically during the country's rise to power during the nineteenth century, may return as the relative position of the country in the global economy continues to decline.

References

Albert, Mathieu, and Daniel Kleinman, eds. 2011. Beyond the Canon: Pierre Bourdieu and Science and Technology Studies. *Minerva* 49 (3): 263–358.

Albert, Mathieu, and Wendy McGuire. 2014. Understanding Change in Academic Knowledge Production in a Neoliberal Era. *Political Power and Social Theory* 27: 33–57.

Allen, Barbara. 2003. *Uneasy Alchemy: Citizens and Experts in Louisiana's Chemical Corridor Disputes*. MIT Press.

Allen, Barbara. 2004. Shifting Boundary Work: Issues and Tensions in Environmental Health Science in the Case of Grand Bois, Louisiana. *Science as Culture* 13 (4): 429–448.

Allen, Barbara. 2005. The Problem with Epidemiology Data in Assessing Environmental Health Impacts of Toxic Sites. *WIT Transactions on Ecology and the Environment* 85: 467–475.

Allen, Barbara. 2014. From Suspicious Illness to Policy Change in Petrochemical Regions. In *Powerless Science? Science and Politics in a Toxic World*, ed. Soraya Boudia and Nathalie Jas. Berghahn.

Alliance for Natural Health USA. 2010. ANH-USA victory! Supplements are Exempted from Codex Language in Food Safety Bill. April 13. www.anh-usa.org.

Alliance for Natural Health USA. 2011. Free Speech about Natural Health Science—It's Time to Fight Back! March 29. www.anh-usa.org.

Althusser, Louis. 1984. *Essays on Ideology*. Verso.

American Legislative Exchange Council. 2016. Membership. www.alec.org.

Amenta, Edwin, Neal Caren, Elizabeth Chiarello, and Yang Su. 2010. The Political Consequences of Social Movements. *Annual Review of Sociology* 36: 287–307.

Ansolabehere, Stephen, and James M. Snyder. 2003. Why Is There So Little Money in US Politics? *Journal of Economic Perspectives* 17 (1): 105–130.

Arthur, Mikaila. 2009. Thinking Outside the Master's House: New Knowledge Movements and the Emergence of Academic Disciplines. *Social Movement Studies* 8 (1): 73–87.

Barkan, Steven. 1984. Legal Control of the Southern Civil Rights Movement. *American Sociological Review* 49 (4): 552–565.

Barley, Stephen. 2010. Building an Institutional Field to Corral a Government: A Case to Set an Agenda for Organization Studies. *Organization Studies* 31 (6): 777–805.

Barnes, Barry, and R. G. A. Dolby. 1970. The Scientific Ethos: A Deviant Viewpoint. *Archives Européennes de Sociologie* 11: 3–25.

Bartosiewicz, Petra, and Marissa Miley. 2013. The Too Polite Revolution: Why the Recent Campaign to Pass Comprehensive Climate Change Legislation Failed. Presented at Symposium on the Politics of America's Fight Global Warming, Columbia University School of Journalism. Available at www.journalism.columbia.edu.

Bass, Scott, ed. 2011. *Dietary Supplement Regulation: A Comprehensive Guide*. Food and Drug Law Institute.

Bateson, Gregory. 1955. A Theory of Play and Fantasy. *Psychiatric Research Reports* 2: 39–51.

Batt, Sharon. 2015. A Community Fractured: Canada's Breast Cancer Movement, Pharmaceutical Company Funding, and Science-Related Advocacy. In *The Public Shaping of Medical Research: Patient Associations, Health Movements, and Biomedicine*, ed. Wilhelm Viehöver, Peter Wehling, and Sophia Koenen. Routledge.

Bauer, Raymond, Pool Ithiel de Sola, and Lewis Anthony Dexter. 1963. *American Business and Public Policy: The Politics of Foreign Trade*. MIT Press.

Beck, Ulrich. 1992. *Risk Society: Towards a New Modernity*. SAGE.

Beck, Ulrich. 1997. Subpolitics: Ecology and the Disintegration of Institutional Power. *Organization & Environment* 10 (1): 52–65.

Beck, Ulrich. 1999. *World Risk Society*. Blackwell.

Beck, Ulrich. 2000. *What Is Globalization?* Blackwell.

Ben-David, Joseph, and Randall Collins. 1966. Social Factors in the Origins of a New Science: The Case of Psychology. *American Sociological Review* 31 (4): 451–465.

Benedict, Ruth. 1934. *Patterns of Culture*. Houghton Mifflin.

Benford, Robert, and David Snow. 2000. Framing Processes and Social Movements: An Overview and Assessment. *Annual Review of Sociology* 26: 611–639.

Benjamin, Regina. 2013. Forward. In *Community-Based Participatory Health Research: Issues, Methods, and Translation to Practice*, ed. Daniel Blumenthal, Selina Smith, Ronald Braithwaite, and Ralph DiClemente. Springer.

Berman, Elizabeth Popp. 2012. *Creating the Market University: How Academic Science Became an Economic Engine*. Princeton University Press.

Berman, Elizabeth Popp. 2014. Field Theories and the Move toward the Market in US Academic Science. *Political Power and Social Theory* 27: 193–222.

Bijker, Weibe. 2010. How is Technology Made? That Is the Question. *Cambridge Journal of Economics* 34 (1): 63–76.

Bimber, Bruce. 1996. *The Politics of Expertise in Congress: The Rise and Fall of the Office of Technology Assessment*. State University of New York Press.

BioInitiative Working Group. 2012. *BioInitiative Report: a Rationale for Biologically-based Public Exposure Standard for Electromagnetic Fields Radiation*. www.bioinitiative .org.

Bourdieu, Pierre. 1975. The Specificity of the Scientific Field and the Social Conditions for the Progress of Reason. *Social Science Information* 14 (6): 19–47.

Bourdieu, Pierre. 1977. *Outline of a Theory of Practice*. Cambridge University Press.

Bourdieu, Pierre. 1981. *The Political Ontology of Martin Heidegger*. Stanford University Press.

Bourdieu, Pierre. 1990. Animadversiones in Mertonem. In *Robert Merton: Consensus and Controversy*, ed. John Clark, Celia Modgil, and Sohan Midgil. Falmer.

Bourdieu, Pierre. 1991. The History of Scientific Reason. *Sociological Forum* 6 (1): 3–26.

Bourdieu, Pierre. 1993. *Sociology in Question*. SAGE.

Bourdieu, Pierre. 1998. *Acts of Resistance: Against the Tyranny of the Market*. New Press.

Bourdieu, Pierre. 2001. *Science of Science and Reflexivity*. University of Chicago Press.

Bourdieu, Pierre. 2005. *The Social Structures of the Economy*. Polity Press.

Brown, Phil. 1992. Popular Epidemiology and Toxic Waste Contamination: Lay and Professional Ways of Knowing. *Journal of Health and Social Behavior* 33 (3): 267–281.

Brown, Phil. 2003. Qualitative Methods in Environmental Health Research. *Environmental Health Perspectives* 111 (14): 1789–1798.

Brown, Phil. 2007. *Toxic Exposures: Contested Illnesses and the Environmental Health Movement*. Columbia University Press.

Brown, Phil, and Edwin Mikkelsen. 1990. *No Safe Place: Toxic Waste, Leukemia, and Community Action*. University of California Press.

Brown, Phil, Julia Brody, Rachel Morello-Frosch, Jessica Tovar, Ami Zota, and Ruthann Rudd. 2012. Measuring the Success of Community Science: The Northern California Household Study. *Environmental Health Perspectives* 120 (3): 326–331.

Brown, Phil, Stephen Zavestoski, Sabrina McCormick, et al. 2000. A Gulf of Difference: Disputes over Gulf War Related Illnesses. *Journal of Health and Social Behavior* 42: 235–257.

Brulle, Robert. 2014. Institutionalizing Delay: Foundation Funding and the Creation of US Climate-Change Counter-movement Organizations. *Climatic Change* 122: 681–694.

Bullard, Robert, Glenn Johnson, and Angel Torres, eds. 2004. *Highway Robbery: Transportation Racism and New Routes to Equity*. South End Press.

Burgess, Anthony. 2002. Comparing National Responses to Perceived Risks from Mobile Phone Masts. *Health Risk & Society* 4 (2): 175–188.

Burgess, Anthony. 2003. Review of *The Precautionary Principle in the Twentieth Century*. *Health Risk & Society* 5 (1): 105–107.

Callon, Michel. 1986. Some Elements of a Sociology of Translation: Domestication of the Scallops and Fisherman in St. Breiuc Bay. In *Power, Action, and Belief: A New Sociology of Action?* ed. John Law. Routledge.

Callon, Michel. 1998. *The Laws of the Markets*. Blackwell.

Callon, Michel. 2007. What Does It Mean to Say that Economics is Performative? In *Do Economists Make Markets? On the Performativity of Economics*, ed. Donald MacKenzie, Fabian Muniesa, and Lucia Siu. Princeton University Press.

Cameron, Ewan, and Linus Pauling. 1978. Supplemental Ascorbate in the Supportive Treatment of Cancer: Reevaluation of Prolongation of Survival Times in Terminal Human Cancer. *Proceedings of the National Academy of Sciences* 75 (9): 4538–4542.

Camic, Charles. 2011. Bourdieu's Cleft Sociology of Science. *Minerva* 49 (3): 275–293.

Campbell, John. 2005. Where Do We Stand? Common Mechanisms in Organizations and Social Movements Research. In *Social Movements and Organizational Theory*, ed. Gerald Davis, Doug McAdam, Richard Scott, and Mayer Zald. Cambridge University Press.

Center for Responsive Politics. 2016a. Chemical and Related Manufacturing. www.opensecrets.org.

Center for Responsive Politics. 2016b. Energy/Natural Resources. www.opensecrets
.org.

Center for Responsive Politics. 2016c. Environment. www.opensecrets.org.

Center for Responsive Politics. 2016d. Green Tech Action Fund. www.opensecrets
.org

Center for Responsive Politics. 2016e. Top Industries Giving to Congress, 2012 Cycle. www.opensecrets.org.

Chabot, John, Wei-Yang Tsai, Robert Fine, Chunxia Chen, Carol Kumah, Karen Antman, and Victor Grann. 2009. Pancreatic Proteolytic Enzyme Therapy Compared with Gemcitabine-based Chemotherapy for the Treatment of Pancreatic Cancer. *Journal of Clinical Oncology* 28 (12): 2058–2063.

Chang, Ha-Joon. 2008. *Bad Samaritans: The Myth of Free Trade and the Secret History of Capitalism.* Bloomsbury.

Citizens for Responsibility and Ethics in Congress. 2013. Natural Cash: Fracking Industry Contributions to Congress. www.citizensforethics.org.

Clarke, Adele. 1998. *Disciplining Reproduction: Modernity, American Life Sciences, and "the Problems of Sex."* University of California Press.

Clawson, Dan, Alan Neustadtl, and Denise Scott. 1992. *Money Talks: Corporate PACs and Political Influence.* Basic Books.

Clynes, Tom. 2012. The Battle. *Popular Science,* July: 36–43, 80.

Coley, Jonathan, and David Hess. 2012. Green Energy Laws and Republican Legislators in the United States. *Energy Policy* 48 (1): 576–583.

Collins, Harry. 1983. An Empirical Relativist Programme in the Sociology of Scientific Knowledge. In *Science Observed,* ed. Karin Knorr Cetina and Michael Mulkay. SAGE.

Collins, Harry. 1985. Changing Order: Replication and Induction in Scientific Practice. *Sage.*

Collins, Harry. 2000. Surviving Closure: Post-Rejection Adaptation and Plurality in Science. *American Sociological Review* 65 (6): 824–845.

Collins, Harry. 2004. *Gravity's Shadow: The Search for Gravitational Waves.* University of Chicago Press.

Collins, Harry, and Robert Evans. 2002. The Third Wave of Science Studies: Studies of Expertise and Experience. *Social Studies of Science* 32 (2): 235–296.

Collins, Harry, and Robert Evans. 2007. *Rethinking Expertise.* University of Chicago Press.

Collins, Harry, and Steven Yearley. 1992. Epistemological Chicken. In *Science as Practice and Culture*, ed. Andrew Pickering. University of Chicago Press.

Corburn, Jason. 2005. *Street Science: Community Knowledge and Environmental Health Justice*. MIT Press.

Cordner, Alissa, and Phil Brown. 2015. A Multisector Alliance Approach to Environmental Social Movements: Flame Retardants and Chemical Reform in the United States. *Environmental Sociology* 1 (1): 69–79.

Coutard, Oliver, ed. 1999. *The Governance of Large Technical Systems*. Routledge.

Culbert, Michael. 1974. *Freedom from Cancer*. Simon and Schuster.

Daly, Herman. 1990. Toward Some Operational Principles of Sustainable Development. *Ecological Economics* 2 (1): 1–6.

Daly, Herman. 1996. *Beyond Growth: The Economics of Sustainable Development*. Beacon .

Daniels, George. 1967. The Pure Science Ideal and Democratic Culture. *Science* 156 (3783): 1699–1705.

Darnton, Robert. 1968. *Memserism and the End of the Enlightenment in France*. Harvard University Press.

Davis, Gerald, and Peter Anderson. 2008. Social Movements and Failed Institutionalization: Corporate (Non)Response to the AIDS Epidemic. In *The SAGE Handbook of Organizational Institutionalism*, ed. Royston Greenwood, Christine Oliver, Roy Suddaby, and Kertin Sahlin. SAGE.

Delborne, Jason. 2008. Transgenes and Transgressions: Scientific Dissent as Heterogeneous Practice. *Social Studies of Science* 38 (4): 509–541.

Delborne, Jason, Jen Schneider, Ravtosh Bal, Susan Cozzens, and Richard Worthington. 2013. Policy Pathways, Policy Networks, and Citizen Deliberation: Disseminating the Results of the World Wide Views on Global Warming in the USA. *Science & Public Policy* 40 (3): 378–392.

Delicado, Ana, Raquel Rego, Cristina Palma Conceição, Inês Pereira, and Luís Junqueira. 2014. What Roles for Scientific Associations in Contemporary Science? *Minerva* 52 (4): 439–465.

Della Porta, Donatella. 1995. *Social Movements, Political Violence, and the State*. Cambridge University Press.

Della Porta, Donatella, and Sidney Tarrow. 2004. *Transnational Protest and Social Activism: People, Passions, and Power*. Rowman and Littlefield.

Diamond, Jared. 2005. *Collapse: How Societies Choose to Fail or Succeed*. Viking.

Diani, Mario. 2003. The Terrestrial Emporium of Contentious Knowledge. *Mobilization* 8 (1): 109–112.

Dickinson, Janis, Rick Bonney, and Richard Louv. 2012. *Citizen Science: Public Participation in Environmental Research.* Comstock.

DiMaggio, Paul. 1991. Constructing an Organizational Field as a Professional Project: US Art Museums, 1920–1940. In *The New Institutionalism in Organizational Analysis,* ed. Walter Powell and Paul DiMaggio. University of Chicago Press.

Douglas, Mary. 1992. *Risk and Blame: Essays in Cultural Theory.* Routledge.

Downey, Gary. 1988. Structure and Practice in the Cultural Identities of Scientists: Negotiating Nuclear Wastes in New Mexico. *Anthropological Quarterly* 61 (1): 26–38.

Downey, Gary, and Joseph Dumit, eds. 1997. *Cyborgs and Citadels: Anthropological Interventions in Emerging Sciences and Technologies.* School for American Research Press.

Drori, Gili, and John Meyer. 2006. Global Scientization: An Environment for Expanded Organization. In *Globalization and Organization: World Society and Organizational Change,* ed. Gili Drori, John Meyer, and Hokyu Hwang. Oxford University Press.

Dunlap, Riley, and Aaron McCright. 2011. Organized Climate Change Denial. In *Handbook of Climate Change and Society,* ed. John Dryzek, Richard Norgaard, and David Schlosberg. Oxford University Press.

Earle, Jennifer. 2011. Political Repression: Iron Fists, Velvet Gloves, and Diffuse Control. *Annual Review of Sociology* 37:261–284.

Eglash, Ron, Jennifer Croissant, Giovanna de Chiro, and Rayvon Fouché, eds. 2004. *Appropriating Technology: Vernacular Science and Social Power.* University of Minnesota Press.

Eglash, Ron, Audrey Bennett, Casey O'Donnell, Sybillyn Jennings, and Margaret Cintorino. 2006. Culturally Situated Design Tools: Ethnocomputing from Field Site to Classroom. *American Anthropologist* 108 (2): 347–362.

Ellenberger, Henri. 1970. *The Discovery of the Unconscious.* Basic Books.

Elzen, Boele, Frank Geels, Cees Leeuwis, and Barbara van Mierlo. 2011. Normative Contestation in Transitions "in the Making": Animal Welfare Concerns and System Innovation in Pig Husbandry. *Research Policy* 40 (2): 263–265.

Epstein, Steven. 1995. The Construction of Lay Expertise: AIDS Activism and the Forging of Credibility in the Reform of Clinical Trials. *Science, Technology & Human Values* 20 (4): 408–437.

Epstein, Steven. 1996. *Impure Science: AIDS, Activism, and the Politics of Knowledge*. University of California Press.

Eubanks, Virginia. 2011. *Digital Dead End: Fighting for Social Justice in the Information Age*. MIT Press.

Evans, John, and Michael Evans. 2008. Religion and Science: Beyond the Epistemological Conflict Narrative. *Annual Review of Sociology* 34: 87–105.

Eyerman, Ron, and Andrew Jamison. 1991. *Social Movements: A Cognitive Approach*. Pennsylvania State University Press.

Fischer, Frank. 2005. Are Scientists Irrational? Risk Assessment in Practical Reason. In *Science and Citizens: Globalization and the Challenge of Engagement*, ed. Melissa Leach, Ian Scoones, and Brian Wynne. Zed.

Fischer, Frank. 2009. *Democracy and Expertise: Reorienting Policy Inquiry*. Oxford University Press.

Fligstein, Neil. 1990. *The Transformation of Corporate Control*. Harvard University Press.

Fligstein, Neil, and Doug McAdam. 2012. *A Theory of Fields*. Oxford University Press.

Foster, John Bellamy, Brett Clark, and Richard York. 2010. *The Ecological Rift: Capitalism's War on the Earth*. Monthly Review Press.

Foucault, Michel. 1970. *The Order of Things*. Vintage.

Foucault, Michel. 2008. *The Birth of Biopolitics: Lectures at the Collège de France, 1978–1979*. Palgrave Macmillan.

Fraser, Nancy. 1997. *Justice Interruptus: Critical Reflections on the "Postsocialist" Condition*. Routledge.

Frickel, Scott. 2004. *Chemical Consequences: Environmental Mutagens, Scientist Activism and the Rise of Genetic Toxicology*. Rutgers University Press.

Frickel, Scott. 2014. Not Here and Everywhere: The Non-Production of Scientific Knowledge. In *Routledge Handbook of Science, Technology, and Society*, ed. Daniel Kleinman and Kelly Moore. Routledge.

Frickel, Scott, and Michelle Edwards. 2014. Untangling Ignorance in Environmental Risk Assessment. In *Powerless Science? Science and Politics in a Toxic World*, ed. Nathalie Jas and Soraya Boudia. Berghahn.

Frickel, Scott, and Neil Gross. 2005. A General Theory of Scientific/Intellectual Movements. *American Sociological Review* 70 (2): 204–232.

Frickel, Scott, and Abby Kinchy. 2015. Lost in Space: Geographies of Ignorance in Science and Technology Studies. In *Routledge International Handbook of Ignorance Studies*, ed. Matthias Gross and Linsey McGoey. Routledge.

Frickel, Scott, Rebekah Torcasso, and Annika Anderson. 2015. The Organization of Expert Activism: Shadow Mobilization in Two Social Movements. *Mobilization* 20 (3): 305–323.

Frickel, Scott, Sahra Gibbon, Jeff Howard, Joana Kempner, Gwen Ottinger, and David J. Hess. 2010. Undone Science: Social Movement Challenges to Dominant Scientific Practice. *Science, Technology & Human Values* 35 (4): 444–473.

Friedland, Roger, and Robert Alford. 1991. Bringing Society Back in: Symbols, Practices, and Institutional Contradictions. In *The New Institutionalism in Organizational Analysis*, ed. Walter Powell and Paul DiMaggio. University of Chicago Press.

Fuenfschilling, Lea, and Bernhard Truffer. 2014. The Structuration of Sociotechnical Regimes: Conceptual Foundations from Institutional Theory. *Research Policy* 43 (4): 772–791.

Galbraith, John Kenneth. 1952. *American Capitalism: The Concept of Countervailing Power*. Houghton Mifflin.

Galbraith, John Kenneth. 1983. *The Anatomy of Power*. Houghton Mifflin.

Galluci, Maria. 2013. Renewable Energy Standards Target of Multi-Pronged Attack. *Inside Climate News*, March 19. insideclimatenews.org.

Gauld, Alan. 1968. *The Founders of Psychical Research*. Schocken.

Geels, Frank. 2002. Technological Transitions as Evolutionary Reconfiguration Processes: A Multi-Level Perspective and a Case Study. *Research Policy* 31 (8–9): 1257–1274.

Geels, Frank. 2005. The Dynamics of Transitions in Socio-technical Systems: A Multilevel Analysis of the Transition Pathway from Horse-drawn Carriages to Automobiles (1860–1930). *Technology Analysis and Strategic Management* 17 (4): 445–476.

Geels, Frank. 2011. The Multilevel Perspective on Sustainability Transitions: Responses to Seven Criticisms. *Environmental Innovation and Societal Transitions* 1 (1): 24–40.

Geels, Frank. 2014. Regime Resistance against Low-carbon Energy Transitions: Introducing Politics and Power into the Multi-level Perspective. *Theory, Culture & Society* 31 (5): 21–40.

Geels, Frank, and Johan Schot. 2007. Typology of Sociotechnical Transition Pathways. *Research Policy* 36 (3): 399–417.

Geertz, Clifford. 1973. *The Interpretation of Cultures*. Basic Books.

Gieryn, Thomas. 1983. Boundary-Work and the Demarcation of Science from Non-Science. *American Sociological Review* 48 (6): 781–795.

Gieryn, Thomas. 1994. Boundaries of Science. In *Handbook of Science and Technology*, ed. Sheila Jasanoff, Gerry Markle, James Peterson, and Trevor Pinch. SAGE.

Giugni, Marco. 1998. Was it Worth the Effort? The Outcomes and Consequences of Social Movements. *Annual Review of Sociology* 24: 371–393.

Goffman, Erving. 1974. *Frame Analysis: An Essay on the Organization of Experience.* Harper and Row.

Gonzalez, Nicholas. 2009. The Truth about the NIC-NCCAM Clinical Study. www.dr-gonzalez.com.

Gonzalez, Nicholas. 2012. *What Went Wrong: The Truth Behind the Clinical Trial of the Enzyme Treatment of Cancer.* New Spring.

Goodwin, Jeff, and James Jasper. 2004a. Caught in a Winding, Snarling Vine: The Structural Bias of Political Process Theory. In *Rethinking Social Movements: Structure, Meaning, and Emotion*, ed. Jeff Goodwin and James Jasper. Rowman and Littlefield.

Goodwin, Jeff, and James Jasper. 2004b. Trouble in Paradigms. In *Rethinking Social Movements: Structure, Meaning, and Emotion*, ed. Jeff Goodwin and James Jasper. Rowman and Littlefield.

Gordon, Scott. 2009. *Controlling the State: Constitutionalism from Ancient Athens to Today.* Harvard University Press.

Goyal, Madhav, Sonal Singh, Erica M. S. Sibinga, et al. 2014. Meditation Programs for Psychological Stress and Well-Being: A Systematic Review and Meta-Analysis. *Journal of the American Medical Association* 174 (3): 357–368.

Greenwood, Jeremy. 2007. Citizens, Science, and Bird Conservation. *Journal für Ornithologie* 148 (Suppl 1): S77–S124.

Greenwood, Justin. 2011. *Interest Representation in the European Union.* Palgrave Macmillan.

Gross, Matthias. 2010. *Ignorance and Surprise: Science, Society, and Ecological Design.* MIT Press.

Gross, Matthias, and Linsey McGoey, eds. 2015. *Routledge International Handbook of Ignorance Studies.* Routledge.

Gross, Neil. 2013. *Why Are Professors Liberal and Why Do Conservatives Care?* Harvard University Press.

Gupta, Akhil, and James Ferguson. 1997. *Culture, Power, Place: Explorations in Critical Anthropology.* Duke University Press.

Guston, David. 2001. Boundary Organizations in Environmental Policy and Science: An Introduction. *Science, Technology & Human Values* 26 (4): 399–408.

Guthman, Julie. 2000. Raising Organic: An Agro-ecological Assessment of Grower Practices in California. *Agriculture and Human Values* 17 (3): 257–266.

Habermas, Jürgen. 1989. *The Structural Transformation of the Public Sphere: An Inquiry into a Category of Bourgeois Society*. MIT Press.

Habermas, Jürgen. 1992. Further Reflections on the Public Sphere. In *Habermas and the Public Sphere*, ed. Craig Calhoun. MIT Press.

Hadorn, Gertrude, Holger Hoffmann-Riem, Susette Biber-Klemm, Walter Grossen-bacher-Mansuy, Dominque Joye, Christian Pohl, Urs Wiessmann, and Elisabeth Zemp. 2008. *Handbook of Transdisciplinary Research*. Springer.

Hagstrom, Warren. 1965. *The Scientific Community*. Basic Books.

Halffman, Willem, and Mieke van Hemert. 2010. *WP5: CSO's Interventions into Agri-Environmental Issues. Final report, FP7 Science in Society Programme*. Radboud University.

Halfon, Saul. 2010. Confronting the WTO: Intervention Strategies in GMO Adjudication. *Science, Technology & Human Values* 35 (3): 307–329.

Hansen, James. 2009. *Storms of My Grandchildren: The Truth about the Coming Climate Catastrophe and Our Last Chance to Save Humanity*. Bloomsbury.

Haraway, Donna. 1989. *Primate Visions*. Routledge.

Harding, Sandra. 1998. *Is Science Multicultural? Postcolonialisms, Feminisms, and Epistemologies*. Indiana University Press.

Harding, Sandra. 2008. *Sciences from Below: Feminisms, Postcolonialities, and Modernities*. Duke University Press.

Harding, Sandra. 2015. *Objectivity and Diversity: Another Logic of Scientific Research*. University of Chicago Press.

Harremöes, Paul, David Gee, Malcolm MacGarvin, Andy Stirling, Jane Keys, Brian Wynne, and Sofia Vaz. 2002. *The Precautionary Principle in the Twentieth Century*. Earthscan.

Harvey, David. 2005. *A Brief History of Neoliberalism*. Oxford University Press.

Haveman, Heather, Rao Hayagreeva, and Srikanth Paruchuri. 2007. The Winds of Change: The Progressive Movement and the Bureaucratization of Thrift. *American Sociological Review* 72 (1): 117–142.

Hayden, Dolores. 1980. What Would a Non-Sexist City Be Like? *Signs* 5 (3 supplement): S170–S187.

Hess, David J. 1991. *Spirits and Scientists*. Pennsylvania State University Press.

Hess, David J. 1995. *Science and Technology in a Multicultural World*. Columbia University Press.

Hess, David J. 1997. *Can Bacteria Cause Cancer?* New York University Press.

Hess, David J. 1999. *Evaluating Alternative Cancer Therapies*. Rutgers University Press.

Hess, David J. 2004a. CAM Cancer Therapies in Twentieth-century North America: Examining Continuities and Change. In *The Politics of Healing*, ed. Robert Johnston. Routledge.

Hess, David J. 2004b. Medical Modernization, Scientific Research Fields, and the Movement for Complementary and Alternative Cancer Therapies. *Sociology of Health & Illness* 26 (6): 695–709.

Hess, David J. 2004c. Organic Agriculture and Food in the US: Object Conflicts in a Health-Environmental Social Movement. *Science as Culture* 13 (4): 493–514.

Hess, David J. 2005. Technology- and Product-Oriented Movements: Approximating Social Movement Studies and STS. *Science, Technology & Human Values* 30 (4): 515–535.

Hess, David J. 2006. Antiangiogensis Research and the Dynamics of Scientific Research Fields: Historical and Institutional Perspectives in the Sociology of Science. In *The New Political Sociology of Science*, ed. Scott Frickel and Kelly Moore. University of Wisconsin Press.

Hess, David J. 2007a. *Alternative Pathways in Science and Industry*. MIT Press.

Hess, David J. 2007b. Crosscurrents: Social Movements and the Anthropology of Science and Technology. *American Anthropologist* 109 (3): 463–472.

Hess, David J. 2007c. What Is a Clean Bus? Object Conflicts in the Greening of Urban Transit. *Sustainability: Science, Practice, and Policy* 3 (1): 45–58.

Hess, David J. 2009a. *Localist Movements in a Global Economy*. MIT Press.

Hess, David J. 2009b. The Potentials and Limitations of Civil Society Research: Getting Undone Science Done. *Sociological Inquiry* 79 (3): 306–327.

Hess, David J. 2010a. Environmental Reform Organizations and Undone Science in the United States: Exploring the Environmental, Health, and Safety Implications of Nanotechnology. *Science as Culture* 19 (2): 181–214.

Hess, David J. 2010b. Sustainable Consumption and the Problem of Resilience. *Sustainability: Science, Practice, & Policy* 6 (2): 1–12.

Hess, David J. 2011a. Bourdieu and Science and Technology Studies: Toward a Reflexive Sociology. *Minerva* 49 (3): 333–348.

Hess, David J. 2011b. Electricity Transformed: Neoliberalism and Local Energy in the United States. *Antipode* 43 (3): 1056–1057.

Hess, David J. 2011c. To Tell the Truth: On Scientific Counterpublics. *Public Understanding of Science* 20 (5): 627–641.

Hess, David J. 2012a. *Good Green Jobs in a Global Economy*. MIT Press.

Hess, David J. 2012b. The Green Transition, Neoliberalism, and the Technosciences. In *Neoliberalism and Technosciences: Critical Assessments*, ed. Luigi Pellozzoni and Marja Ylönen. Edward Elgar.

Hess, David J. 2013a. Industrial Fields and Countervailing Power: The Transformation of Distributed Solar Energy in the United States. *Global Environmental Change* 23 (5): 847–855.

Hess, David J. 2013b. Neoliberalism and the History of STS Theory: Toward a Reflexive Sociology. *Social Epistemology* 27 (2): 177–193.

Hess, David J. 2013c. Sustainable Consumption, Energy, and Failed Transitions: The Problem of Adaptation. In *Innovations in Sustainable Consumption: New Economics, Socio-Technical Transitions, and Social Practices*, ed. Maurie Cohen, Halina Brown, and Philip Vergragt. Edward Elgar.

Hess, David J. 2013d. Transitions in Energy Systems: The Mitigation-Adaptation Relationship. *Science as Culture* 22 (2): 197–203.

Hess, David J. 2014a. Smart Meters and Public Acceptance: Comparative Analysis and Governance Implications. *Health Risk & Society* 16 (3): 243–258.

Hess, David J. 2014b. Sustainability Transitions: A Political Coalition Perspective. *Research Policy* 43 (2): 278–283.

Hess, David J. 2014c. When Green Became Blue: Epistemic Rift and the Corralling of Climate Science. *Political Power and Social Theory* 27: 123–153.

Hess, David J. 2015a. Beyond Scientific Consensus: Scientific Counterpublics, Countervailing Industries, and Competing Research Agendas. In *The Public Shaping of Medical Research: Patient Associations, Health Movements, and Biomedicine*, ed. Peter Wehling, Willy Viehöver, and Sophia Koenen. Routledge.

Hess, David J. 2015b. Public as Threats? Integrating Science and Technology Studies (STS) and Social Movement Studies (SMS). *Science as Culture* 24 (1): 69–82.

Hess, David J. 2015c. Undone Science and Social Movements: A Review and Typology. In *Routledge International Handbook of Ignorance Studies*, ed. Matthias Gross and Lindsey McGooey. Routledge.

Hess, David J. 2016. Forthcoming. The Politics of Niche-Regime Conflicts: Distributed Solar Energy in the United States. *Environmental Innovation and Societal Transitions*.

Hess, David, and Jonathan Coley. 2014. Wireless Smart Meters and Public Acceptance: The Environment, Limited Choices, and Precautionary Politics. *Public Understanding of Science* 23 (6): 688–702.

Hess, David J., and Scott Frickel. 2014. Introduction: Fields of Knowledge and Theory Traditions in the Sociology of Science. *Political Power and Social Theory* 27: 1–30.

Hess, David J., and Quan D. Mai. 2014. Renewable Electricity Policy in Asia: A Qualitative Comparative Analysis of Factors Affecting Sustainability Transitions. *Environmental Innovation and Societal Transitions* 12: 31–46.

Hess, David J., and Quan D. Mai. 2015. The Convergence of Economic Development and Energy Transition Policies in State-government Plans in the United States. *Sustainability: Science, Practice, and Policy* 11 (1): 5–20.

Hess, David J., and Brian Martin. 2006. Backfire, Repression, and the Theory of Transformative Events. *Mobilization* 11 (2): 249–267.

Hess, David J., Quan D. Mai, and Kate Pride Brown. 2016. Red States, Green Laws: Ideology and Renewable Energy Legislation in the United States. *Energy Research and Social Science* 11: 19–28.

Hessen, Boris. 1971. *The Social and Economic Roots of Newton's Principia*. Howard Fertig.

Hilgartner, Stephen. 2000. *Science on Stage: Expert Advice as Public Drama*. Stanford University Press.

Hirsh, Richard. 1999. *Power Loss: The Origins of Deregulation and Restructuring in the American Electric Utility System*. MIT Press.

Hoffmann-Riem, Holger, and Brian Wynne. 2002. In Risk Assessment, One Has to Admit Ignorance. *Nature* 416 (March 14): 123.

Hornberger, George M., David J. Hess, and Jonathan Gilligan. 2015. Water Conservation and Hydrological Transitions in American Cities. *Water Resources Research* 51 (6): 4635–4649.

Hughes, Thomas. 1983. *Networks of Power: Electrification in Western Society, 1880–1930*. Johns Hopkins University Press.

Hughes, Thomas. 1987. The Evolution of Large Technological Systems. In *The Social Construction of Technological Systems*, ed. Wiebe Bijker, Thomas Hughes, and Trevor Pinch. MIT Press.

International Agency for Research on Cancer. 2011. IARC Classifies Radiofrequency Electromagnetic Fields as Possibly Carcinogenic to Humans. IARC Press Release 208. www.iarc.fr.

Irwin, Alan. 1995. *Citizen Science: A Study of People, Expertise, and Sustainable Development*. Routledge.

Irwin, Alan. 2006. The Politics of Talk: Coming to Terms with the "New" Scientific Governance. *Social Studies of Science* 36 (2): 299–320.

Jacques, Peter, Riley Dunlap, and Mark Freeman. 2008. The Organization of Denial: Conservative Think Tanks and Environmental Skepticism. *Environmental Politics* 17 (3): 349–385.

Jaffee, Daniel. 2012. Weak Coffee: Certification and Co-Optation in the Fair Trade Movement. *Social Problems* 59 (1): 94–106.

Jamison, Andrew. 2006. Social Movements and Science: Cultural Appropriations of Cognitive Praxis. *Science as Culture* 15 (1): 45–59.

Jasanoff, Sheila. 1990. *The Fifth Branch: Science Advisers as Policymakers*. Harvard University Press.

Jasanoff, Sheila, and Sang-Hyun Kim. 2013. Sociotechnical Imaginaries and National Energy Policies. *Science as Culture* 22 (2): 189–196.

Jasper, James. 1997. *The Art of Moral Protest: Culture, Biography, and Creativity in Social Movements*. University of Chicago Press.

Jasper, James. 1998. The Emotions of Protest: Affective and Reactive Emotions in and Around Social Movements. *Sociological Forum* 13 (3): 397–424.

Jasper, James, and Jane Poulsen. 1995. Recruiting Strangers and Friends: Moral Shocks and Social Networks in Animal Rights and Anti-Nuclear Protests. *Social Problems* 42 (4): 493–512.

Johnston, Hank. 2009. Protest Cultures: Performance, Artifacts, and Ideations. In *Culture, Social Movements, and Protest*, ed. Hank Johnston. Ashgate.

Johnston, Hank, and Bert Klandermans. 1995. The Cultural Analysis of Social Movements. In *Social Movements and Culture*, ed. Hank Johnston and Bert Klandremans. University of Minnesota Press.

Jones, Candace, Eva Boxenbaum, and Callen Anthony. 2013. The Immateriality of Material Practices in Institutional Logics. *Institutional Logics in Action. Research in the Sociology of Organizations* 39A:51–75.

Kaufman, Marc. 2005. Dalai Lama Gives Talk on Science. *Washington Post*, November 13.

Keck, Margaret, and Kathryn Sikkink. 1998. *Activists Beyond Borders: Advocacy Networks in International Politics*. Cornell University Press.

Kempner, Joanna. 2015. The Production of Forbidden Knowledge. In *Routledge International Handbook of Ignorance Studies*, ed. Matthias Gross and Linsey McGoey. Routledge.

Kempner, Joanna, Clifford Perlis, and Jon Merz. 2005. Forbidden Knowledge. *Science* 307: 854.

Kern, Florian, and Adrian Smith. 2008. Restructuring Energy Systems for Sustainability? Energy Transition Policy in the Netherlands. *Energy Policy* 36 (11): 4093–4103.

Kinchy, Abby. 2010. Epistemic Boomerang: Expert Policy Advice as Leverage in the Campaign against Transgenic Maize in Mexico. *Mobilization* 15 (2): 179–198.

Kinchy, Abby. 2012. *Seeds, Science, and Struggle: The Global Politics of Transgenic Crops*. MIT Press.

Kinchy, Abby. 2014. Political Scale and Conflicts over Knowledge Production: The Case of Unconventional Natural-Gas Development. In *Routledge Handbook of Science, Technology, and Society*, ed. Daniel Kleinman and Kelly Moore. Routledge.

Kinchy, Abby, Kirk Jalbert, and Jessica Lyons. 2014. What Is Volunteer Water Monitoring Good For? Fracking and the Plural Logics of Participatory Science. *Political Power and Social Theory* 27: 259–289.

Kinchy, Abby, Daniel Kleinman, and Roby Autry. 2008. Against Free Markets, Against Science? Regulating the Socio-Economic Effects of Biotechnology. *Rural Sociology* 73 (2): 147–179.

Kind, Peter. 2013. *Disruptive Challenges: Financial Implications and Strategic Responses to a Changing Retail Electric Business*. Edison Electric Institute.

King, Brayden. 2008. A Political Mediation Model of Corporate Response to Social Movement Activism. *Administrative Science Quarterly* 53 (3): 395–421.

King, Brayden, and Sarah Soule. 2007. Social Movements as Extra-Institutional Entrepreneurs: The Effects of Protests on Stock Price Returns. *Administrative Science Quarterly* 52 (3): 412–443.

Kitschelt, Herbert. 1986. Political Opportunity Structures and Political Protest: Anti-Nuclear Protest in Four Democracies. *British Journal of Political Science* 16 (1): 57–85.

Klawiter, Maren. 2008. *The Biopolitics of Breast Cancer: Changing Cultures of Disease and Activism*. University of Minnesota.

Klein, Naomi. 2014. *This Changes Everything: Capitalism v. the Climate*. Simon and Schuster.

Kleinman, Daniel L., and Abby Kinchy. 2003. Why Ban Bovine Growth Hormone? Science, Social Welfare, and the Divergent Biotech Policy Landscapes in Europe and the United States. *Science as Culture* 12 (3): 375–414.

Kleinman, Daniel L., and Abby Kinchy. 2007. Against the Neoliberal Steamroller? The Biosafety Protocol and the Regulation of Agricultural Technologies. *Agriculture, Food, and Human Values* 24 (2): 195–206.

Kleinman, Daniel L., and Steven Vallas. 2001. Science, Capitalism, and the Rise of the "Knowledge Worker": The Changing Structure of Knowledge Production in the United States. *Theory and Society* 30 (4): 451–492.

Knorr Cetina, Karin. 1981. *The Manufacture of Knowledge*. Pergamon.

Koopmans, Ruud. 1993. The Dynamics of Protest Waves: West Germany, 1965–1989. *American Sociological Review* 58 (5): 637–658.

Koopmans, Ruud. 1997. Dynamics of Repression and Mobilization: The German Extreme Right in the 1990s. *Mobilization* 2 (2): 149–164.

Koopmans, Ruud. 2004. Political Opportunity Structure: Some Splitting to Balance the Lumping. In *Rethinking Social Movements: Structure, Meaning, and Emotion*, ed. Jeff Goodwin and James Jasper. Rowman and Littlefield.

Kriesi, Hanspeter. 2004. Political Context and Opportunity. In *The Blackwell Companion to Social Movements*, ed. David Snow, Sarah Soule, and Hanspeter Kriesi. Blackwell.

Krimsky, Sheldon. 2000. *Hormonal Chaos: The Scientific and Social Origins of the Environmental Endocrine Hypothesis*. Johns Hopkins University Press.

Kuhn, Thomas. 1970. *The Structure of Scientific Revolutions*. University of Chicago Press.

Laird, Frank. 2001. *Solar Energy, Technology Policy, and Institutional Values*. Cambridge University Press.

Lamprou, Anna. 2010. Nanotechnology Regulation: Policies Proposed by Three Organizations for the Reform of the Toxic Substances Control Act. Studies in Sustainability Series, Chemical Heritage Foundation. www.chemheritage.org.

Lamprou, Anna, and David J. Hess. 2016. Forthcoming. Finding Political Opportunities: Civil Society, Industrial Power, and the Governance of Nanotechnology in the European Union. *Engaging Science, Technology, and Society*.

La Porte, Todd, ed. 1991. *Social Responses to Large Technical Systems: Control or Anticipation*. Kluwer.

Latour, Bruno. 1987. *Science in Action*. Harvard University Press.

Latour, Bruno, and Steve Woolgar. 1986. *Laboratory Life: The Social Construction of Scientific Facts*. Princeton University Press.

Lave, Rebecca. 2014. Neoliberal Confluences: The Turbulent Evolution of Stream Mitigation Banking in the US *Political Power and Social Theory* 27: 59–88.

Layne, Linda, Sharra Vostral, and Kate Boyer, eds. 2010. *Feminist Technology*. University of Illinois Press.

Leach, Melissa, and James Fairhead. 2002. Manners of Contestation: "Citizen Science" and "Indigenous Knowledge" in West Africa and the Caribbean. *International Social Science Journal* 54 (173): 299–311.

Leydesdorff, Loet, and Janelle Ward. 2005. Science Shops: A Kaleidoscope of Science-Society Collaborations in Europe. *Public Understanding of Science* 14 (4): 353–372.

Lindblom, Charles, and Edward Woodhouse. 1992. *The Policy-Making Process*. Prentice-Hall.

Livingston, Virginia Wuerthele-Caspé, and Eleanor Alexander Jackson. 1965. An Experimental Biologic Approach to the Treatment of Neoplastic Disease. *Journal of the American Women's Medical Association* 20 (9): 858–866.

Lounsbury, Michael. 2005. Institutional Variation in the Evolution of Social Movements. In *Social Movements and Organizational Theory*, ed. Gerald Davis, Doug McAdam, Richard Scott, and Mayer Zald. Cambridge University Press.

Lubitow, Amy. 2013. Collaborative Frame Construction in Social Movement Campaigns: Bisphenol-A and Scientist-Activist Mobilizations. *Social Movement Studies* 12 (4): 429–444.

Lukes, Steven. 1974. *Power: A Radical View*. Macmillan.

MacKenzie, Donald. 1978. Statistical Theory and Social Interests: A Case Study. *Social Studies of Science* 8 (1): 35–83.

MacKenzie, Donald. 1981. Interests, Positivism, and History. *Social Studies of Science* 11 (4): 498–501.

Markle, Gerald, and James Peterson. 1980. *Politics, Science, and Cancer: The Laetrile Phenomenon*. American Association for the Advancement of Science.

Martin, Brian. 1996. Sticking a Needle into Science: The Case of Polio Vaccines and the Origin of AIDS. *Social Studies of Science* 26 (2): 245–276.

Martin, Brian. 2007. *Justice Ignited: The Dynamics of Backfire*. Rowman & Littlefield.

Martin, Brian, Ann Baker, Clyde Manwell, and Cedric Pugh, eds. 1986. *Intellectual Suppression*. Angus and Robertson.

Martin, Emily. 1991. The Egg and the Sperm: How Science Has Constructed a Romance Based on Stereotypical Male-Female Roles. *Signs* 16 (3): 485–501.

Marx, Gary. 1979. External Efforts to Damage or Facilitate Social Movements: Some Patterns, Explanations, Outcomes, and Complications. In *The Dynamics of Social Movements*, ed. Mayer Zald and John McCarthy. Winthrop.

Marx, Karl. 1970. *The German Ideology*. International Publishers.

Marx, Karl. 2011. *Capital: A Critique of Political Economy*, volume 1. Dover.

Masco, Joseph. 2006. *The Nuclear Borderlands: The Manhattan Project in Post–Cold War New Mexico*. Princeton University Press.

Mayer, Brian. 2008. *Blue-Green Coalitions: Fighting for Safe Workplaces and Healthy Communities*. Cornell University Press.

Mayer, Brian. 2009. Cross-Movement Coalition Formation: Bridging the Labor-Environmental Divide. *Sociological Inquiry* 79 (2): 219–239.

McAdam, Doug. 1982. *Political Process and the Development of Black Insurgency, 1930–1970*. University of Chicago Press.

McAdam, Doug, and W. Richard Scott. 2005. Organizations and Movements. In *Social Movements and Organizational Theory*, ed. Gerald Davis, Doug McAdam, Richard Scott, and Mayer Zald. Cambridge University Press.

McAdam, Doug, and Sidney Tarrow. 2011. Introduction: Dynamics of Contention Ten Years On. *Mobilization* 16 (1): 1–10.

McAdam, Doug, John McCarthy, and Mayer Zald, eds. 1996. *Comparative Perspectives on Social Movements: Political Opportunities, Mobilizing Structures, and Cultural Framings*. Cambridge University Press.

McAdam, Doug, Sidney Tarrow, and Charles Tilly. 2001. *Dynamics of Contention*. Cambridge University Press.

McCammon, Holly, Courtney Muse, Harmony Newman, and Teresa Terrell. 2007. Movement Framing and Discursive Opportunity Structures: The Political Successes of the US Women's Jury Movements. *American Sociological Review* 72 (5): 725–749.

McCarthy, John. 1996. Constraints and Opportunities in Adopting, Adapting, and Inventing. In *Comparative Perspectives on Social Movements: Political Opportunities, Mobilizing Structures, and Cultural Framings*, ed. Doug McAdam, John McCarthy, and Mayer Zald. Cambridge University Press.

McCarthy, John, and Meyer Zald. 1977. Resource Mobilization and Social Movements: A Partial Theory. *American Journal of Sociology* 82 (6): 1212–1241.

McCormick, Sabrina. 2006. The Brazilian Anti-Dam Movement: Knowledge Contestation as Communicative Action. *Organization & Environment* 19 (3): 321–346.

McCormick, Sabrina. 2009. *Mobilizing Science: Movements, Participation, and the Remaking of Knowledge*. Temple University Press.

McCormick, Sabrina. 2012. After the Cap: Risk Assessment, Citizen Science, and Disaster Recovery. *Ecology and Society* 17 (4): 31.

McCright, Aaron, and Riley Dunlap. 2010. Anti-Reflexivity: The American Conservative Movement's Success in Undermining Climate Science and Policy. *Theory, Culture & Society* 27 (2–3): 100–133.

McFarland, Andrew. 2004. *Neopluralism: The Evolution of Political Process Theory*. University Press of Kansas.

Meadowcroft, James. 2011. Engaging with the Politics of Sustainability Transitions. *Environmental Innovation and Societal Transitions* 1: 70–75.

Melucci, Alberto. 1980. The New Social Movements: A Theoretical Approach. *Social Science Information* 19 (2): 199–226.

Melucci, Alberto. 1996. *Challenging Codes: Collective Action in the Information Age*. Cambridge University Press.

Merton, Robert. 1970. *Science, Technology and Society in Seventeenth-Century England*. Howard Fertig.

Merton, Robert. 1973. *The Sociology of Science*. University of Chicago Press.

Metz, W.D. 1977. Solar Thermal Electricity: Power Tower Dominates Research. *Science* 197 (July 22): 353–356.

Meyer, David S., and Suzanne Staggenborg. 1996. Movements, Countermovements, and the Structure of Political Opportunity. *American Journal of Sociology* 101 (6): 1628–1660.

Meyer, David S., and Suzanne Staggenborg. 2008. Opposing Movement Strategies in US Abortion Politics. *Research in Social Movements, Conflicts and Change* 28: 207–238.

Mims, Forrest, III. 1999. Amateur Science—Strong Tradition, Bright Future. *Science* 284 (5411): 55–56.

Mirowski, Philip, and Edward Nik-Khah. 2007. Markets Made Flesh: Performativity, and a Problem in Science Studies, Augmented with Consideration of FCC Auctions. In *Do Economics Make Markets? On the Performativity of Economics*, ed. Donald MacKenzie, Fabian Muniesa, and Lucia Siu. Princeton University Press.

Mirowski, Philip, and Esther-Mirjam Sent. 2008. The Commercialization of Science and the Response of STS. In *The Handbook of Science and Technology Studies*, ed. Edward Hackett, Olga Amsterdamska, Michael Lynch, and Judy Wajcman. MIT Press.

Mizruchi, Mark. 2013. *The Fracturing of the American Corporate Elite*. Harvard University Press.

Mohl, Raymond. 2003. The Second Ghetto Thesis and the Power of History. *Journal of Urban History* 29(3): 243–256.

Mohl, Raymond. 2004. Stop the Road: Freeway Revolts in American Cities. *Journal of Urban History* 30 (5): 674–706.

Monahan, Torin. 2010. *Surveillance in the Time of Insecurity*. Rutgers University Press.

Moore, James, and Tom Rubin. 2008. Train Wreck. *Los Angeles Times*, January 13.

Moore, Kelly. 1996. Organizing Integrity: American Science and the Creation of Public Interest Science Organizations, 1955–1975. *American Journal of Sociology* 101 (6): 1592–1627.

Moore, Kelly. 2006. Powered by the People: Scientific Authority in Participatory Science. In *The New Political Sociology of Science*, ed. Kelly Moore and Scott Frickel. University of Wisconsin Press.

Moore, Kelly. 2008. *Disrupting Science: Social Movements, American Scientists, and the Politics of the Military, 1945–1975*. Princeton University Press.

Moore, Kelly, Daniel L. Kleinman, David J. Hess, and Scott Frickel. 2011. Science and Neoliberal Globalization: A Political Sociological Approach. *Theory and Society* 40 (5): 505–532.

Moore, R. Lawrence. 1977. *In Search of White Crows: Spiritualism, Parapsychology, and American Culture*. Oxford University Press.

Morello-Frosch, Rachel, Julia Brody, Phil Brown, Rebecca Altman, Ruthann Rudel, and Carla Pérez. 2009. Toxic Ignorance and Right-to-Know in Biomonitoring Results Communication: A Survey of Scientists and Study Participants. *Environmental Health* 8 (6).

Moss, Ralph. 1996. *The Cancer Industry*. Equinox.

Moss, Ralph. 2005. Patient Perspectives: Tijuana Cancer Clinics in the Post-NAFTA Era. *Integrative Cancer Therapies* 4 (1): 65–86.

Moss, Ralph. 2011. A Visit to the Tijuana Cancer Clinics. *Townsend Letter for Doctors and Patients*, April. Available at www.townsendletter.com.

Mulkay, Michael. 1976. Norms and Ideology in Science. *Social Science Information* 15 (4–5): 637–656.

Mullins, Nicholas. 1972. The Development of a Scientific Specialty: The Phage Group and the Origins of Molecular Biology. *Minerva* 10 (1): 52–82.

Mumford, Lewis. 1964. Authoritarian and Democratic Technics. *Technology and Culture* 5 (1): 1–8.

National Institute for Money in State Politics. 2016a. No on 23: Californians to Stop Dirty Energy Proposition. www.followthemoney.org.

National Institute for Money in State Politics. 2016b. Proposal 12-3: Electricity from Renewable Energy Resources. www.followthemoney.org.

Natural Resources Defense Council. 1998. Exhausted by Diesel: How America's Dependence on Diesel Emissions Threatens Our Health. www.nrdc.org.

Nelkin, Dorothy. 1994. Scientific Controversies: The Dynamics of Public Disputes in the United States. In *Handbook of Science and Technology*, ed. Sheila Jasanoff, Gerry Markle, James Peterson, and Trevor Pinch. SAGE.

Nelkin, Dorothy, ed. 1992. *Controversy: Politics of Technical Decisions*. SAGE.

Nelson, Richard, and Sidney Winter. 1982. *An Evolutionary Theory of Economic Change*. Belknap.

Noble, David. 1977. *American by Design: Science, Technology, and the Rise of Corporate Capitalism*. Oxford University Press.

Noble, David. 1984. *Forces of Production: A Social History of Industrial Automation*. Knopf.

Obach, Brian. 2015. *Organic Struggle: The Movement for Sustainable Agriculture in the United States*. MIT Press.

O'Donovan, Orla, and Kathy Glavanis-Granthan. 2005. Patients' Organizations in Ireland: Challenging Capitalist Biomedicine? Final Report to the Royal Irish Academy. www.ria.ie.

Office of Technology Assessment. 1990. *Unconventional Cancer Treatments*. US Government Printing Office.

Oil Change International. 2013a. 112th (2011–2012) House votes. dirtyenergymoney.com.

Oil Change International. 2013b. 112th (2011–2012) Senate votes. dirtyenergymoney.com.

Olzak, Susan, Maya Beasley, and Johan Oliver. 2003. The Impact of State Reforms on Protest against Apartheid in South Africa. *Mobilization* 8 (1): 27–50.

Opp, Karl-Dieter, and Wolfgang Roehl. 1990. Repression, Micromobilization, and Political Protest. *Social Forces* 69 (2): 521–547.

Oreskes, Naomi, and Erik Conway. 2010. *Merchants of Doubt: How a Handful of Scientists Obscured the Truth on Issues from Tobacco Smoke to Global Warming*. Bloomsbury.

Organic Consumers Association. 2015. SOS: OCA's Ongoing Campaign to Safeguard Organic Standards. www.organicconsumers.org.

Ottinger, Gwen. 2010. Buckets of Resistance: Standards and the Effectiveness of Citizen Science. *Science, Technology & Human Values* 35 (2): 244–270.

Ottinger, Gwen. 2013. *Refining Expertise: How Responsible Engineers Subvert Environmental Justice Challenges*. NYU Press.

Oudshoorn, Nellie, and Trevor Pinch, eds. 2003. *How Users Matter: The Co-Construction of Users and Technology*. MIT Press.

Page, Benjamin, Larry Bartels, and Jason Seawright. 2013. Democracy and the Policy Preferences of Wealthy Americans. *Perspectives on Politics* 11 (1): 51–73.

Panofsky, Aaron. 2014. *Misbehaving Science: Controversy and the Development of Behavior Genetics*. University of Chicago Press.

Peck, Jamie, and Adam Tickel. 2002. Neoliberalizing Space. *Antipode* 34 (3): 380–404.

Peck, Jamie, and Adam Tickel. 2007. Conceptualizing Neoliberalism: Thinking Thatcherism. In *Contesting Urban Futures: Decentering Neoliberalism*, ed. Helga Leitner, Eric Sheppard, Kristin Sziarto, and Anant Maringanti. Guilford.

Peoples, Clayton. 2010. Contributor Influence in Congress: Social Ties and PAC Effects on US House Policymaking. *Sociological Quarterly* 51 (4): 649–677.

Perrault, Thomas. 2006. From the *Guerra Del Agua* to the *Guerra Del Gas*: Resource Governance, Neoliberalism and Popular Protest in Bolivia. *Antipode* 38 (1): 150–172.

Phadke, Roopali. 2008. People's Science in Action: The Politics of Protest and Knowledge Brokering in India. In *Technology and Society: Building Our Sociotechnical Future*, ed. Deborah Johnson and James Wetmore. MIT Press.

Pichardo, Nelson. 1997. New Social Movements: A Critical Review. *Annual Review of Sociology* 23: 411–430.

Pignataro, Anthony. 2010. Big Green's Opaque Funding. *CalWatchdog*, June 10.

Pinch, Trevor. 2010. The Invisible Technologies of Goffman's Sociology: From Merry-Go-Round to the Internet. *Technology and Culture* 51 (2): 409–424.

Pinch, Trevor, and Wiebe Bijker. 1987. The Social Construction of Facts and Artifacts: Or How the Sociology of Science and the Sociology of Technology Might Benefit Each Other. In *The Social Construction of Technological Systems*, ed. Wiebe Bijker, Thomas Hughes, and Trevor Pinch. MIT Press.

Piven, Frances Fox, and Richard Cloward. 1978. *Poor People's Movements: Why They Succeed and How They Fail*. Vintage.

Polanyi, Karl. 1944. *The Great Transformation: The Political and Economic Origins of Our Time*. Farrar and Rinehart.

Polletta, Francesca. 2004. Culture Is Not Just in Your Head. In *Rethinking Social Movements: Structure, Meaning, and Emotion*, ed. Jeff Goodwin and James Jasper. Rowman and Littlefield.

Polletta, Francesca. 2009. Storytelling in Social Movements. In *Culture, Social Movements, and Protest*, ed. Hank Johnston. Ashgate.

Powell, Maria, and Daniel Kleinman. 2008. Building Citizen Capacities for Participation in Nanotechnology Decision-Making: The Democratic Virtues of the Consensus Conference Model. *Public Understanding of Science* 17 (3): 329–348.

Rao, Hayagreeva, and Martin Kenny. 2008. New Forms as Settlements. In *Handbook of Organizational Institutionalism*, ed. Royston Greenwood, Christine Oliver, Roy Suddaby, and Kerstin Sahlin-Andersson. SAGE.

Ravetz, Jerome. 2005. The Post-Normal Science of Safety. In *Science and Citizens: Globalization and the Challenge of Engagement*, ed. Melissa Leach, Ian Scoones, and Brian Wynne. Zed.

Reece, Ray. 1979. *The Sun Betrayed: A Report on the Corporate Seizure of US Solar Energy*. South End.

Richards, Evelleen. 1981. *Vitamin C and Cancer: Medicine or Politics?* St. Martin's Press.

Rip, Arie, and René Kemp. 1998. Technological Change. In *Human Choice and Climate Change*, volume 2, ed. Steve Rayner and Elizabeth Malone. Batelle.

Robinson, Joanna. 2013. *Contested Water: The Struggle against Water Privatization in the United States and Canada*. MIT Press.

Rose, Nikolas. 1999. *The Powers of Freedom: Reframing Political Thought*. Cambridge University Press.

Rose, Nikolas, Pat O'Malley, and Mariana Valverde. 2006. Governmentality. *Annual Review of Law and Social Science* 2: 83–104.

Rothschild, Joan, ed. 1999. *Design and Feminism: Revisioning Spaces, Places, and Everyday Things*. Rutgers University Press.

Sarewitz, Daniel. 2004. How Science Makes Environmental Controversies Worse. *Environmental Science & Policy* 7 (5): 385–403.

Schnaiberg, Allan, and Kenneth A. Gould. 1994. *Environment and Society: The Enduring Conflict*. St. Martin's Press.

Schneiberg, Marc. 2007. What's on the Path? Path Dependence, Organizational Diversity and the Problem of Institutional Change in the US Economy, 1900–1950. *Socio-economic Review* 5 (1): 47–80.

Schneiberg, Marc, and Michael Lounsbury. 2008. Social Movements and Institutional Analysis. In *The SAGE Handbook of Organizational Institutionalism*, ed. Royston Greenwood, Christine Oliver, Roy Suddaby, and Kertin Sahlin. SAGE.

Schneiberg, Marc, and Sarah Soule. 2005. Institutionalization as a Contested, Multilevel Process: The Case of Rate Regulation in American Fire Insurance. In *Social Movements and Organizational Theory*, ed. Gerald Davis, Doug McAdam, Richard Scott, and Mayer Zald. Cambridge University Press.

Schneiberg, Marc, Marissa King, and Thomas Smith. 2008. Social Movements and Organizational Form: Cooperative Alternatives to Corporations in the American Insurance, Dairy and Grain Industries. *American Sociological Review* 73 (4): 635–667.

Schumacher, Ernst. 1973. *Small Is Beautiful: Economics As If People Mattered.* Harper and Row.

Schurman, Rachel. 2004. Fighting "Frankenfoods": Industry Opportunity Structures and the Efficacy of the Anti- Biotech Movement in Western Europe. *Social Problems* 51 (4): 243–268.

Scoones, Ian. 2005. Contentious Politics, Contentious Knowledges: Mobilising against GM Crops in India, South Africa, and Brazil. Institute for Development Studies, University of Sussex. www.ids.ac.uk.

Scott, James. 1987. *Weapons of the Weak: Everyday Forms of Peasant Resistance.* Yale University Press.

Scott, Pam, Evelleen Richards, and Brian Martin. 1990. Captives of Controversy: The Myth of the Neutral Social Researcher In Contemporary Scientific Controversies. *Science, Technology & Human Values* 15 (4): 474–494.

Scott, W. Richard, Martin Ruef, Peter Mendel, and Carol Caronna. 2000. *Institutional Change and Healthcare Organization: From Professional Dominance to Managed Care.* University of Chicago Press.

Seidman, Steven. 2013. *Contested Knowledge: Social Theory Today.* Wiley-Blackwell.

Seifert, Franz, and Helga Torgersen. 1997. How to Keep Out What We Don't Want: An Assessment of "Sozialverträglichkeit" under the Austrian Genetic Engineering Act. *Public Understanding of Science* 6 (4): 301–327.

Seyfang, Gill, and Adrian Smith. 2007. Grassroots Innovation for Sustainable Development: Towards a New Research and Policy Agenda. *Environmental Politics* 16 (4): 584–603.

Shwom, Rachel. 2011. A Middle-range Theorization of Energy Politics: The Struggle for Energy-Efficient Appliances. *Environmental Politics* 20 (5): 705–726.

Slaughter, Sheila, and Larry Leslie. 1997. *Academic Capitalism: Politics, Policies, and the Entrepreneurial University.* Johns Hopkins University Press.

Slaughter, Sheila, and Gary Rhoades. 2004. *Academic Capitalism and the New Economy: Markets, State, and Higher Education.* Johns Hopkins University Press.

Smelsner, Neil. 1962. *Theory of Collective Behavior.* Free Press.

Smith, Adrian, and Rob Raven. 2012. What Is Protective Space? Reconsidering Niches in Transitions to Sustainability. *Research Policy* 41 (6): 1025–1036.

Smith, Adrian, Mariano Fressoli, and Hernán Thomas. 2014. Grassroots Innovation Movements: Challenges and Contributions. *Journal of Cleaner Production* 63 (January): 114–124.

Smith, Adrian, Mariano Fressoli, Dinesh Abrol, Elisa Arond, and Adrian Ely. 2016. *Grassroots Innovation Movements.* Routledge.

Snow, David, and Robert Benford. 2000. Comment on Oliver and Johnston: Clarifying the Relationship between Framing and Ideology. *Mobilization* 5 (1): 55–60.

Snow, David, E. Burke Rochford, Steven Worden, and Robert Benford. 1986. Framing Alignment Processes, Micromobilization, and Movement Participation. *American Sociological Review* 51 (4): 464–481.

Snow, David, Robert Benford, Holly McCammon, Lyndi Hewitt, and Scott Fitzgerald. 2014. The Emergence, Development, and Future of the Framing Perspective: 25+ Years Since Frame Alignment. *Mobilization* 19 (1): 23–45.

Soule, Sarah. 2010. *Contentious Politics and Corporate Social Responsibility.* Cambridge University Press.

Soule, Sarah. 2012. Targeting Organizations: Contentious and Private Politics. *Research in the Sociology of Organizations* 34: 261–285.

Star, Susan Leigh, and James Griesemer. 1989. Institutional Ecology, "Translations," and Boundary Objects. *Social Studies of Science* 19 (3): 387–420.

Stephens, Jennier, Elizabeth Wilson, and Tarla Peterson. 2015. *Smart Grid (R)evolution: Electric Power Struggles.* Cambridge University Press.

Stirling, Andy. 2007. Risk, Precaution and Science: Towards a More Constructive Policy Debate. *EMBO Reports* 8: 309–315.

Stirling, Andy. 2008. *Final Report: European Commission FP7 Expert Advisory Group on Science in Society.* European Commission. Available at ec.europa.eu.

Stirling, Andy. 2015. Power, Truth, and Knowledge Democracies in Europe. In *Future Directions for Scientific Advice in Europe*, ed. James Wildson and Robert Doubleday. Centre for Science and Policy.

Stocking, S. Holly, and Lisa Holstein. 2015. Purveyors of Ignorance: Journalists as Agents in the Social Construction of Scientific Ignorance. In *Routledge International Handbook of Ignorance Studies*, ed. Matthias Gross and Linsey McGoey. Routledge.

Strathern, Maryilyn. 2000. *Audit Cultures: Anthropological Studies in Accountability, Ethics, and the Academy*. Routledge.

Stratmann, Thomas. 2002. Can Special Interests Buy Congressional Votes? Evidence from Financial Services Legislation. *Journal of Law & Economics* 45 (2): 345–373.

Stratmann, Thomas. 2005. Some Talk: Money in Politics. A (Partial) Review of the Literature. *Public Choice* 124 (1–2): 135–156.

Summerton, Jane. 1994. *Changing Large Technical Systems*. Westview.

Suryanarayanan, Sainath, and Daniel L. Kleinman. 2014. Beekeepers' Collective Resistance and the Collective Politics of Pesticide Resistance in the United States. *Political Power and Social Theory* 27: 89–122.

Tarrow, Sidney. 2011. *Power in Movement: Social Movements and Contentious Politics*. Cambridge University Press.

Tatum, Jesse. 1995. *Energy Possibilities*. State University of New York Press.

Tatum, Jesse. 2000. *Muted Voices*. Associated University Presses.

Tilly, Charles. 1978. *From Mobilization to Revolution*. Addison-Wesley.

Tilly, Charles, Louise Tilly, and Richard Tilly. 1975. *The Rebellious Century: 1830–1930*. University of Chicago Press.

Titarenko, Larissa, John McCarthy, Clark McPhail, and Boguslaw Augustyn. 2001. The Interaction of State Repression, Protest Form, and Protest Sponsor Strength during the Transition from Communism in Minsk, Belarus, 1990–1995. *Mobilization* 6 (2): 129–150.

Torres, Susana. 1999. Expanding the Urban Design Agenda: A Critique of New Urbanism. In *Design and Feminism: Revisioning Spaces, Places, and Everyday Things*, ed. Joan Rotschild. Rutgers University Press.

Touraine, Alaine. 1992. Beyond Social Movements? *Theory, Culture & Society* 9 (1): 125–145.

Trenberth, Kevin. 2012. Check with Climate Scientists for Views on Climate. *Wall Street Journal*, February 1.

US Department of Agriculture. 2015. Organic Market Overview. www.ers.usda.gov.

US House of Representatives. 2011. Discretionary Spending Recommendations Offered by the Following Members of the House Committee on Science, Space, and Technology: Rep. Ralph M. Hall, Rep. F. James Sensenbrenner, Rep. Lamar Smith, Rep. Judy Biggert, Rep. W. Todd Akin, Rep. Michael McCaul, Rep. Steven Palazzo, Rep. Andy Harris, and Rep. Randy Hultgren. October 14. science.house.gov.

US Senate. 2014. The Chain of Environmental Command: How a Club of Billionaires and Their Foundations Control the Environmental Movement and Obama's EPA. Committee on Environment and Public Works, Minority Staff Report. www .epw.senate.gov.

Vallas, Steven, and Daniel Lee Kleinman. 2008. Contradiction, Convergence, and the Knowledge Economy: The Confluence of Academic and Commercial Biotechnology. *Socio-economic Review* 6 (2): 283–311.

van Broekhuizen, Pieter, and Lucas Reijnders. 2011. Building Blocks for a Precautionary Approach to the Use of Nanomaterials: Positions Taken by Trade Unions and Environmental NGOs in the European Nanotechnologies Debate. *Risk Analysis* 31 (10): 1644–1657.

Van Dyke, Nella, and Holly McCammon, eds. 2010. *Strategic Alliances: Coalition Building and Social Movements.* University of Minnesota Press.

Vasseur, Michael. 2014. Convergence and Divergence in Renewable Energy Policy in US States from 1998 to 2011. *Social Forces* 92 (4): 1637–1657.

Veblen, Thorstein. 1921. *The Engineers and the Price System.* W. B. Heubsch.

Verbong, Gert, and Frank Geels. 2007. The Ongoing Transition: Lessons from a Socio-technical, Multi-level Analysis of the Dutch Electricity System (1960–2004). *Energy Policy* 35: 1025–1037.

Wachelder, Joseph. 2003. Democratizing Science: Various Routes and Visions of Dutch Science Shops. *Science, Technology & Human Values* 28 (2): 244–273.

Wahlström, Mattias, and Abby Peterson. 2006. Between the State and the Market: Expanding the Concept of "Political Opportunity Structure." *Acta Sociologica* 49 (4): 363–377.

Waidzunas, Tom. 2013. Intellectual Opportunity Structures and Science-Targeted Activism: Influence of the Ex-Gay Movement on the Science of Sexual Orientation. *Mobilization* 18 (1): 1–18.

Warner, Michael. 2002. *Publics and Counterpublics.* Zone Books.

Weber, Klaus, Hayagreeva Rao, and L. G. Thomas. 2009. From Streets to Suites: How the Anti-Biotech Movement Affected German Pharmaceutical Firms. *American Sociological Review* 74 (1): 106–127.

Weber, Max. 1978. *Economy and Society: An Outline of Interpretive Sociology*. University of California Press.

Weinberg, Adam, David Pellow, and Allan Schnaiberg. 2000. *Urban Recycling and the Search for Sustainable Community Development*. Princeton University Press.

Welsh, Ian, and Brian Wynne. 2013. Science, Scientism and Imaginaries of Publics in the UK: Passive Objects, Incipient Threats. *Science as Culture* 22 (4): 540–566.

White, Robert. 1999. Comparing State Repression of Pro-State Vigilantes and Anti-State Insurgents: Northern Ireland, 1972–75. *Mobilization* 4 (2): 189–202.

Williams, Logan D. A. 2013. Three Models of Development: Community Ophthalmology NGOs and the Appropriate Technology Movement. *Perspectives on Global Development and Technology* 12 (4): 449–475.

Williamson, Thad, David Imbroscio, and Gar Alperovitz. 2002. *Making a Place for Community: Local Democracy in a Global Era*. Routledge.

Winner, Langdon. 1977. *Autonomous Technology*. MIT Press.

Winner, Langdon. 1986. *The Whale and the Reactor: A Search for Limits in an Age of High Technology*. University of Chicago Press.

Wisler, Dominique, and Marco Giugni. 1999. Under the Spotlight: The Impact of Media Attention on Protest Policing. *Mobilization* 4 (2): 171–187.

Woodhouse, Edward, and Steve Breyman. 2005. Green Chemistry as a Social Movement? *Science, Technology & Human Values* 32 (3): 199–222.

Woodhouse, Edward, David J. Hess, Steve Breyman, and Brian Martin. 2002. Science Studies and Activism: Possibilities and Problems for Reconstructivist Agendas. *Social Studies of Science* 32 (2): 297–319.

Woolgar, Steve. 1981a. Critique and Criticism: Two Readings of Ethnomethodology. *Social Studies of Science* 11 (4): 504–514.

Woolgar, Steve. 1981b. Interests and Explanation in the Social Study of Science. *Social Studies of Science* 11 (3): 365–394.

World Commission on Economic Development. 1987. *Our Common Future*. Oxford University Press.

Wynne, Brian. 1982. *Rationality and Ritual: The Windscale Inquiry and Nuclear Decisions in Britain*. British Society for the History of Science.

Wynne, Brian. 1995. Public Understanding of Science. In *Handbook of Science and Technology Studies*, ed. Sheila Jasanoff, Gerald Markle, James Petersen, and Trevor Pinch. SAGE.

Wynne, Brian. 1996. Misunderstood Misunderstandings: Social Identities and Public Uptake of Science. In *Misunderstanding Science? The Public Reconstruction of Science and Technology*, ed. Alan Irwin and Brian Wynne. Cambridge University Press.

Wynne, Brian. 2005. Risk as Globalizing " Democratic' Discourse? Framing Subjects and Citizens. In *Science and Citizens: Globalization and the Challenge of Engagement*, ed. Melissa Leach, Ian Scoones, and Brian Wynne. Zed.

Wynne, Brian. 2007. Public Engagement as a Means of Restoring Public Trust in Science: Hitting the Notes, but Missing the Music? *Community Genetics* 9 (3): 211–220.

Yates, Frances. 1972. *The Rosicrucian Enlightenment*. Routledge.

Yearley, Steven. 1992. Green Ambivalence about Science. *British Journal of Sociology* 43 (4): 511–532.

Yearley, Steven. 2005. *Making Sense of Science: Understanding the Social Study of Science*. SAGE.

Yearley, Steven. 2011. Citizen Engagement with the Politics of Air Quality: Lessons for Social Theory, Science Studies, and Environmental Sociology. In *Governing the Air: The Dynamics of Science, Policy, and Citizen Interaction*, ed. Rolf Kidskog and Gören Sundqvist. MIT Press.

Zald, Meyer, and Roberta Ash. 1966. Social Movement Organizations: Growth, Decay, and Change. *Social Forces* 44 (3): 327–341.

Zwerman, Gilda, Patricia Steinhoff, and Donatella della Porta. 2000. Disappearing Social Movements: Clandestinity in the Cycle of New Left Protest in the US, Japan, Germany, and Italy. *Mobilization* 5 (1): 85–104.

Index